FEARLESS

A Jewish boy in Nazi Germany

Robert Middelmann

I dedicate this book to my Oma, the cornerstone of my life, and to my children, Marie, Bobby, Gloria and Barry, who have always brought me great joy.

ACKNOWLEDGEMENTS

I want to thank my beloved wife, Dorothy Beavington, for her support and guidance through the process of writing my life story. It was a labour of love. I also want to thank my son, Bobby, and his wife, Melanie, for preparing the book for publication and their daughter Rebecca Green for the editing.

CHAPTER 1

Summer, 1931. I wake up when I feel someone slip into bed with me. I'm only four, but I recognize Bruno, a family friend. He clutches on to me under the eiderdown quilt and I feel his heartbeat pounding like a ticking bomb in my back. Bruno whispers in my ear, "Be quiet, Robert, don't move." I hear the door open, and two tall men in dark uniforms come in with flashlights. My mother enters behind them. "Don't wake up the boy," she pleads. I pretend to be asleep, but I see them look under my bed and inside my closet. They leave, and after a bit, Bruno cautiously gets up and silently slips out the door. The next day, Mama explained to me that the SS were chasing Bruno Betnatski, a leader in the Communist party, and they had seen him heading for our house, which led them to suspect he might be hiding there. Mama let him in, and told him to quickly climb into bed with me. That took a lot of courage, because she could have been in a lot of trouble with the SS. If they caught one small inkling of the truth, it could result in a public beating, or death. The SS, short for Schutzstaffel, were the ruthless thugs of Adolf Hitler's totalitarian regime. One of Hitler's primary goals was to destroy the Communist Party, making Bruno a prime target. Hitler also sought to enslave, dehumanize, scapegoat, and execute those he viewed as "Others." During World War II, the SS carried out mass executions of Jews, communists, gypsies, and partisans. Bruno escaped to Poland and came to thank us for saving his life after the war ended. I felt proud that I was able to keep quiet and help him survive.

The early 1930s were full of excitement and awe for a boy like me. Our home became a safe meeting place for the resistance, including the communists and others who opposed the Nazis. I grew up as an only child, surrounded by adults from many nations who felt safe to express their opinions in our home. I was a participant in fascinating conversations about politics, religion, history, and the fight for freedom. It wasn't until later that I truly understood the gravity of the danger my family was in during the time of Hitler and the Nazi regime.

I was born into a family of candy makers who were also smugglers, socialists, and survivors. Prostitutes helped raise me and became my beloved aunties. My mother hated my father, who was often savagely violent toward her and I, and on one occasion I had to stop them from actually murdering each other. My Dutch Oma was my safe nest, and her love saved me from the bitterness and violence of my parent's marriage. It was soon apparent that I had a fearless, adventuresome, and independent spirit. At the age of four, I accidentally discovered that my father, Otto Schulte-Middelmann, was not truly my father, and my biological father was actually a Polish Jew with whom my mother had had an affair. This made me half Jewish at a time when it was perilous and vulnerable to be Jewish in Germany. I kept that secret to myself for 25 years. In our family, we knew the necessity of keeping secrets to survive. My mother, Maria, was in labour for three long days before I finally agreed to be born. It was 6 am on July 10th, 1927. Part of the delay was likely due to my weight of 11 lbs and my laughably large and square head. This was the beginning of my life at Muehlen Strasse 15, Herne, Germany, in the Ruhr Valley.

My mother was 28 when she gave birth to me. She had been married for 11 years to Otto, which was a marriage of convenience, not love. She looked like a frightened fawn in her wedding photo, while Otto looked like an arrogant and smug autocrat. Mama had to sit in a chair for the photo because she was much taller than Otto, who was almost a midget at 4'8". What a tragic marriage it would turn out to be, filled with violence, betrayal, and hatred. She looked delicate and ethereal in her wedding photo, with thick, dark hair, light skin, and luminescent brown eyes. Mama had a great love for music and history, which she passed on to me. She was intelligent, humorous, extremely hard-working and unusually open in talking with me. At a very young age, I learned about sex, abortion, and childbirth from Mama. I am grateful that she was progressive in this, as I learned a great deal of knowledge from her that helped me later in life as I was able to help the midwife during the birth of my first child.

Otto was 38 when I was born and apparently delighted at my arrival. He desperately wanted a male heir to carry on the family candy business, and I was the answer to his dreams for the future. He loved my mother, but was abusive and violent to her. I believe he had some kind of mental illness, because his mood could change in an instant, and he would suddenly go into a rage. When this happened, he had the adrenaline-fuelled strength of five men and was extremely dangerous. We would run to a neighbour's house to be safe from his rages. At least we had an early warning signal moments beforehand; when going into a rage, his tongue would stick out of the right side of his mouth and we would run for our lives. Otto seemed to have a Napoleon Complex because he always had to be the one in control and "top dog." He always had an arrogant look on his face and presented himself as a man of substance who was better than others. I remember him as a classy dresser, with an elegant top hat and a silver tipped cane. When he went out on the town, he had the biggest cigar and the most expensive gold and opal rings and cufflinks. Otto had a public persona which was very different from his private one. I saw him as my protector, although he was also often my abuser. When I was five, some kids beat me up. I shouted, "Just you wait, when my Papa grows up he'll show you!" They just laughed at me. Neighbourly women would often comment to Mama how lucky she was to have a husband like Otto. They didn't know she was living in hell with a violent husband.

I was extremely close to my Oma, my mother's mother, Gertrude Arens. She was born in 1860 in Hatert, Gelderland, the Netherlands. Her family were poor migrant farm workers who had never been to school. Gertrude's mother died giving birth to her, and there were now five children for her father to raise. When she was twelve, her father brought his family to Germany where the coal mining industry was booming. Gertrude was clever and innovative. She found a job as a maid for a rich family, of the surname Barts, in Cologne. Her pay was five marks per month, which would be like $1.25 in today's standards. For the first time in her life, she slept in a bed, and instead of wooden clogs, she had shoes made of leather. This family treated her with love and kindness, but Oma told me that she cried herself to sleep at night for the first week because she didn't understand German. Then Sunday came, and she went to a large Catholic church with the Barts. She told me, "Peace came back into my heart when I heard the priest chanting in Latin."

Gertrude missed her family but was content living with the kind Barts family. She worked hard to be a good maid. She was determined to learn to read and write, so when the Barts children did their homework, she studied along with them. When Gertrude was 23, she went to celebrate Mardi Gras and met a handsome miner, Wilhelm Kirschfink, from Hoengen. They fell deeply in love and were married soon thereafter. They decided to move to Herne-Baukau, in the Ruhr Valley, where a new coal mine shaft was being sunk. Wilhelm took a job as a contract miner. They were able to save enough money to build a house with a general store in front and living quarters in the back. Gertrude ran the store, and over the next few years, gave birth to four children; Willie, Gerard, Robert, and my mother, Maria. They had a loving and successful marriage until Wilhelm started to drink to excess. Sadly, because of his alcoholism, he died at the age of 38 due to kidney failure. This tragedy left poor Gertrude a lonely widow, with four young children to care for on her own. Maria was only two years old.

Oma continued to run the store, but her heart was too kind. If customers said they couldn't pay her, she let them have groceries on credit. As a result, she lost the entire business and was forced to declare bankruptcy. In the end, all she had left was a horse and buggy. Willie was the eldest child, about 12-years-old. He helped his mother pick up fruit and vegetables from nearby farms and sell them in town door-to-door. In the winter, they sold fish from the buggy. Her three sons all went to work underground in the coal mines at 16 to help support the family. When the First World War broke out in 1914, all her sons had to serve the Kaiser. Her youngest son, Robert, was killed at age 19 near Verdun, France. It was a terrible heartbreak for Gertrude, one that she never forgot. I was named after my uncle Robert. Her other sons, Willie and Gerhard, survived. With her sons in the war, Gertrude was in desperate need of money, and one solution was for Maria to marry a man who could provide for her financially. That is how my mother came to marry Otto Schulte-Middelmann when she was only 17. Gertrude saw it as a good match, because Otto was well established financially. Shortly after the wedding, Otto was drafted into the army, which again left Gertrude and Maria in a difficult financial position.

The government ordered that all young women must work, so Maria found a job in Essen at the Krupp ammunition factory. The work was hard and the factory was freezing cold. There was a great shortage of food, so Gertrude devised a plan to start smuggling. She would cross the Dutch border near Elten at night through rough bush land. She would then buy groceries in Holland and carry as much as she could back across the border in order to sell them for a higher price in town. She soon became connected with locals at the border and began to smuggle Indonesian spices that brought a better profit and were easier to carry. Whenever Gertrude got caught by the Dutch border patrol, she told them she was a Dutch widow who needed to feed her starving children. Conversely, when she was caught by the Germans, her story was that she was a poor widow whose three brave sons were fighting for Germany. Both versions of her life softened the hearts of the border guards, and they would let her go. Gertrude was a devout Catholic and never wanted to commit the sin of lying. However, she was also practical. She would say to herself, "God understands." Her ingenuity and courage were truly something to behold.

When the war ended in 1918, Gertrude had been so successful in her smuggling business that she had enough money to buy a house. That is the house where I was eventually born. Gertrude, Maria, and Otto decided to build a candy factory in the back yard and live together as a family. Oma was 67 when I was born. She had long tresses of snow-white hair that she wore in a graceful bun. Her body was completely covered by long dark dresses that made her look like a Greek widow. Oma's skin was as brown as shoe leather and gave her the appearance of a gypsy. Her intense smouldering eyes were like two pieces of coal. Those eyes never missed a thing. She had huge peasant hands with fingers like giant Polish sausages, and a loving heart that drew many to her door. Oma was honest, humorous, and was known for helping others. She was likewise renowned for her intelligence, wit, and thorough knowledge of politics. Oma believed in justice for all and was a true humanitarian. The family candy business did well until the 1929 Wall Street crash and the start of the Great Depression. Oma mortgaged her house to keep the candy business afloat, but people didn't have enough money to buy bread, let alone candies. They had to shut the factory down and find another solution to their financial problems. The factory had two sections with individual entrances. My parents and Oma decided to rent out these sections. The left wing became living quarters for Communists, while the right wing was rented to Orthodox Russian Jews for their synagogue. They also rented out three rooms downstairs, and four rooms upstairs to eight prostitutes.

These fascinating women treated me like family, and I referred to them as my beloved aunties. They had all come to prostitution through dire economic need. Lotti and Maria were sisters who had grown up in a Catholic orphanage together. At the age of 14, they were placed in a convent to become nuns against their will. They didn't want to be nuns, and one night they climbed out the window and ran away. Maria was 16, and Lotti was 14 at the time of their grand escape. They both became prostitutes and came to live in our house a few years later. They did very well, as they were extremely beautiful and sweet-natured. Erna had an interesting history as well. She was tiny, striking in appearance, and trained as an exotic dancer. She had travelled Germany with her pet boa constrictor and performed to large crowds. However, with the financial collapse, men could no longer afford a ticket to see Erna and her snake. Because of this, she also turned to prostitution to survive. During the five years these aunties lived in our home, the vice squad would turn up regularly to try to get evidence to arrest the women. One day, Erna was arrested by the head of the vice squad. He fell madly in love with her, and they later married and had eight children. Lotti and Maria also made good marriages. Lotti's husband was an electrical engineer who was disowned by his family when he married Lotti, and Maria married a city clerk. Both sisters had long and happy marriages. God bless the prostitutes. They were among the few people who had money for rent to help my family survive. Other people wouldn't rent to them due to their chosen profession, but my parents were happy to do so. These beautiful and loving women helped save Oma's house and our factory.

As the only child of the house I had the position of a "crown prince." These exotic ladies of the night treated me with love, tenderness, and spoiled me terribly. I called them all Tante, which means auntie. My eight aunties were Lotti, Erna, Friedel, Josefa, Vera, Maria, Leni, and Thelma. Lotti and Erna were my favourites, but I grew to love all of them as family. As a toddler, I'd crawl up the stairs on all fours to visit them. They were always delighted to see me and gave me fancy chocolates or drops of French perfume behind my ears. I joined them for tea, and they taught me high-class table manners and how to eat properly with a fork and knife. They adored "little Robert," and I adored them in return. I still remember how beautiful they looked in their elegant clothes, how heady their perfume was, and how perfect their nails. Those aunties taught me a great deal, and probably inspired in me a lifelong love and passion for women. I was turning two when they first came to live with us. I was a picky eater and didn't want to eat healthy food like spinach and turnips, which frustrated Mama and Oma to no end. Tante Lotti asked if she could take over my feeding and convince me to eat my vegetables. She lined up a stuffed cat, monkey, and a teddy bear and pretended to feed each of them a small morsel. "One for the cat, one for the monkey, one for the bear, and one for little Robert." I was so fascinated by this unique dinner party with the animals that I opened my mouth wide to take in my healthy morsel from Tante Lotti's clever hand.

Leni had a sweet and loving heart. She became pregnant at 18 by a client who was a school teacher. Being Catholic, she did not consider abortion as an option, and gave birth in our home. Leni named her daughter Ruth. She was an exceptionally beautiful child, with big blue eyes and buoyant masses of blonde curls. I was enchanted by her. She became something like a sister to me and was doted on by everyone in the house. Ruth had a sweet nature, just like her mother, and was always laughing and full of joy. I had always wanted a sibling, so I was delighted to have this playmate just one year younger than me. When she was two, we were playing marbles outside. It was a warm day and we were having great fun. Ruth was always such a good-natured girl, and I absolutely adored her. Suddenly and without warning, she started to choke and collapsed to the ground. I frantically ran in to tell Mama, who called Leni. They took Ruth to the hospital, where she died the next day from diphtheria. I was heartbroken, and that deep and inexplicable sadness has stayed in my heart ever since. Leni was inconsolable, and everyone in the house was devastated by the untimely loss of this angelic child.

Leni never got over the loss of Ruth. After the war, she met a British soldier. They fell madly in love and moved to England. They never had children, but she was happy in her marriage to a kind man. I was truly blessed to have these kind and loving aunties, as my family life was a tumultuous one of bitterness and violence. My father's rages and his brutality caused my mother's hatred to increase with every passing day. I received love from my Oma and my aunties, but never from my mother. She never showed me physical affection. I always felt that I was just a nuisance and a burden to her, a burden she resented and never wanted. Much later in life, I realized how desperately unhappy she must have been to be married to such a violent and abusive man. She worked her fingers to the bone, and still had to care for a child at the end of the day. With this understanding, I was finally able to forgive her for her aloofness and find compassion for my mother.

The Communists renting the left wing would often hold meetings that I was allowed to attend. That was an exciting allowance for me. I was fascinated by their music and lyrics, such as "The Internationale will win our human rights." This song, "The Internationale," was the rallying song of the early Communists during World War I. The musicians at these meetings played guitars and mandolins with great passion and helped to instigate my lifelong love of music. Every evening, the Russian Jews had a gathering, and I happily attended and learned their religious customs. They often had tea with Oma in the evening, and I hungrily listened to the lively discussions. I realize now how fortunate I was to be exposed to all these different political and religious values, and how much I learned as a very young child. This immersion in such a rich diversity of human customs helped sculpt the open-minded person I am today.

Mama and Papa were always busy, and it was Oma who nurtured and cared for me. I shared a bed with her until I was five years old, and she was my first deep familial heart connection. She was hard working, devout, funny, and wise. Oma was firm in disciplining me, but never laid a hand on me physically. I adored her. One time I was naughty and she said, "If you were my boy, I would give you a good thrashing!" I immediately burst into tears. "What do you mean? I'm not your boy?" I was consumed with pain by the thought that she didn't consider me to be her boy. Oma quickly understood my literal interpretation of her cutting words. She took me in her arms, hugged and kissed me, and reassured me that I was, indeed, her boy. Papa and I also developed a heart connection when I was young. He would take me for walks and carry me on his shoulders. I knew he loved me deeply and would always be there for me despite his bad temper.

I learned by the age of three that I had a knack for making people laugh. In order to entertain the neighbours, I would go out on the street and mimic members of my family. The women would hang out their windows while waiting for the show. I would stagger about like a drunk, and they all knew that was my Uncle Willy. I would then walk like a Prussian drill sergeant with heavy steps, and they recognized this as my portrayal of my mother. Next, I would walk with my head held high like an aristocrat, swinging an imaginary walking cane, and they knew that was meant to be Otto. However, the imitation that got the most laughs was the one I did of my beloved Oma. I would walk with my arms hanging heavy while lumbering side to side like an unwieldy monkey. The neighbours would roar with laughter and mirth. They all loved Oma, but they also loved and appreciated my Commedia del Arte slapstick representation of her.

When I was four, I went with Oma on a streetcar to go to her friend's funeral. I was curious about death. Even though I experienced Ruth's passing, I hadn't realized that dying was a universal experience for everything alive. "Why did she die, Oma?" She looked kindly at me. "She was very old, Robert, and when people get old they die." I was stricken by this thought as I knew my beloved Oma was considered old. "But you won't die, Oma." She looked down at me with her wise eyes. "Yes, I will, everyone dies." I was horrified. This concept had never entered my youthful consciousness until that moment. Sitting across from us was a pretty little girl about my age. She had platinum blonde hair, and I had admired her pink socks, black patent shoes, and frilly pink dress. She smiled sweetly at me when we made eye contact. Suddenly, a terrible awareness came into my mind. "But that little girl won't die, will she Oma?" Oma glanced at the pretty little child and looked at me sadly. "Yes, she will, Robert." I was heartbroken and burst into uncontrollable tears. I couldn't stop thinking how Oma would die, and how that sweet little girl would die. It was all too much for me, I couldn't bear it. That anguish stayed with me for a long, long time.

One day I went to town with other boys during the "Parade of Nazis." There were many SS men watching the parade. One boy said, "My Papa is a member of the Nazi Party!" An SS man smiled at him and gave him a candy to show his approval. Then the SS man asked me, "What about your father, little boy?" Impulsively, I proudly exclaimed, "My Papa is a Communist!" I was naively expecting a candy, but the SS man took off his leather shoulder belt and gave me a whipping instead. I learned that day not to publicly discuss Papa's affiliation with the Communist Party ever again. It was yet another secret for me to keep. My juvenile brain was becoming burdened with the weight of family secrets. My parents continued to make candies in half of our basement, even though they didn't have a proper license to do so. This had to be done covertly so they wouldn't get in trouble with the authorities. The other half of the basement was boarded off, and Mama raised her pigs there. There were increased bouts violence in the streets, with constant battles between the Nazis and the Communists. The unmistakable sound of gunfire was often heard echoing throughout the town of Herne. With my wellbeing in mind, my parents decided I would be safer at Uncle Gerard's and Aunt Anna's place out in the country. They were Communists and lived in a commune between Wanne-eikel and Bochum, No. 25 Dorstener Strasse. Eight families lived there, and each had an equally portioned piece of land on which to grow vegetables. They also had chickens, sheep, pigs, and pigeons. There was great happiness and harmony in the commune. They were all peaceful and kind people who loved the land and valued family.

Gerard and Anna had two daughters, Trudi and Else. They were my older cousins and they pampered and fussed over me whenever I visited. I had a wonderful time with them, as we played house together with their dolls. My time with Uncle Gerard and his family was one of the happiest times of my life. The relaxed and loving aura of serenity in the commune was a welcomed sharp contrast to the tension and violence at home. When the Summer was over, Papa had me balance on the spokes of his back tire and doubled me on his bicycle all the way back home. I was sad to leave, but I had become homesick for my Oma, the unbreakable cornerstone of my life. It wasn't Mama or Papa I missed, it was Oma. She taught me so much. She didn't have book learning, but she had the kind of ripened wisdom that you can't learn in school. Oma was spiritual and taught me that we are all God's children and we have to love one another. She always believed in peace and love over war and hate. I don't recall ever hearing Oma say one bad word about anyone. She valued the power of the goodness in people over their mistakes. Oma told me that I had nothing to fear in life as long as I followed the path of God. "When you connect with God, cross yourself and say, 'In the name of the Father, the son, and the Holy Spirit,' you will be protected by God's armour and nothing can harm you."

I took Oma's words to heart, and in honouring them, I have bravely faced the entirety of my life without fear. Despite having lost my faith in the Christian aspect of these teachings when I was 18, I still kept this belief of being protected. Oma taught me how to be fearless. She was famous for her delightful sense of humour and

20

her wise sayings. Once she told me, "God gave us ten commandments, but the 11th is the most important." "What is the 11th commandment, Oma?" She replied, with a mischievous twinkle in her eye, "Do not get caught!" One of her more amusingly vulgar sayings was, "One pussy has more pull than 20 horses." I wish I had paid more attention to one of her more serious and soulful sayings. She told me, "See people as they are, and not how you want them to be." It would have saved me a lot of agony and heartache if I had taken that saying to heart from the beginning.

When I returned home from the commune, I found that our house had been vandalized with anti-Semitic slogans such as, "Die Juden sind unser Unglueck," which means, "The Jews are our misfortune." We were a Catholic family, but it was well known that we had Communists and Jews among our inner circle of friends. Still, I was able to look past this deplorable act, because I was overjoyed to have my Oma back and could sleep safely in her arms again. I always felt safe with Oma. She provided me with a safe nest during times of turmoil and danger. The Nazis were gaining strength but were not yet in power. Soon after my return, Uncle Willy was severely beaten by three SS men directly in front of our house. Mama called for help, and my father ran outside and started fighting them like a wild maniac. When my father went into a rage, he became indestructible. He had the strength of many men and knew how to fight. He finally won the fight by delivering some well-placed kicks directly in the groins of the SS men. I was so proud of my father, who was only 4'8", for being able to drive off these tall SS men.

The next day, I boisterously went downtown and bragged that my father had beaten up three SS men. Two men took offense to my proclamation, grabbed me by the collar, and gave me a good beating. I was still learning that I should keep my mouth shut in this new dystopian world of Nazis.

CHAPTER 2

We had rented out our factory and most of the house, so we just had the kitchen and one bedroom left for our family. Consequently, we all now slept together in one large bed. Our candy business had been very successful right up until the financial crisis crash of 1929. One reason my parents' business did as well as it did was as a result of the support and influence from a man named Leo Neuberger. Papa hired him in 1925 as the "idea man." He was an Ashkenazi Jew from Galicia, Southern Poland, who had come to Germany after the First World War. He married a Protestant woman and had a son and a daughter with her. Leo was tall, charismatic, handsome, and a known womanizer who captivated many women with his charm, intelligence, and sarcastic wit. Even though he lived in the nearby town of Bochum, he was often in Herne romancing the married women of the town. Leo was a dedicated Communist who was active politically and quite outspoken in his views. This was dangerous and ill-advised, but he didn't seem to care. He was highly respected for his clever problem-solving skills and astute business sense. He knew our business was in trouble and that my parents were struggling financially. Because of this, he came into our house carrying several heavy boxes one day. They contained a variety of moulds for making lollipops. Leo showed me and Papa the designs, including bears, monkeys, Indian chiefs, and sailors. Leo told Papa, "These will sell like hotcakes! Give it a try." Papa was dubious, but was willing to take a chance, and I was soon allowed to stir the sugar in the copper pot

only woman he visited. One day, I heard Mama tell Uncle Willie, "Frau Markmann says Otto Schulte-Middelmann is her best customer." Even though I was young, I was aware that Frau Markmann was a well-known prostitute in Herne. It was too much for me to process, so I withdrew emotionally from my parents and turned more to Oma and Uncle Willie for affection in their stead.

By nature, I was a mischievous and adventurous child. I was a street performer at the age of three, and by the time I was four, I had become the established town prankster. One of my favourite pranks was to pick up horse droppings from the streets, put them in a bag, and place them on our neighbours' doorsteps. I would entice other boys to join me in these pranks. My friends and I would hide and then watch the person open the door, open the bag, and discover the putrid surprise. We would burst out with laughter and run away giggling. Mama started getting complaints, and Papa would give me a beating, but I still kept on with my pranks. I got bored easily and could always come up with another prank to amuse myself. In desperation, Mama decided to try to get me enrolled in kindergarten early to get me off the streets and out of her hair. She succeeded, and I started school when I was four years old. It was a Catholic school and the nuns were kind to me. However, I found the other children terribly boring. They didn't seem to have the same mischievous ways that I had, and were instead very passive and obedient. To me, they seemed to be lacking in intelligence and most uninteresting.

I told Mama I wanted to quit school, but she wouldn't allow it. I was horrified to think I was stuck with these boring babies, but I realized I would have to make the best of it. To make that school year bearable, I began to hang out with older boys. I would follow them to soccer games, bicycle races, and into the country for adventures. This drove Mama crazy, because I would disappear in the morning every weekend, and not return home until late at night. More beatings from Papa didn't dissuade me from my adventures. I was always curious, and one day I saw many men gathering at a local betting station. They were betting on international horse races. This looked exciting, so I started to sneak in to observe what was going on. Mama found out and gave me strict instructions not to go there, so inevitably I just went all the more often. These visits resulted in one of the most important lessons of my life over time. I saw how sad and desperate these men were, how they despaired when they lost the bet, and how they always came back again and again in a cycle of addiction. They were stressed out, broke, and poorly dressed. I knew with certainty that I disliked gambling after witnessing its detrimental nature. At the age of four, I knew that I didn't want to end up like those sad and desperate men at the betting station. I managed to get through that year at kindergarten with my pranks, escapades, and sporting events keeping me entertained enough that I could bear my monotonous peers at school. I was glad when the school year ended, and I would finally be free again.

On my fifth birthday, July 10th, 1932, Mama baked me a special chocolate cake. Later that day, I visited one of the lovely ladies upstairs, Tante Edith, who was sipping on a glass of Samos wine. "It's your birthday, Robert, have a little sip." I took the wine glass and drank it all down. It tasted delicious, and I felt a bit of a thrill. I decided I should go to see Uncle Willie, who always had a good supply of liquor. He had a gift for me, a bottle of Dortmunder Union Beer. I was delighted and guzzled it down, much to Uncle Willie's amusement. Later, when I tried to cross the yard to go home, I felt dizzy and fell flat on my face. Mama found me, and as one might imagine, was extremely furious with her brother for getting me stumbling drunk on my 5th birthday. That was likely my first step on the long and melancholy road to alcoholism. It has been a lifelong battle that has brought great sorrow and pain to me, as well as my wife and children. I see it as the curse of our extended family, as several generations of men in both the Dutch and German ancestors on Oma's side became alcoholics. My maternal grandfather died much too young at 38 because of the sickness alcohol brings. My addiction brought me to the brink of death more than once.

On January 30, 1933, I was cheerfully throwing rocks into puddles and getting soaking wet in the rain. I heard our neighbours cheering and saw them leaning out their windows and waving. One woman shouted joyfully, "Hitler has won the election!" They were cheering because Adolph Hitler had just become the new chancellor of Germany. My heart filled with sadness and I was overcome with a dreadful sense of foreboding. I ran home to find many of our tenants and friends gathered with Oma around the radio. Some were weeping, and all were in great distress. Our tenants, who were politically active Communists, were extremely frightened. They expected to be arrested at any moment, and knew the future would have them walking on eggshells. Right after becoming chancellor, Hitler passed a law that all political activists of the opposition were to be arrested and sent to the Oranienburg concentration camp. On February 1st, police officers came to our home at 4 a.m. and arrested two of our tenants, Emil and Otto Voelkop. Emil was 17, and his father, Otto, was in his forties. A year later, they were released, and they told my parents they had been tortured and beaten mercilessly. During the next few days, several men we knew were arrested and taken to an abandoned factory nearby. I decided to go there to find out what was going on. I saw a big steel gate with tall SS men guarding it, and a towering wall. Our whole family viewed Hitler as an evil man, and the Nazis as his savage thugs. It was undescribably distressing to realize that many people we knew not only supported Hitler, but saw him as some sort of Messiah come to save Germany. We had to be careful not to draw the attention of the SS and lay low during this dangerous time. Many of our communist friends had to find ways to escape arrest, seek safety by crossing the border, or disappearing altogether.

In September 1932, I was enrolled in grade one at the Kaiser Wilhelm Catholic School. I was only five but was able to easily pass the entrance test. This was a little more interesting than kindergarten, but I was still bored by what I saw as the mechanically normative ways of the other children. I had always been surrounded by adults; having learned a lot about politics, history, and religion. I just couldn't relate to these children who seemed to know nothing beyond the drivel that was fed to them. By then, it was obvious that I had inherited a gift for linguistics, and that I could communicate in several languages. Sadly, I had no desire to communicate with these mundane and tedious children. I still felt safe in my family and protected by them. I knew that I was half Jewish, and that Jews were being treated more and more like subhumans. My Jewish friends had to go to be transferred to a school designated for Jews and was controlled by the Nazis. Mama explained to me that Jews were no longer allowed to go to public places like parks, theatres, and restaurants. She also said that Jewish students could no longer attend high school or university. It just seemed terribly unfair to me, and I couldn't understand why all this was happening. I didn't feel afraid for myself just yet, as the secret of my heritage was still well kept. Also, I knew that as long as Mama kept giving Frau Israel food, she would keep our secret to herself. Mama had found a way to protect me.

Alas, danger found another route in which to plague me. The Catholic Church was powerful and did not approve of my family renting to communists, Jews, and prostitutes. The church decided I was in an "unfit" home and applied to the city officials to have me removed from my parents' care to be sent to a Catholic orphanage far from Herne. Mama found out and warned me about what the Church was planning. "If you see a public health nurse approaching you at school, I want you to quickly run to Uncle Gerard's commune and hide there." I decided to prepare myself. During recess, I practiced my escape over and over in my mind. My plan was to climb out the window, slide down the drainpipe, and run as fast as I could the five miles to Uncle Gerard's home. Now that I had my plan, I was no longer afraid. I knew I was a much faster runner than the overweight school nurse. One day, our classroom door opened, and the public health nurse came in with the principal. I had already readied myself to leap out the window when the teacher announced that we were all getting a vaccination. I relaxed and lined up with the other students for the needle.

My grade one teacher, Mr. Hollenbeck, was a jolly fellow who often played the fiddle and taught us singing. Mama came to school one day and asked him how I was doing. "Robert is doing fine. He is extremely smart and is a child who is "wissbegierig." That word describes a person who is "greedy for knowledge." His reply made Mama happy and proud. Now that I was five, I wanted to earn a little pocket change. I needed to keep busy all the time, or else I became restless. My designated job to help the family was to go from door to door, pulling a wagon, to collect kitchen clippings to feed our pigs. That was unpaid work, of course. I wanted to make real money, so I came up with the idea of offering a watchful eye over people's bikes for a penny each. I had observed over time that bikes often got stolen while people were shopping, so I knew there was a lucrative demand for bike security. This business scheme was a huge success. Once I collected 100 pennies, I cashed them in for a silver mark at the store and took it to Oma, who served as my banker. My goal was to have enough money to buy Oma, Mama, and Papa special Christmas gifts. When the time came, I bought the best Indonesian coffee that money could buy for my beloved Oma, French perfume for Mama, and Havana cigars for

with me, and the words stuck like sandpaper in my throat when I tried to say them. We were also commanded to raise our right arms in the Nazi salute. My family knew we had to go along with this in order to stay alive. Sometimes you have to "howl with the wolves," as they say. Out of fear, no one dared go against this decree. There were big parades held on the weekends, and at night, the brown shirts marched through the streets singing and carrying torches in a show of power and intimidation. It seemed as though the majority of the German people were deceived into thinking Hitler was essentially the new Messiah, and some even believed he had been sent by God to save us. This, of course, put our family in peril. We grudgingly feigned ourselves as Hitler supporters, and kept silent about our many associations with Jews and communists in order to survive.

CHAPTER 3

In the summer of 1933, I turned six, and my parents decided to send me to Papa's brother, Uncle Joseph. I was more than happy to go, since my home was filled with boiling resentment and violence. Mama hated Papa with a deep bitterness that struck at my heart. Papa loved his wife, but his brutality had irrevocably destroyed their marriage. He still went out most nights to see other women, and Mama was relieved to see him go. Papa treated Mama like a slave; demanding work from her at all times. He was a perfectionist, and nothing could ever satisfy his unachievable standards. Mama received nothing but constant callous criticism from him, and I never once heard Papa praise her for all her hard work. It would be a relief to spend the summer away from the toxic atmosphere that permeated through my broken home. Uncle Joseph lived with his wife, Elizabeth, in Hannoversch-Muenden, lower Saxony. It was a beautiful thousand-year-old town surrounded by forest. They were childless and happy to have me stay with them.

Uncle Joseph had been injured in WWI and was on a disability pension. He'd suffered a brain injury and could no longer do his work as an orthopedic cobbler. I loved being immersed in nature, and for Uncle Joseph, nature was his therapy. We would go on hikes in the early morning, and sometimes he would tell me tragic stories about the Battle of Verdun, France. He had survived, but many hadn't, such as Oma's youngest son, Robert. We would pick berries and mushrooms and spend magical hours in the forest while he taught me about the plants and animals. He was a dedicated pacifist with a kind and gentle soul. Aunt Elizabeth had a heart of gold and treated me with great kindness. With her being a gourmet cook and me a growing boy with a passion for food, she was the perfect aunt. Despite being physically disabled and needing crutches, she worked hard and made a loving home for Uncle Joseph. I had my guitar with me and was able to make them laugh at my songs from the Ruhr. That was a special summer, and my love of nature and food increased greatly. I missed Oma but was not looking forward to returning to my unhappy family home at the end of August.

August 29th, 1933, I got home and went to town to see my friends. There were groups of older kids going to Market Square. Their parents were with them and everyone seemed in a festive mood. Many of the boys were wearing their Hitler Youth uniforms. I asked one of them, "Where are you going?" He replied with great excitement, "To the Rally in Nuremberg!" It sounded like fun. "Can I come?" He looked me over. "Sure, but you'll need a blanket." I ran home as fast as I could to retrieve one for what seemed to be an adventure. "I'm going to see the rally," I told Mama. She erroneously thought I was playing another one of my fantasy games. "I need a blanket, Mama." She retrieved an old army blanket for me, and I ran back quickly to the Market Square, where there were several trucks with open backs and canopies over top of them. A teenage boy shouted to me, "Here, give me your hand and I'll pull you up!" Before I could climb up, one of the mothers grabbed me and pulled me back. "Where's your mother?" "Home." She looked sternly at me. "Go home, you can't go without your parent's consent." I ran home once more. "Mama, you have to go to the square and sign so I can go to the rally in Nuremberg." Mama was taken aback. "Are you out of your mind? That is a Nazi rally, and it's 500 kilometres south of here!" I was bewildered, as I thought it was some sort of festival, and I simply wanted to join the fun with the other boys. Now I understood that I would have been going right into the hands of our enemy. Thank God for mothers, eh? This little half-Jewish boy was saved from going to a Nazi rally by a vigilant mother who recognized my childish naïveté and sent me home.

Our family never suffered absolute poverty, but many families did. One day at school, I saw a boy who looked undernourished and ill. He was shivering from the cold and never played with the rest of the boys. I was warm with a wool sweater handmade by Aunt Ann. "Would you like to have my sweater?" He looked at me, wide-eyed, and took it gladly. The next day he said, "My mother wants you to come home with me this afternoon. She wants to meet you." I went with him after school to his house. It was a dilapidated wooden shack with holes rotted in the floor. His mother was a widow with seven children, and they all lived together in that one room. I was rattled by their extreme poverty. Their makeshift beds were lumpy burlap bags filled with straw. I sat on a wooden bench in the corner, and the mother came over to me with a heart-warming smile. "You are a very good boy. Thank you." When I got home, I told Mama about giving my sweater away, and asked if I could take some candy for the family. She smiled warmly at my generosity and gave me a big bag of candies to give to the boy the next day.

Mama would always talk openly with me about sex and women's reproductive health. She treated me more like an adult than a child and would share shocking stories and gossip with me. As she could never share with Papa, perhaps I was his replacement. One day, when I was seven, she said, "I have something to show you, Robert." She had a serious look and told me it was a "lehrreich," which means "rich learning." Mama took me into the basement and showed me a shoe box. When she opened it, there was a dead baby inside. I could see it was a girl and was aghast to see the body was a dark commingling of red and blue in colour. I felt saddened, but Mama said, "The baby didn't suffer. The woman who rents one of our upstairs rooms lost the baby, and tonight her husband will take it to the morgue and sneak it into one of the coffins." I was a little baffled by how nonplussed Mama was while telling me this, holding the box with the dead baby in her arms. "This is part of your education, Robert, to know these things." Mama's education for me started early, and in later years I appreciated her openness. When my first child was born, I was able to help with the birth, and understood the labour and delivery due to my Mama's efforts to provide me with "lehrreich." Of course, I was also taught a rich amount about life by my beautiful aunties who coddled and spoiled me. One of the prostitutes, Edith, looked just like the actress Marlene Dietrich. I noticed that she always went to high mass on Sunday at St. Bonifatius. I found that curious, as it seemed to be counterintuitive to her profession. One day I asked her, "Tante Edith, why do you go to high mass?" She looked at me, her enchanting blue eyes filled with amusement. "Because, little Robert, I find my best customers there!"

One night I was having a bath in the kitchen in our portable tin bathtub, when Mama noticed deep purple bruises on my bottom. "Where did you get those bruises?" Reluctantly, I told her. "The teacher beat me with a bamboo stick." She looked at me sternly. "What did you do?" I was embarrassed but had to confess. "...I pinched a girl's bum." Mama tried to stifle her laughter. I had an overwhelming crush on Edeltraut Funke, a girl in my class. She had long, blonde braids, and had the most lovely rounded bottom. In my youthful unworldliness, I just couldn't resist pinching it. Mama surprised me with her lack of anger. "That teacher was too severe. I'm going to make a complaint." I was absolutely horrified by the notion of this. It would just make things worse for me at school. "Please, Mama, don't do that," I begged. She finally agreed not to complain, and I was greatly relieved. Oma also saw the bruises and saved me once again with her ingenuity. She really was my guardian angel. Oma took a thick patch from an old Ulster winter coat and sewed it into my pants. Now I was well protected against future beatings with the dreaded bamboo cane. Both Oma and I knew there would likely be more beatings because of my impulsive and mischievous ways.

I was always eager to learn more about our family. One day I asked Mama about Papa's family, the Schulte-Middelmanns. "Papa's father, Theodor, was a wealthy farmer who owned a hotel, bowling alley, pub, and restaurant in Herne-Sodinggen. They were a devout trips, cooked meals over the fire, and told stories around the campfire at night. I made friends in the Hitler Youth, but I felt sick to my stomach when anti-Semitic songs were sung with lyrics such as, "Wenn das Judenblut vom Messer spritzt dann gehts nochmal so gut." In English that is, "When the Jewish blood runs off our swords, things will be twice as good." In order to keep my secret, I would pretend to mouth these vile words. Luckily, I was a popular boy, which helped ensure that my secret heritage would not be discovered. As a member of the Hitler Youth, I passed for a strong and athletic Aryan boy that could always make the others laugh with my silly jokes.

At age 11, I was still a prankster and drove my mother crazy. Neighbours complained to her about my outlandish behaviour. In addition to dealing with my tomfoolery, she was overworked and always exhausted. Papa and Mama were constantly fighting, and she could never escape his terrible fits of rage. One day, I must have done one prank too many, and Mama's patience was pushed over the edge. She began to cry and then she screamed at me, "I wish you had died when you fractured your skull!" It felt as though an electric charge had just rocketed down my spine, and I stood there, dumbstruck. In my state of hurt, I thought with certainty, "I don't have a mother anymore." There was a powerful sense of loss, but also an equally powerful sense that I now had to be strong and independent. What Mama said that day could never be unsaid and changed our relationship for the rest of our lives. I felt a deep bitterness towards her. Any real consanguinity I had with my mother died that day. Indeed, it confirmed my longstanding suspicions that I was an unwanted child who she viewed as just another burden. I had been abandoned by Leo, who never showed any fatherly feelings toward me. Now I found myself emotionally abandoned by my mother. My loyalty was to Otto, who loved me as a father. Leo was still working for Papa and would stay in the evenings to discuss politics with Oma. Whenever he was near, I could see that Mama would blush and seem to glow. She behaved like a newly infatuated teenage girl and it made me feel ashamed. When Papa was there, she would have a bitter and hard look on her face that radiated vibes of animosity toward him. Oma was the only one I could truly trust, and the only emotional insurance I had when all others had failed me.

Papa always wanted me to aspire to improve myself and to become a refined and scholarly gentleman. However, that was the furthest thing from my mind. I just wanted to hang out with my friends, make mischief, and have adventures. Sports were a passion for me, and I won many long-distance races in my Hitler Youth group. Music enthralled me, but I had no interest in learning how to play an instrument. Of course, Papa had other ideas. One summer day, a fine violin arrived at our door with a handsome gypsy who was desperate to help his mother. He told Papa that his mother was ill and in a Catholic hospital, but they were going to move her where she wouldn't receive such good care. If he was able to pay them, she could stay where she was, and he was willing to sell his precious violin for the sake of his mother. In his hands he tenderly held a beautiful violin, the wood gleaming golden in the sun. "It is a very fine connections moved to England, Holland, and the United States. They all lost their business licences and had to sell at a great loss.

There was an international agreement that each Jewish family could send one child by kindertransport to England. Many families did this, finding it hard to decide which child to send away. It was such an impossible and terrible decision for one to make. It reminds me of the book by William Styron, "Sophie's Choice," where she is told by a SS officer that she can save only her little son or her daughter, and she must choose. If she doesn't choose, he will kill them both. Some Jewish fathers we knew escaped to Switzerland. They left their families behind believing, falsely, that a highly cultured nation like Germany would not harm women and children. If only that had been true.

There was a major change in the school system that was suddenly enacted. Catholic and Protestant schools were eliminated, and there were now only public schools. Our new teachers spread hateful vitriol during classes. The crucifix in our class was replaced by a large portrait of Adolph Hitler. It became much more difficult for me in school to behave with any normalcy. I had to live two lives, a false public one, and my true self at home with my family. At school I had to pretend to be a Nazi follower, say "Heil Hitler," and sing all the Nazi songs. I had to be vigilant at every moment and never make a slip. It was a despondent time for me. My biological father was murdered by the Nazis, and the father that was raising me was a violent and sick man. I felt that I no longer had a mother. It was a formidable world, and I no longer felt safe anywhere except with Oma, who was my safe nest in this world gone mad.

Otto and Anna Maria Schulte-Middelmann 1915

Robert one year old 1928

Oma with her Grandchildren in front of her house on Muhlenstrase 1931, L to R - Else, Elsbeth, Robert, Trudi

Robert's first excursion by train 1930

boy, I believed that Hitler would soon lose the war. Also, I was still a devout Catholic at this time, and believed that God would protect us. Oma was my spiritual mentor and taught me that evil never wins out. I dreaded returning to school where I had to pretend to be a counterfeit of myself, a boy who feigned to love Hitler. The next day, my teacher made an announcement. "The final battle has begun, and our victory over Judaism is on the horizon." We were all assembled in the school yard and were told to sing the National Anthem along with the new Nazi national anthem, "die Fahne hoch", which means "raise the Swastika flag." I remember having an intense revelation that my life had changed forever, and that I needed to be tenacious to survive this new and treacherous world.

An order came to arrest all Polish men. Sadly, one of our neighbours, 19-year-old Josef Jostalski, was arrested on his way to work at the coal mine. He was born in Herne, but his father never applied for German citizenship. In jail, they told him that if he became a German citizen, he could get out of jail and join the army. He readily signed the papers to secure his freedom. Two years later, he lost his life in Russia. He was admirable, steadfast, and far too young to die. Nevertheless, so many young men of good heart were dying for Hitler's war. If he had refused to sign, he would have ended up in a concentration camp. We heard of many who met this fate. In the pubs in Herne, there were large signs on the wall saying, "POLNISCH PRECHEN VERBOTEN." The Polish language was now forbidden to be spoken in public everywhere in Germany.

Later in life, I realized how much worry and stress my mother must have endured over my Jewish heritage and the need to keep it secret. My parents would have done anything to protect me. The only person outside the family who was aware of my background was Frau Israel. She is the one that I overheard asking Mama when she was going to tell me that Leo was my real father when I was four. Over the years, I became aware that Mama was being blackmailed by her to keep the secret. Frau Israel would often visit Mama and receive pork roasts, chocolates, and many other items that we had acquired from the black market. It seemed to me that she gave her so many of our resources that it was beyond regular generosity or friendship. I also wondered what other neighbours thought about our family's dealings with Frau Israel, and if they wondered about my paternity because of it. Papa was very small in stature at 4 ft 8 inches. My mother was not tall, either. And yet, I had grown to six feet by the time I was 12. Uncle Leo had been the tall, handsome, and charismatic family friend and employee. He was a known womanizer and bedded many married women in Herne. I wonder if neighbours ever put two and two together and came up with Robert. I'll never know. Mama had to give up a lot of our food to ensure that our secret was never revealed.

Papa's rages were becoming more unpredictable and deadly. Anything could set him off, and then we had to escape his attention at all costs to avoid his wrath. One day we were all working in the candy factory and Papa went into a rage, picked up a 30 lb bag of sugar, and hurled it right at Mama. We were distracted and missed the tell-tale warning signal of his emerging tongue. By this time, I had started trying to protect Mama from being beaten. I would hold Papa back by restraining him with all the strength I could possibly muster so that Mama could run and hide. We had to be vigilant all the time. One minute Papa would be sitting quietly at the piano playing Beethoven, and the next minute he would be in a rage, projecting his anger physically unto us. This was almost a daily event, and we became so used to it that it seemed normal. But, of course, it wasn't normal. However, it was indeed our normal. Papa's rages were also sometimes aimed at our staff, customers, and even the police. Whenever he ended up incarcerated for assaulting and seriously injuring others, he would repent by being a model prisoner and would be released early for good behaviour. One of the worst assaults that I witnessed happened when I was three. A bailiff came to our house to confiscate our couch, because Papa had refused to pay his taxes. Papa's tongue came out, he moved the couch away from the wall, grabbed the poor bailiff, and threw him behind the couch. Then, to my horror, Papa smashed the couch against the wall repeatedly, breaking the bailiff's ribs and seriously injuring him. Screaming in agony, the bailiff stumble-ran out of the house as best as he was able in his traumatized state. The police soon arrived, and Papa went to jail for assault. The police were always at our house, which influenced my great distaste for authority.

Every night, our family would gather around the radio and listen to BBC London and Radio Moscow. We knew how dangerous this was, but we had a deep need to learn what was actually happening in the war, rather than listen to the Nazi propaganda. It was announced that anyone listening to a foreign radio station was guilty of treason, a crime punishable by death. I realize now the extraordinary amount of courage that Oma, Papa, and Mama had in order to defy this order. Many Nazi sympathizers reported their neighbours for violating such laws, and for speaking against the Nazis. They could then be declared "enemies of the state" and sent straight to the gallows. I knew how to keep our family secrets and never spoke of what we heard on the radio. Radio Moscow often expressed more dark humour than the British. When Chamberlain, as Britain's Minister of Foreign Affairs, signed the agreement to give Czechoslovakia to Germany, Radio Moscow commented that he should have been a pastor in a remote country village. When we tuned into the BBC, we would hear the Morse code for the letter "V", for victory, and then, "This is London Calling," in German. Those times under the woolen blanket gathered around Oma's radio were some of the only times in my childhood when I felt our family was united. Ironically, sharing a common enemy brought our dysfunctional family together in solidarity each night. Otherwise, the air around us was fraught with resentment and violence.

The air raids started in 1939. The targets were mostly industrial sites. Every city in Germany built air raid shelters with steel enforced concrete. One was built just a block from our home by French prisoners of war (POW, for short) and tradesmen from Italy. I was a curious child and loved meeting people from other countries and learning new languages. Soon, I was doing shopping for the Italian tradesmen. As the Italians were allies, I could do that without fearing reprisal. However,

I also networked with the French POW's despite the harsh consequences dealt to any German who fraternized with the French. My curiosity carried heavier influence than my fear. All citizens were living on ration books, but our family had good connections, and I was able to sneak some food to the French prisoners who were virtually starving. They were grateful for my help, and I quickly picked up French from speaking with them.

Once a month, the French POW's were given coupons and taken by bus to the brothel in Bochum. The guards were easy-going, and I could bribe them with chocolate in order to bring food to the French. Easter was coming, and I felt sympathy towards them for being imprisoned away from their families. I wondered what I could do to give them a treat for Easter. I asked Mama, and we came up with a plan to boil an egg for each of the 30 prisoners. Then, I would sneak into their changing room and put an egg in each pair of clogs. They left their clogs in the changing room when they put on their work boots necessary for working on the construction site. On Good Friday, I had effectively played my part as the Easter bunny. I was happy to think how pleased they would be when they went to put on their clogs. Eggs were precious and highly valued at the time. The French prisoners were very grateful for the aid they received from my family. One of the prisoners with whom I was closer to painted a special watercolour portrait of me at age 13 that I still have to this day. It hangs on my wall as a reminder of our friendship. Later on, my kindness toward these prisoners saved me from a long prison term in France. In the spring of 1941, I graduated from grade eight. By then, I could communicate in French, Italian,

Polish, Dutch, and German. The government ordered that everyone who had reached the age of 14 must help Germany by becoming part of the work force. Many boys and girls went into the coal mines or the factories. I was lucky, as I could work in my family's candy factory. This was a great relief to me, as I dreaded going into the coal mines. The black market was now booming due to the shortages of food, clothing, tobacco, and other coveted items. My family was well connected with many other businesses, and we could obtain needed items by trading. Candy and chocolate were not widely available, but were highly desired, so we were in a beneficial position to barter. The almost nightly air raids had become a way of life. That summer, I volunteered for the Hitler Youth Harvest Camp to work on a farm near the village of Mantinghausen. I enjoyed the hard work and made friends with the other boys. One day, we went to the village and a friend took a photo of me in my Hitler Youth uniform. When I saw the photo I thought, "Swastika on the outside and Star of David on the inside."

My secret was still safe. In the fall, I volunteered to be on the Hitler Youth Rescue Team. We reported to the police station at 8pm twice a week. We had all been trained in first aid as a part of being in the Hitler Youth. One time in particular, we helped a family by saving their furniture from a burning house. We were proud of our work to help others. Almost everyone went to the air raid shelters at night to sleep. Mama told me that sometimes babies were born in the shelters. My family all went to the shelter, but I decided I wanted to sleep in my own bed and refused to go. Mama pleaded with me, but I was adamant in my decision. I firmly believed I would survive the war and didn't want to be stuck in a claustrophobia-inducing bomb shelter with so many others when I could sleep peacefully in my own bed instead. For years, I slept right through the bombings and woke up refreshed and rested.

Looters were shot on the spot by patrolling police. It was becoming clear that the morale of the German people was now quite low. Neighbours were spying on each other to gain favor with authorities. There was a palpable climate of fear and paranoia. Jewish families, communists, and foreigners were all being sent to concentration camps. Life in Herne was completely unrecognizable now compared to the Herne in which I was born. You couldn't trust anyone, and you had to be constantly on your guard. In the summer of 1941, the unbelievable happened. Germany invaded Russia. We thought that Hitler had lost his mind and would now lose the war. Food rations became starvation rations. Even our family, with all its connections, was finding it difficult to gather enough food to survive. Mama came up with a daring plan. If she was caught, she would be labelled an "enemy of the people" and sent to a concentration camp, or worse. Her plan was to buy one pig every week from a cattle agent for a black market price and slaughter the pig in our basement. She knew that if she did this at night, when the bombs were dropping and the anti aircraft cannons sounded, that the squeals of the pig would not be heard by listening ears.

Mama recruited me to help her. We slaughtered a pig every week and had no problem selling the meat the next day. Now we had enough food for our family, and we could help our friends who were starving as well. There was a very high risk of being caught, but my mother was a clever woman in addition to being a brave one. We weren't close, but I respected her daring and intelligence. We often engaged in long talks about life, love, sex, history, and politics. I felt sorry for Mama because she had a loveless marriage. One day I asked her, "Mama, have you ever been loved?" She gave me a long look. "Yes, Robert, before you were born, there was a salesman who worked for us. His name was Bergmann. We fell in love and met secretly. We even went away for a week to the summer resort, Bestwig. Frau Israel also had a secret lover, and they would join us there." "What happened?" Mama looked sad as she reminisced. "It all ended when Otto got a hint of what was happening and fired him immediately." I was happy to know that at least Mama had experienced real love at some point in her life.

A special midnight mass was always held on Christmas Eve at St. Bonifatius, the church I faithfully attended. I was a devout Catholic, like my Oma, and was even an altar boy. It was a forlorn and depressing time in Germany. Many sons, brothers, and fathers were dying in Russia as a result of Hitler's megalomania. We personally knew countless families who had lost loved ones. Christmas Eve, 1941, I was on my way to mass when I ran into some older boys. They asked me to come with them to visit the local brothel, Im Winkel, which was in the neighbouring city of Bochum. With my usual imprudence, I decided to skip mass and join them. Growing up with so many benevolent and loving prostitutes who had treated me like family had left me with a great curiosity about brothels. Here was my chance to satisfy my curiosity. In front of the brothel there was a large sign, "Eintritt Fuer Deutsche Verboten." That translated to, "This brothel is off limits for Germans." The prostitutes were from France and were there to service foreigners only. Additionally, you had to be 18 to enter, and I was only 14. However, I was quite tall for my age, and spoke fluent French thanks to the French POW's I had befriended. All the other boys, who were actually older than me, were turned away because they only spoke German. By dangling a cigarette from my lips and standing very tall, I was able to bluff my way into the brothel. I was already trying to appear older than I was with my Humphrey Bogart hat and a royal blue long winter coat. That outfit helped me effortlessly fool the patrolling policemen who were making sure that Germans did not enter the French brothel.

Inside the brothel, there were five different women who offered their services. I noticed a woman with dark and curly hair who was dressed in an enticing two-piece black bathing suit and was smiling charmingly at me. She had a perfect figure, large breasts, and long, shapely legs. I fancied her above the rest, and she told me her name was Christine. "I'm only 14," I blurted out nervously. She smiled tenderly. "Who cares, I'm 36, come with me." She took me into a room, held out her hand, and told me to pay five marks. I was feeling a bit bolder now. "I'll give you ten if we can both be in the nude." Christine seemed extremely amused by this naïve yet charismatic young boy. She agreed and examined my penis for any discharge or symptoms of transmittable diseases. After that, she washed my genitals in a small bowl with soap that consisted of purple crystals with antiseptic qualities that were dissolved in the warm water. Christine then disrobed and washed her pubic area. I was impressed by her rigorous cleanliness routine and intrigued. She seemed to be humoured by this curious and blithesome young boy.

Christine became my tutor in the sexual arts. Afterwards, I asked her to tell me about herself. "I'm from Bordeaux. My mother thinks that I work in a factory here in Bochum. I make good money and I send my mother enough for her to survive." We chatted a bit, and then Christine gave me an appraising glance. "You are a tall young man. When you grow up, you can become a great man like Hitler." She said this in such a way that I could clearly see she was merely saying what might be expected from a German boy and was veiling her disgust for Hitler's regime. I took a chance and spoke my own truth to her. "I'm antifascist and I resist the Nazis as much as I can." She made it clear that she was pleasantly surprised and delighted by my reply. "I'll be back next week, Christine," I announced enthusiastically. "All right, Robert, I'll see you then," she replied, with a sweet smile. In 1941, I chose to spend that Christmas Eve with the enchanting Christine instead of attending my traditional midnight mass.

That night changed my life and launched me into a blissfully clandestine adventure. I decided that I would save my money all week so that I could spend Saturday evenings at the brothel. The fact that these ladies were French only enriched this escapade of mine, as I had long been fascinated by French culture and their language. Every Saturday night for the next year, I would arrive at the brothel with my ten marks, having told my parents that I was going to the movies. All week I waited with great anticipation for Saturday night to come. The police never caught on to who I really was, a 14-year-old German disguised as a Frenchman. If I didn't make the ten marks during the week, I would steal one of my Mama's salami sausages and bring that with me instead. For my first six visits there, I chose to be with Christine, but then I became braver and began to request the services of the other women. They were all beautiful and gracious women who seemed to be quite charmed by my eagerness and youth. They all loved Mama's sausages, and I became quite a hit at the brothel. I would also take them candies which I would sometimes give as a tip for their services. They became quite fond of me, and I was learning a great deal from these lovely French ladies of the night, as well as improving my fluency in French.

In order to become even more fluent in French, I found a tutor named Erik Finkler who gave me private lessons. He previously taught in the school that was entirely secular and without religion. Communists, socialists, and Jews would send their children to that school. When Hitler seized power in 1933, these schools were shut down and the teachers had their licences revoked. They lost their professions and were desperate to find work in order to survive. Mr. Finkler soon discovered my talent for languages and added English and Latin to my lessons. I progressed quickly in all my classes. "Why don't you enroll in the academic program, Robert?" I had wanted to do this, but thought that I had missed my chance, as you had to apply at age ten to attend high school. High school, in Germany, was somewhat comparable to choosing University over a tradesman career.

Mr. Finkler was tutoring high school students. "Robert, within a year I could bring you up to their level." Papa gave me time off work to study. He was proud of my effort and wanted me to be more educated. His dream was that I would one day take over the management of the candy factory and handle all of the accounts and administrative tasks. However, this was not my dream. Instead, I wanted to join the merchant marine. On the day of my high school admissions exam, I excelled in French, Latin, and English, but I failed German. This may seem strange, but I had learned German from my Oma, who spoke a mix of Dutch, Ruhr German, and a dialect from Cologne. I also was unable to pass Algebra, a subject I had always struggled with. These failures were devastating to me, but I decided to try again and study even harder than before. I was determined to get into high school.

In 1942, Jews were rounded up and moved into buildings that were off limits to non-Jews. In the winter of that year, the first involuntary transport of Jews was sent to Libau, Latvia, for what was called "resettlement." The news soon leaked out all of them were callously machine-gunned down by Latvian SS upon their arrival. Some of my friends were among the mindlessly executed. The entire Blumental family, the parents and three children, was massacred. Mr. Blumental was our local butcher, who was a magnanimous man who gave away surplus meat to the poor and extended credit to many. His son, Heinz, was one of my close friends. There was one group of Jews left to go with the last exodus from Herne to Riga. I began going to the Jewish building almost nightly to take them food. The building was originally for four families, but now housed 12 families crammed into tight quarters. Jews had ration books, but it only supplied half of the food that the non-Jews' ration books provided. They were starving, and I knew I had to take the risk of going there to help these desperate families survive. I also helped by going out and selling their belongings for them in order to secure some money for them.

My family had always helped others when they could with food and other necessities. There was one family, the Rosenbergs, that I was particularly fond of. Mr. Rosenberg had been a decorated hero in World War I and had received the Iron Cross medal for bravery. He and his wife had four children, a daughter, and three younger brothers. Mr. Rosenberg had been arrested on Kristallnacht and sent to Oranienburg concentration camp. A few months later, he was miraculously released, and knew he had to leave Germany in order to save his life. He made it to Britain and joined the British forces to fight the Nazis. There was an international agreement that decreed that one child of every Jewish family could go on the "kindertransport" to England to be placed with foster parents. The Rosenbergs had an impossible choice to make. They chose their middle child, Karl, who was 12 at the time. They believed that he was old enough to still remember the family, while young enough to be able to adapt to the new environment. It was a monstrous choice for any parent to forced to make. Karl was fortunate and was assigned to loving foster parents. He joined the military cadets and later ended up in the Jewish Legion, a unit in the British army, and served under Field Marshall Montgomery. Sixty-three years later, we would meet again in Australia.

The daughter, Irene, was a great beauty and well-known as a talented dancer. She was spirited, brave, and I found her enchanting. We became close, and soon I was hopelessly infatuated. I was 15, and Irene was two years older and much more sophisticated. She didn't take me seriously at all and thought of me more like a younger brother. I was desperate to save her, and asked Mama if she would be willing to hide her in our home. My mother wanted to do this but knew that anyone caught providing refuge to Jews would be executed. It would put our whole family at risk. In the end, Irene's mother made the decision. "It is an impossible situation. If Irene is missing, our whole family will be hung by the Nazis." So, Irene had to go on the transport with her family. There was no other option, and there was nothing I could do to influence the situation. It was absolutely heartbreaking for me. I felt powerless and terribly sad.

It wasn't until later that I discovered the truth about these "resettlements." In reality, they were all sent to the Riga concentration camp. Mama and I brought them woolen blankets and non-perishable food for the long train trip. We stayed with them until late at night. Before we left, Irene said, "Robert, I give you this as a goodbye present, so that you will remember me." It was an empty bottle of "Jardin de Paris" in the shape of the Eiffel tower. Irene's mother pointed to a large framed portrait on the wall. It was her husband, seated on a horse, as a high-ranking German officer in WWI. "I want the SS to get a good hard look at that," she said bitterly. At 4:00 a.m., the SS came with trucks to take all 12 families away. We knew in our hearts that we would never see them again. It was around that same time that Frau Israel passed away. She had blackmailed my mother to keep my paternal lineage a secret for the past 15 years. Otto finally said to me, bitterly, "She is taking our secret into the grave. I had to support two families all these years, mine and hers. I never asked Mama, but I understood what was going on."

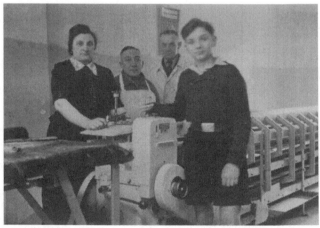

Robert's parents, uncle Fritz and Robert in the candy factory 1940, inauguration of the latest machine from Magdeburg

Robert and his Mother 1941

Robert in uniform, Hitler Youth 1941

*Drawing of Robert (14 yrs old) by a French
Prisoner of War, 1941*

The French Prisoner of War on the left, Louis Le Blanc, who drew the portrait of Robert

CHAPTER 5

I was determined to do whatever I could to fight the Nazis and made alliances with a few others to form a youth resistance group. These groups, called Edelweisspiraten, were forming all over Austria and Germany. They supported the allies, assisted deserters from the German army, and were opposed to the Nazi regime. Piraten stands for "pirates" in English. In order to show we were members of this group, we boldly wore a small metal pin of the flower. Hans and I were in the Hitler Youth and had become friends. We pinned the Edelweiss flower on to our ski hat, which was part of our Hitler Youth uniform. We placed it right next to the swastika pin, so that it would be hidden in plain sight. It was a reckless and precarious gesture, but it made us feel brave and confident. Ours was a small group of five, but we were whole-heartedly dedicated to making life difficult for the Nazis. Hans, who was also half-Jewish, Simon and Gilbert, who were French, and Ria, a French girl of Czech parentage who worked as an interpreter. We were all young, but I was the youngest at 15.

It was riveting to finally be making plans to fight against the Nazis. We met every night at the Zur Klause, which was a pub close to the railway station on Main Street. After a couple of weeks, two Gestapo agents came into the pub and demanded our identification papers. I happened to be sitting at the next table to the others and the Gestapo didn't realize I was part of the group. They took me outside for questioning. "What are you doing hanging around foreigners?" I knew I had to bluff my way out of this dicey predicament. "I'm a high school student, and I want to improve my French." They saw from my ID that I was a member of the Hitler Youth, and that seemed to appease them enough to ease up on me. One of them gave me a warning, "We'll let you go this time, but don't let us catch you with foreigners again." That was when we decided to move to an obscure little cafe at the far end of the town to exchange news and make our plans. It felt fulfilling to plot against the fascists and find ways to show our resistance, as if we were born to do so.

I didn't let my parents know what I was doing, because I knew they would try to stop me, despite sharing the same beliefs. We made posters by hand in my bedroom. They had antiwar slogans like, "NIEDER MIT HITLER," which was "Down with Hitler!" Additionally, we wrote "SCHLUSS MIT DEM KRIEG RETTET EUCH!" which translated to, "End the War and Save Yourselves!" We wrote about the concentration camps and how innocent people were sent to die there. We then went out at night during the blackout and hung these posters all over town. People were allowed to be out on the streets during blackout. There was no curfew. We knew how hazardous it was to be putting up these posters, but we didn't care. With the arrogance and innocence of youth, we believed we could outsmart the enemy. And we did. The posters were in rolls hidden under our coats. We had wire to tie the posters to the bars over the store windows. We hung the posters in haste when no one could be detected nearby and took off running when the job was done.

The posters were not representative of the full extent of our insurrection. We also painted these slogans on the last streetcar, which would be the first one out in the morning and carry our message to the masses. This was far more dangerous, and there was a bigger risk of being caught. In one of our planning sessions, we decided to burn down the Hitler Youth Office. Hans and I volunteered for the mission. We had been forced to be part of the Hitler Youth and were both half-Jews. This would be our poetic revenge. We bought two cans of gasoline in a service station and went to the location with Simon. He waited nearby to keep watch. We were pleasantly surprised to find the main door had been accidentally left unlocked. Hans and I entered and went in different directions to splash the gasoline throughout the building. When we came out, and everything was thoroughly saturated, Simon threw a flaming torch into the building. We then ran like Jesse Owens himself, and I looked back to see the whole building engulfed in flames. It burned completely and satisfyingly to the ground. Perhaps of no relation, it was subsequently announced that wearing the Edelweiss pin was illegal, and Hans and I reluctantly removed them from our hats.

By word of mouth, we learned that there was going to be a gathering of youth resistance groups in Essen in the fall of 1942. Under the guise of it being a music festival, the Edelweisspiraten members gathered in Essen to connect with each other secretly and gain strength. I went with Hans and Ria to the festival. The music itself was a rebellion on its own, as the lyrics were all about peace and solidarity. We felt we were part of something bigger than the confines of our group, and that others also wanted peace as much as we did. Many of us discreetly made fun of Hitler whenever we could get away with it safely. One joke making the rounds was about two Austrians looking at a globe. Rudy asks, "What are all those pink areas?" Josef replies, "Those are England and all her colonies." "And what about those purple areas?" "Those are France and her colonies." "Well, what is that great big green area?" "That's Canada." "Okay, and what about that enormous orange area?" "That's Russia." At this point Rudy pointed at a tiny brown spot on the globe. "...and this little thing?" Franz replied, "That is Germany!" Rudy became pensive with his eyes darting side to side and then very quietly whispers, "...Do you think Hitler knows?" Then we would all share a good laugh. If you were caught telling such a joke, however, you would be sent to a concentration camp. We did it regardless, as it was one of our small acts of rebellion and defiance.

When we returned from Essen, we discovered that Simon and Gilbert had been arrested by the Gestapo. The waitress in the cafe where we would meet told us that the Gestapo came in and took our friends away. They were sent to the Buchenwald concentration camp. The gravity of the consequences we would face if we were also caught began to sink in. Soon after I returned, Papa discovered the protest posters in my bedroom and two revolvers that I had hidden there. He confronted me with conflicted emotions. "I am proud of your spirit and ideals, but this is dangerous. If the Nazis find out, they will take the whole family away to a concentration camp or worse." Papa took the handguns and made me burn the posters. In order to break the spirit of the rebellious German youth, the government opened detention camps for youth who were thought to be lacking loyalty to the

Nazi movement. It was a brutal boot camp and your head would be shaved to humiliate and dehumanize you. Some of my acquaintances were sent there for punishment. I personally managed to avoid being caught, as I had learned throughout my childhood to present a false mask to the world in order to survive.

At 15, I was not only leading the life of an active member of the fascist resistance, but I had fallen deeply in love. I had hidden this from my parents, as I knew they would say I was too young. It was the fearless Ria who had captured my wild heart. She was 19, born in Lille, France, of Czechoslovakian immigrants. On our first meeting, she proudly showed me that she had been a card-carrying member of the French Communist Youth. Ria was uncommonly beautiful, with high cheek bones, light brown hair, and a self-confident manner. Her accent was intoxicating and unique, a mix of French and Slavic tones. She was petite, but physically strong and maintained a powerful presence. I admired her passion and dedication to our cause. On our second meeting with the group, she took a small mirror out of her purse to touch up her lipstick. "See my mirror." She turned it over. "You can even write on the back of it." I took the mirror and instantly wrote on the back "Je t'aime, Robert" as I slipped it back in her purse. The next night, I picked her up at the train station as she came from Castrop, a town that was 15 km away. She had a sly grin and said, in a teasing way, "Did I show you my mirror yet?" She then handed it to me, looking at me with bright and smiling eyes, and I saw that she had written "Moi je t'aime aussi." We both looked at one another and relished in the powerful bond that was developing between us. That is how Ria became my first real love. I fell deeply, madly, and passionately in love with this brave, beautiful, and delightfully unusual French woman.

This was one of the most exhilarating, thrilling, and jeopardous times of my life. Ria and I were in love, risking our lives daily to show our resistance to the Nazis. We were in the throes of madness, a madness of love and of fighting for a noble but potentially fatal cause. As soon as I could sneak away, I took the train to Castrop to be with Ria. She had a small attic room which she rented from a family. We made love for hours, revelling in this new-found passion we shared. I took the last train home in a state of indescribable euphoric bliss. Oma was still up, because she could never sleep soundly until I came home. She lied to Papa, saying that I came home shortly after he went to bed at 10 p.m., even though I didn't get home until after two in the morning. Oma knew what was going on, but never said a word. I took every chance I could to see Ria. Eventually, Mama became suspicious. I had always told my good friend, Hans, about my life, so naturally I had told him about my love for Ria and about our secret meetings. Hans was 18 and was likewise infatuated with Ria. I didn't realize that he was upset that an upstart 15-year-old like me had beaten him to this French beauty. I was unaware of his jealousy and what it might possess him to do. He did the unthinkable and told my mother everything that was going on. It was the ultimate betrayal. Every time I shared with him about my beautiful love affair, he would relay every single word to my mother, when all along I had believed him to be my confidante.

A few weeks later, Mama informed me she knew all about Ria and had told Papa. At the time, I didn't know who had betrayed me. Papa came in and spoke firmly. "If you get her pregnant, that child will be entitled to inherit from your estate." Of course, Papa always thought of the money first. I was busted with no room for denial. They told me that I now had a curfew of 9 p.m., to which I reluctantly agreed. It was the only time in my life that I saw my parents in agreement. Now, I had to figure out a plan on how to weasel around the restriction of this curfew. I had to think long and hard to overcome this obstacle. Nothing was going to stop me from seeing Ria. I remembered that I had established a friendly partnership with some farmers that I had worked for when I was 13. Mr. and Mrs. Hoppe lived near Guetersloh, about 150 km away from Herne. I told my parents that I was going to visit the Hoppe family and stay with them for three days. My plan was that I would stay one night, and then I would still have two nights to go to Castrop to be with my beloved Ria. My ingenious plan was successful.

Because I loved to learn new languages, I was intrigued by Ria who spoke fluent French, Czech, Russian, German, and Polish. She worked in Castrop and Herne as an interpreter in factories which used slave workers from other countries. I took any chance I could to see her. We became closer and talked about a future together in a free country some day. She told me about her childhood, and that her father and uncle had both fought against Franco in Spain. We spent time walking and sharing our dreams of toppling the Nazi regime. I told her about my parent's unhappy marriage, my estrangement from my mother, and my unshakable love for my dearest Oma. I had come to trust Ria completely and decided to tell her that I was the result of my mother's affair with a Polish Jew. It was a profound relief to share the secret that had burdened me for so many years. I had never shared that secret with anyone else before. By now, I truly believed that Ria was to be my life partner. Other than Oma, I had never felt such a profound and deep connection with anyone as I did with Ria.

My clandestine meetings with Ria carried on for six ecstatic months. One day, however, Mama said, "Robert, I need you to go to the hardware store and get rat traps. Come back right away." This was perfect, because Ria's train was coming into Herne in half an hour, and the hardware store was right near the train station. I got the rat traps and ran breathlessly to the station. Ria was surprised and delighted to see me. "Let's go someplace quiet," I said. We went down into a tunnel below the tracks and walked arm and arm, kissing and hugging, delighted to have this unexpected gift of a meeting. Suddenly, I heard heavy and familiar footsteps in the tunnel. "That's my mother," I exclaimed, with a downtrodden heart. We turned to face her. "Don't you feel ashamed to be going with a 15-year-old boy?" Ria looked baffled. "He told me he was 18!" Then they both turned and looked at me, united in their frustration. I felt ganged up on with my mother and my girlfriend both glaring at me with annoyance. "Robert, I'm going home. I will see you there shortly." Mama walked away, at least giving me the chance to shamefully say goodbye to her by sending non-perishable food items and cigarettes to the prison guard who would bring it in for her. She could use these items to barter for what resources she needed. Every week I sent a parcel to the guard, including a pound of coffee and other items for the guard herself to show my gratitude for her help. During her time in jail, Ria made friends with a local woman who had been caught smuggling. They were released at around the same time, and she assisted Ria in getting across the border into Belgium.

Several weeks later, I received a letter from Liege, Belgium, stating that she was safe. She sent her love, and again wrote of our promise to meet when the war was over. I missed her terribly and dreamed longingly of the day when we would meet again. At least she was safe, and the Gestapo would not hurt her. Ria was a brave, intelligent, and fierce woman who was an unwavering survivor. She already had a false identity as a Belgian woman and had made alliances with several people who shared her political ideals. Our resistance group was very lucky that we were never caught in the act. Not all youth who resisted were quite so fortunate. Some were imprisoned, tortured, and hung. At the end of the war, I learned that Hans, Simon, and Gilbert had all miraculously survived Buchenwald. They were bright and resourceful young men who were determined to live. They survived by taking a job that was essential for the efficient running of the camp. It was a ghastly job that no one wanted, but my friends saw it as their only way of living to speak of the horror. The job was to transport all of the corpses to the crematorium. These were prisoners who had died of starvation, typhoid, dysentery, suicide, or were murdered by the guards. Hundreds of prisoners were dying every week. My friends knew that if they did this work, they would be given extra rations. It was a wretched job, but it kept them alive.

My relationship with the French prisoners of war continued to be a close one. Every day, I brought them news about the war which I had learned from listening to the forbidden foreign stations. One of the prisoners, Abel Cerilot, had become a good friend. He approached me one day and asked me to help him escape. "I need civilian clothes, Robert, and a map of Western Europe." I knew this was a risky endeavour, but I was determined to help him. I brought him my own pants, sweater, jacket, and one of my school maps. Soon, I heard that he had managed to escape. I didn't know until a year after the war ended that he had successfully made it back home. A letter arrived from Abel thanking me for my help and inviting me to visit him in France. I was happy to know that I had been able to help him return safely home.

The prisoners that remained were still building bomb shelters. The construction boss, Vincent Dickmann, gave me money to buy bread and meat on the black market for the workers. My family networked well, and I knew how to obtain the food. The French were grateful for my help. Many of the prisoners were smokers and were desperate for a smoke. They asked me if I could help them. Always wanting to assist, I devised a plan of how to do this. Albert was a man in his 80s who was renting an attic room in our house. He had a compulsion to collect cigarette butts in the street and had been doing this for years. His large closet was packed to the bomb shelter. Many nights I slept right through the bomb explosions and anti-aircraft canons without waking. My parents were worried for my safety, but with the infamous arrogance of youth, I believed I was invincible.

As a member of the Hitler Youth, I had to report to the police station once a week and stay the night there. We were part of a rescue team that would help people who were trapped in burning houses or buried in the rubble from the air raids. They had bunk beds for us, and the station also served as an underground bomb shelter. My family was happy that I was safe at least one night a week. On July 10th, my 16th birthday, I reported for duty. At 4:00 a.m., a bomb hit just across the street from our home. It obliterated every house on that side of the block. Our house was partially demolished as well, and the roof was completely gone. When I got home later, I found that a piece of the bomb had gone through the attic wall and cut straight through the middle of my bed. I felt I had cheated the devil again. The house directly across from ours was reduced to nothing but a pile of rubble. An elderly Polish couple lived there, and they had never gone to the shelter. We started digging there first, and I found an arm sticking out of the rubble. I thought it was Adam Figolla, the Polish gentleman who lived there. Two of us went over to help uncover him. We frantically cleared the rubble away from his arm, hoping that it wasn't too late to save him. I reached for his arm when the area around it had been cleared and pulled. The arm came easily, but it was not attached to his body. Adam's 14-year-old granddaughter, Lieselotte, was behind me. She screamed, "Opa! Opa!" and began to weep. I felt an incredible sadness for her that her Opa had died in such a gruesome fashion. We worked to clear the debris for the next eight hours and were finally able to rescue Mrs. Figolla. Physically, she only suffered a broken hip.

The house next door was four stories high and had been cleaved in two. Our long-time neighbour, Mrs. Ritterswuerden, was still in bed on the fourth floor. The bed was hanging precariously on the edge, ready to fall at any moment. She was crying for help, but it was a dangerous rescue. Our crew was composed of older men, young boys, and a group of Russian POW's. One of the young Russians said to the officer in charge, "For a bottle of Schnapps, I will go up and get her." The officer quickly agreed, and they put up an extension ladder that just barely reached the crumbling edge of the fourth floor. He was a strong man, and when he got to the top, he put Mrs. Ritterswuderden on his shoulder and brought her safely down. We found out later that five of our neighbours had been killed in the same air raid. They had all been sleeping in their beds, choosing not to go to the bomb shelter, just as I had done so many times before. I again thanked Lady Luck for watching out for me. It seemed as though I had a greater number of lives than a cat.

The house across the street were the bomb hit, there were 5 dead, 10th of July 1943

Robert's parents' house after the bombing on the 10th of july, 1943 (16th Birthday)

CHAPTER 6

Due to the extensive damage that our home had endured, we were forced to move into the factory until it was rebuilt. We were happy to have survived, and quickly adjusted to our new living quarters. Life went on, as they say. In August, all the students were evacuated to safer regions. Our school classes were sent to Treptow, which was a small rural town close to the Baltic Sea in Eastern Pomerania. I was excited about this new chapter of my life and wondered what Treptow would be like. My home life was unbearable, and I was always eager to escape. My only regret was that I couldn't bring my beloved Oma with me. The students and the staff
went by train to Treptow. When I arrived, I found that I was billeted with an elderly childless couple, the Raabs. They had a lovely house at 20 Schleusenweg, and they treated me like a son during my time there.

The local students went to school early in the day while the students from the Herne school went from 2 pm to 7 pm. We enjoyed the warm weather and close proximity to the coast. I loved the beach and the fluid serenity of the ocean. The Raabs gave me a key to the house and I could come and go whenever I wanted. My friends and I would meet and go to the movies together. We quickly discovered that there were plenty of girls who wanted to join us. There was a shortage of young men around, as they had all been drafted into the military. We took advantage of our new freedom and stayed out until all hours. I deeply missed Ria, but I was a passionate and hormonal teenager who wanted to have fun. We felt that there was no yesterday, no tomorrow, and instead lived for the moment, because we didn't know what the future held. I still loved Ria and hoped we would both be alive after the war and find each other again.

The town people soon made complaints about our rambunctious ways, and our school board enacted a curfew from 8 pm to 6 am. We were foiled at first, but my friend Eric and I soon found ways to weasel around the curfew. We disguised ourselves with hats so people wouldn't recognize us, and continued meeting girls and staying out late. Back home, my parents were worried sick about me, and every other day I would receive a letter and a 20 mark bill from Papa. Unfortunately, it was around this time that my smoking became an addiction. One day I was smoking in the school bathroom outside the main building, and got caught by Dr. Siebert, my Latin teacher. He was the most fanatical Nazi at our school. Dr. Siebert scowled at me and told me to follow him inside the school. My heart pounded in my chest and I thought I was in big trouble. He closed the door, and we were alone. It was recess time, and everyone else was outside. "Quickly, let me roll a cigarette." Apparently, he was simply dying for a smoke. My teacher was a fellow addict. I gave him half my tobacco and rolling papers and let out a sigh of great relief. I took off without saying a word. Saved again.

I began stopping at his home once a week to supply him with tobacco. What a funny thing, a Nazi and a Jew doing tobacco deals together because of their mutual addiction. In return, he tutored me in Latin, which I picked up rather quickly. The war was changing

Treptow. A garrison for Romanian army recruits was established at the outskirts of town. Dance halls were converted into military hospitals for wounded soldiers from the Russian front. French prisoners of war ran the barber shops, tailor shops, and worked in bakeries to serve the community. My fluency in French came in handy during this time. I quickly established friendly connections with several of the French prisoners. We started meeting in an attic above a barber shop in the evening, listening to BBC London in French, well aware of the looming danger. In order to keep the sound down, we used Oma's trick and covered our heads and the radio with blankets as we listened.

The people of Treptow were good-natured and treated all foreigners with respect and kindness. Unfortunately, however, their national pride did not allow them to question what Hitler and the Nazis were doing. They had great faith in him and were confident that Germany would win the war. The only information they received came from the propaganda machine in Berlin run by Dr. Josef Goebbels. He had a doctorate in Theology and had been educated by Jesuit monks. Goebbels was an evil genius who was so charismatic and manipulative that he was able to brainwash the people of Germany into believing that the Jews had to be exterminated. In October, orders came that the Herne students were to go to potato farms nearby to harvest the crops for a week. The barns were filled with women and elderly men from the town who worked the fields from sunup to sundown. Their daily diet was mainly small rations of potatoes, and they were exhausted and near starvation. It was back-breaking work, and some of the students had a difficult time doing as they were told. One week turned into three, but I managed to bribe my Latin teacher to say that Papa was ill, so that I would have an excuse to go home. The bribe cost me 100 grams of tobacco, but it was worth it to escape the potatoes. They let me go home for two weeks, and my parents and my beloved Oma were happy and surprised to see me. Dr. Siebert told me that I must get a doctor's letter stating that Papa was seriously ill enough to require my homecoming. That was easy to get, and only cost me a pound of coffee.

I had a lovely time at home being fussed over by Oma, but after a week I was restless and decided to spend the second week in Berlin. There I could escape the tension and violence at home and enjoy the alluring cosmopolitan beauty of Berlin. Not much time passed before I had become in love with this historic and fascinating city. Berliners have great wit and are open-minded toward people different from themselves. I felt at home there, and soon found that many headstrong Berliners had escaped Hitler's giant flock of sheep. It was a heady time for me in this exciting city that was frenetically living on the edge of disaster. I reluctantly returned to Treptow, and was there until a week before Christmas, 1943, when we were told that anyone born in 1927 and 1928 had to report to the anti-aircraft garrison in Bochum. We were allowed to go home and spend Christmas with our families, but we had to report to the garrison on January 5th, 1944. It sounded like fun to me, like another grand adventure. Of course, I didn't have the maturity to understand that this also meant that I would now be part of the war, and thus shooting down the Western allies. I would be helping Hitler's war effort and killing the very people that I wanted to win the war. The innocence and ignorance of youth.

We celebrated our Christmas as best we could. There was a pervasive feeling of sadness about the house, as we all knew that life was about to change for my family. Oma and my parents were worried about what the future would be for me but tried to put up a visage of optimism. During that time, I reflected on my childhood, my family, and my time in the youth resistance. I often thought of Ria and wondered if we would ever meet again to fulfill our dream of building a life together. By the time January 5th came, I could tell that the carefree and fun-loving Robert had evolved into a more serious and mature young man. I was no longer able to escape the sickening reality of this tragic war. How ironic it was; I would be forced to fight against those who stood for the same morals as myself. There seemed to be no way to escape what was to come. I was trapped without alternative options.

On January 5th, I said an emotional goodbye to my family. Oma was distraught and tears glistened in her eyes. She took out a wooden rosary on a chain and gently put it over my head and around my neck. "I gave this rosary to your Uncle Willie in 1914 when he went to war. I told him to bring it back, and he did. Now, I expect you to do the same." I felt honoured that Oma had given me this special rosary and hugged her, trying my best not to cry. Papa, too, had tears brimming in his eyes. "Look after yourself, Robert." Mama looked sad but shed no tears. She was a strong woman. Even though I no longer truly loved her, I respected her. While walking to the streetcar I wondered if I would ever see my family again, especially my beloved Oma. She was now 83 years of age. I wanted nothing more than for this damn war to end, so that I could come back to my Oma. When we arrived at the garrison, we received our air force uniforms, and trucks arrived to take us to our units. My unit was in a farmer's field near Recklinghausen.

The commanding officer was Bernhard Grimm, a young man from Munich. His name was ironic, because he was actually very jolly and friendly. Later on, I found out that he had studied for the priesthood before the war. He gave us a warm reception and helped to calm this unit of nervous 15 and 16-year-old kids. "Our job is to protect the Krupp factory in Bochum that is manufacturing war ammunition. It is an important job for the war effort." Our unit was the fifth battery of the 524th division. After Captain Grimm finished his introduction, a cantankerous sergeant major named Schmidt took over. He informed us of the rules of the unit, and then showed us the dugouts underground with bunk beds for our sleeping quarters. We were close to the enormous anti-aircraft guns that reached ominously towards the sky. Next, they separated us by height and strength. I was put in the stronger group, and we were assigned to operate the heavy guns, 105 mm. The other group was taken away to another dugout, where they would be doing calculations on the anti-aircraft equipment. This equipment was named after the inventor, Professor Malsi.

My group was taken to the anti-aircraft cannons to learn how to operate these weapons and we were given a crash course. Each cannon had a team of nine men to operate it. Our team had a young sergeant in charge, four students, and four Russian POW's. There was a seat for each operator, with a radar screen and a steering wheel. Each member of the team had a specific task. My job was to sit in the seat, follow the commando hand on the screen, and adjust the vertical position. My friend and classmate, Walter, was in charge of the horizontal position. Others were in charge of timing the detonation and troubleshooting. The Russians handled the ammunition and loaded the cannons that were shot off every ten seconds. Each cannon had been assigned a name. I worked on Anton, and the others worked on Bertha, César, and Dora. The names were from an alphabetical list given by the military. The first night experienced our "feuertaufe," which means "baptism by fire." Many bombers flew overhead that night, and we shot at them for hours without hitting a single bomber. I wondered what the allied pilots must think of these children down here shooting at them. Were they fearful, or were they just laughing at these children playing war games?

We all slept in the next day, exhausted from our late-night endeavours. We spent the day cleaning the cannons and lubricating the parts. Over the next few days, I started making friends with the Russians. I had my guitar with me and lent it to them. There was Paul from Kirgistan, Sergei from Moscow, Nocolai from Saparoje, and Gusma, from the Caucasian Mountains. They were an amicable and lionhearted group whose jubilant spirit and soulful music I greatly enjoyed. Every night, while we were on standby, the Russians would start singing and playing music. I joined in, even though it was against the rules. We were not allowed to make friends with the Russian prisoners, as it would make for a bit of a conflict of interest. The others in my unit avoided the Russians, but how could I stay away from these people with their entrancing music? They began to teach me Russian, and I surprised them by singing old communist songs I had learned from Uncle Gerard's commune. The melodies were all Russian, and they were delighted with this young German who knew their ancient songs.

We would sing and smoke Russian "machorka." This consists of the stems of the tobacco leaf rolled in newspaper. We called them "lung torpedoes," as they were strong and deadly. I became close friends with all four Russians and trusted them enough to let them know I was not a Nazi, and that my family was against the war. Sharing my truth brought us even closer. One night, there were several objects on the radar that were not moving. We kept firing at them to no avail. At daylight, we found out that the British had used a clever trick to fool us. All over the field were pieces of aluminum foil that they had scattered out of their planes to deceive the radar.

German planes were protected from being shot down by us with a code that consisted of different colours of flares thrown from the plane. This code changed daily, and we were informed of the new code each day. One night, a low-flying plane came above us and threw out the flares. They were not the right ones for that day. We were undecided on what to do, as it appeared to be a German plane. It came around a second time, this time bombing us. It was actually a British plane playing another trick on us. Luckily, there were no causalities, as the bombs had missed us by 50 metres. We began to realize just how inventive the British pilots could be. The next day, we received orders from headquarters instructing us, "If the code is not correct, fire immediately." A week later, a similar event happened when a lone plane flew above us and didn't throw out any flares. It was an easy target in the searchlight, and we skillfully shot the plane down. The next day, we found out that we had shot down a Fokke Wulf German night fighter. The Russians were especially downtrodden because the vodka that was to be given as a reward when we shot down a plane was certainly not coming for shooting down a German plane. By April, however, our unit had shot down five planes, and we had painted five rings around our cannon to show this achievement.

I was accustomed to being surrounded by Nazis in the Hitler Youth, but now I was living side by side with ardent Nazis. I had been safe at home with my family where I could speak my mind. In contrast, I had to be extremely careful at all times, as I was surrounded by Nazis who could report me for the slightest slip, even in private. Some of the other students criticized me for my camaraderie with the Russians. They weren't aware of my abhorrence of Nazis or my convictions that Hitler would soon lose the war. My friend and classmate, Fritz, was the only one of our Anton crew who may have felt the same way that I did. We never actually talked of our opposition to the Nazis, but I could tell he was not so easily brainwashed by Nazi propaganda like the others. Also, like me, he showed no enthusiasm for the sadistic ways of the SS or the antipathy for Jews that the others expressed. I was comforted to have at least one person who I suspected shared my views, even though we could never speak of it in case we were overheard. It was a beautiful April day when the order came for the entire unit to be transferred. We had to be ready the next day to leave by freight train, with all the cannons and other equipment. Our destination was top secret and there was no time to inform our families. When everything was packed up, we filled boxcars with straw and were ready to go. We climbed into the boxcars, and soon figured out that we were travelling east.

In the morning, the train stopped near Riesa, in Saxony. We got out, and our Russian cooks made us a soup of whatever they could find. Our lunch consisted of soup and a piece of bread. We were growing boys, so we were all left hungry and wanting for more. The next morning, we crossed the border into Czechoslovakia and marvelled at the awe-inspiring beauty of the mountains. When we reached the city of Most, we were told to unload all the equipment and put it on heavy duty transport trucks. The cannons were lifted by large cranes onto the trucks. From there, we travelled by truck into the countryside to a village named Maria Ratschitz. We all made jokes when we heard the odd name of this village, and I was on a roll with churning out a series of gutbusters. Prefabricated huts awaited us, containing double bunk beds, benches, and tables. Our equipment arrived a few hours later and was placed in each corner of the field about 50 metres apart. We could see black smoke billowing into the sky in the distance. We learned that the smoke's origin was an oil refinery that turned out to be the target that we were assigned to protect.

Within two days, we were equipped for action. "German efficiency," I thought wryly at the time. The kitchen and office were in the nearby village of the unfortunately named Maria Ratschitz.

In the Ruhr there had been bombings every night, but it was peacefully quiet here. It was a welcomed reprieve for us. We would run around the field in our shorts and wooden clogs while tossing the football back and forth. Part of the day was spent cleaning and maintaining the equipment, but there were no bombings. We were members of the German air force, the "Luftwaffe," but we were still just kids. Even though I knew it was risky, I was still drawn to the joyful spirit of the Russians and spent even more time with them playing music and joking together. I was eager to learn Russian and fascinated by their rich culture. We were not allowed to enter the Russians' quarters, which consisted of two yurts housing 40 men, but every night I would sneak out and join them after work. I would bring them war news, then we would sing together, smoke machorkas, and laugh at each other's jokes. I knew that what I was doing was ill-advised but felt that my luck would hold. One night, Captain Grimm came in unexpectedly to the yurt to do an inspection. I was trapped, as there was only one exit and that was blocked by the captain. I jumped quickly into some straw used for bedding, and my Russian friends covered me with their blankets. He was always kind and friendly to the Russians. "Do you have any complaints? Is everything all right?" They reassured him everything was fine, and he eventually left after a friendly conversation that seemed to last for an eternity. I sensed that he was not a true Nazi, just a man with a good heart who had studied for the priesthood and was then coerced into joining the air force.

Our unit became a bit of a joke because we were greatly lacking in discipline. We dressed sloppily and acted as though we were kids on a long camping trip. The war seemed far away, and we felt we could just be teenagers having fun. Our little vacation ended abruptly in June 1944, when other antiaircraft units joined us. A ring of 42 units was placed in a circle around the oil refinery. On our right side was a unit with a large cannon of 88 millimetres. On the other side were the largest aircraft cannons, 128 millimetres, mounted on rails. I made contact with the neighbouring unit, which consisted of high school students and Russian POW's. There I met Erwin, a 17-year-old Berliner, who became my close friend. He told me they had been stationed near Auschwitz to protect the I.G. Farben Werke chemical plant. As we got to know each other better, he shared that he had become ill from the stench of the crematorium. I could sense from the emotions in his face and stature that he was not sympathetic to the Nazi cause and had compassion for the inmates in Auschwitz. He was thankful to be away from that unbearably heinous nightmare.

One day, a group of about 30 concentration camp inmates were brought in to dig ditches for underground cable connections. They looked like walking corpses, and several measures had been taken to dehumanize them. Their heads were shaved, and their flesh clung tautly to their bones like old leather. Their striped uniforms were emblazoned with a large E on the back.

106

The "E" was short for "Erziehungslager," meaning Education Camp. These inmates were Germans who were being punished for not pulling their weight to help the Nazi war effort or had voiced any sort of opposition. The SS ran the camp and life was brutal under their regime. When the inmates saw our compost heap, they fell on the scraps like a frenzied flock of seagulls. It was horrifying to see these desperate men reduced to nothing but the innate instinct to survive. We wanted so badly to help them but knew we would be punished if we were caught doing so. I told them we would sneak them food from our kitchen. The Russians immediately got as much food as they could for the men, and they tore at the food like ravenous dogs as soon as the scraps were received. They were brought to work on the dugouts every morning, and I felt great compassion for these victims of the sadistic SS. I gave them tobacco and shared my candies with them. It became my mission to make them laugh each day by telling some of my jokes. If I could get some of them to laugh, it made me feel I was helping these poor souls to survive.

I felt that my Jewish ancestry was successfully concealed and felt safe with my fellow students. One night, however, I realized I had to be more careful with my actions. My friendship with the Russians had brought me to the attention of another student, Mueller, who was a rabid Nazi. Several of us were playing cards one night, and I said something about the musical talents of the Russians. Mueller gave me a cold, calculating look. "I know what they do to Germans." Without thinking I retorted, "I know what we do to people at Auschwitz." A stunned silence followed, and everyone froze. All eyes were on Mueller. He leaned forward and hissed at me, "If we didn't like you so much, Robert, I would make sure you were sent to where you belong!" I knew what he meant by that. I also knew I would have to be more cautious in the future to avoid a striped uniform of my own. My popularity saved me this time, but what about the next? I couldn't risk a next time.

Around the same time, Papa also got himself into a dangerous situation with the Nazis. He had finally rebuilt our home after it had been so badly damaged in the air raids. He paid for all the work out of his own pocket and was flabbergasted when a representative from the revenue office arrived and presented him with a tax bill. He absolutely lost it. "I paid for everything and received no help from the government!" he screamed. He grabbed an iron bar and was ready to kill the man for this offense. "The Fuehrer needs every mark he can get to win the war," the tax man protested. "The Fuehrer can kiss my ass!" was Papa's reply, still wielding his makeshift weapon. The man ran for his life as he shouted, "You'll pay for this!" He was a high-ranking member of the Nazi party. The next day, two Gestapo agents came and took Otto to Gestapo headquarters in Bochum. After three long days in a cell, he was taken for interrogation. Papa was sitting dejectedly in the hallway waiting to be called. He knew he was in dire trouble and chances of leniency in his punishment were quite slim. He had insulted Hitler, meaning he could be declared "an enemy of the people." Such a title meant he could be sent to a concentration camp...or worse.

Unbelievably, though, his old school friend, Heinrich Schneider, came strolling down the hallway just then. "What are you doing here, Otto?" he asked. "I got myself into trouble, terrible trouble!" Otto then told him what he had said to the representative. Heinrich replied, "Don't worry, Otto, I'll help you." Heinrich was an old member of the Nazi party and a Hitler supporter from the beginning. He had the high officer rank of "Obersturmbannfuehrer." He was a useful man to have on your side in this bad situation. He walked into the Gestapo office and returned a half an hour later. "Otto, everything is fine, I took care of it. Go in and face the music and act remorseful." Otto went into the office and the Gestapo interrogator gave him a stern lecture about his behaviour. "Make sure this never happens again!" Otto promised it wouldn't and was told he could go home. He was shaken up and vowed to work harder at buttoning his lip in the future. If it hadn't been for his old friend recognizing him from school, he would be well on his way to a concentration camp rather than the safety of home.

Anti-Aircraft Unit, Czech Republic (July 1944),
All former students of the Pestalozzi Gymnasium Herne,
15-17 years old

CHAPTER 7

All 42 batteries had their own Russian POW's and students. It wasn't long before a black market was established between the batteries. The anti-aircraft units were named FLAK and were known as the most laid-back division in the entire German military. The others made jokes about us, referring to us as clowns. We had little discipline or training in the FLAK units and were looked down upon by the more disciplined military units. Perhaps they overlooked our units because we were made up of teenagers and POW's that were forced to take part. On June 26th, 1944, we heard on the radio that the allied invasion had begun on the beaches of Normandy. This is what the allies called "D Day." The newscaster said that our troops had the enemy pinned down on the beach and that casualties were high. Some of my classmates, who were fanatic Nazis, shouted joyfully, "Now we have our chance to destroy the allied forces on land, and the final battle will be won!" They were jubilant. I too felt jubilant, but my jubilation was the hope that the Nazis would be defeated in this battle. It was forbidden to pass any news to the Russian POW's, but I took the risk and shared the news of the invasion. They thanked me, and I could see how elated they were that they now had hope for their freedom.

My turn came to go on my annual 16 day leave. I went home to celebrate my 17th birthday with my family. Oma's eyes flowed with tears of joy when she saw me at the door. We hugged, and I kissed that wise, sweet face, grateful she was still alive. My parents were happy to see me and pleased that I looked so well. They were still operating the candy factory, but only producing about half of their pre-war candies due to the rationing. The war meant that everything was rationed, and it was difficult or impossible to buy the necessities of life. As a result, the black market was flourishing. My parents and Oma were actively involved in this illegal activity, as was inevitable. My 16 days slipped through my fingers in the blink of an eye, and I knew I didn't want to return to shooting down the planes of the allies I supported. Of course, I also preferred not to die in a bombing by my would-be comrades. A friend had an idea. "Why don't you visit Dr. Rudy Hunold? He'll give you a letter to say you are sick and unable to go back to your unit." Dr. Hunold was a highly respected doctor who also happened to be a closeted homosexual. If the Nazis found out, he would have been sent to a concentration camp or killed. He was an excellent physician with a compassionate heart. I went to see him and asked him if he could help me extend my furlough. "Yes, I can give you a note that you have a kidney infection and need one extra week before you can travel." He risked his livelihood in doing this for me, and I was overwhelmingly grateful. I gave him cigarettes as a sign of thanks and took the note to the local military office to have it stamped and certified. I was overjoyed. I now had seven more days to enjoy with my friends and family. I daydreamed that the war would end before I returned to my unit. Alas, the time finally came when I had to say goodbye. My mother and I were still aloof from each other. I could never forgive her for what she had said to me. Papa became emotional, and I could see he was worried about me. Oma hugged me tightly, and I tried not to weep freely until I had left.

I returned to find my unit was now considered First Battery Division 656. With our new designated number, the discipline became stricter and we all had to smarten up. Soon, an incident happened that brought our unit to the attention of the powers that be, and it changed everything. Herman, our office clerk, had trained a Russian POW to look after the office while he went to the village pub and flirted with the lovely frauleins. This worked well for a time, until one day a high-ranking officer from division headquarters phoned our office. The Russian answered the phone and his accent gave him away. The officer shouted, "Who the hell are you?" The Russian replied, "Russian Vasil." Early the next day, our commanding officer, Captain Grimm, assembled the unit for inspection. He had a sad look on his face. "From now on, we have to play a different tune. Things have to change." He tried to be stern and strike fear into our hearts to incite discipline, but it just wasn't in his nature. Later, we heard that Grimm had been told off by his superiors and was in trouble for his lack of control over his men. Grimm was forced to reprimand Herman, who was quite saddened by the loss of his happy hours at the pub with the girls.

On July 20th, Captain Grimm came into our dugout. Historically, he always greeted us with the international military salute, bringing his right hand firmly to the cap. Instead, this time, he gave the Nazi salute. I was surprised and dismayed. "I have new orders. Today, there was an assassination attempt on the Fuehrer. The Fuehrer survived the attempt, but now the

113

military will be under the control of the SS. Therefore, we must now always give the Nazi salute." He said this without emotion, unadorned and with a face of stone. My heart felt strained for the difficult situation of Captain Grimm. He himself was not a Nazi, but he had no choice but to follow orders. Soon after this announcement, I took a chance and shared this information with the Russians. They were disappointed by the news that Hitler had survived. I, too, was angry that the assassins had failed, and I cursed them. The loyal disciples of the Nazi regime were appalled about this attempt on Hitler's life. On the contrary, I was just upset that they hadn't succeeded in killing him and ending the war.

We had not seen much action since we had left the Ruhr Valley in April, but that all changed by the end of July. It was about noon on a sunny and blistering hot day. We were all dressed in shorts and occupying our time by manoeuvring the equipment. Suddenly, our unit leader received the news that several hundred four-engine bombers, called the Flying Fortresses, were heading our way. They had already passed Dresden and there wasn't much time before they would be upon us. We were told to stand by and get ready for the fray. The Russians began passing the shells for the cannon down our human assembly line. These shells were about 3 feet long, weighed about 80 lbs, and were 105 mm in diameter. They had to pass them all the way from the ammunition dugout to Anton's bunker. We all put our helmets on and heard our sergeant tell us to position the cannon barrels to north northwest. The radar went on, and I followed the commando hand to the required angle to reach the target.

All 42 batteries began firing in unison every ten seconds, inciting chaos. The beautiful blue sky we had been basking under was abruptly filled with dark smoke that choked the sun out of view entirely. The darkness of the war again engulfed us. We could see through the smog that the oil refinery was on fire. The allies were using a system against us called "carpet bombing." The planes flew high to escape our anti-aircraft firing. While safe from our retaliation, their altitude sacrificed their target accuracy. To compensate, they used a carpet system, which meant many of the bombs missed the target. We witnessed three planes on fire that crashed near us and exploded. There were no survivors. Suddenly, I felt a powerful terrifying pressure that threw me violently into the wall of the bunker. I couldn't breathe, and I was suffocating on black smoke. I realized we had been hit by a bomb. It had hit on the opposite side of the cannon, and Anton had shielded me from the impact. My good friend and classmate, Fritz, was seated 4 metres from me (as he was the operator of the horizontal settings.) He was now on the ground and screaming in agony. I saw that he was bleeding heavily. Sergei, my dear Russian friend, was lying lifeless on the ground. His intestines were hanging out in a tangle before him, his body having been eviscerated by the bomb. Sergei was a master of the balalaika and had a beautiful tenor singing voice. He always laughed at my jokes and had shown great courage under fire. We had become close through our mutual love for Russian music. Now, he was dead.

I was in shock, and still unable to breathe in the dense smoke. After a few moments passed, I stood up and realized that my only injury was a shrapnel wound in my leg. The medics arrived and took Fritz away on a stretcher. I hoped he would survive as I stumbled outside the bunker to go to the water tank. My throat was burning immensely, and I soothed it with as much water as I could drink. When I looked up, I saw a parachute coming down in the nearby field. A few of my classmates were already running towards the man who was landing, so I joined them. The first one who reached the crew member said, very politely, in his high school English, "How do you do, sir. Do you have any Woodbine cigarettes?" Woodbines had a special aroma and were a precious commodity on the black market. The man seemed to be in shock and stared wordlessly with his mouth agape. By then, one of our sergeants came, searched him for weapons, and escorted him into a nearby hut. I followed them and offered to serve as an interpreter since I was fluent in English. The sergeant was happy to have me there. He would ask a question in German, and I would translate it into English for the prisoner. I tried to convey to him that I was not his enemy by showing compassion in my face. The first question was, "What is your nationality?" He seemed shaken, confused, and would not reply. The sergeant could see the prisoner was in no shape to be questioned just yet. They kept him there under guard and I left to do repairs on Anton, which had been badly damaged in the explosion.

The news came that my friend Fritz had been taken to a nearby hospital and had had his leg amputated.

I was taken aback by this news. He was one of the most athletic and strong students that I had played soccer and handball with in Herne. I felt a great sadness for his needless loss. Fritz was only 15 years old. Though it was of little recompense, at least the war was over for him. A day later, Captain Grimm made an announcement to the unit. "Anyone who has turned 17 must be discharged and report to the military station in his hometown." He was very emotional. "I wish you all the best, I and thank you for your loyal service. You are about to become real soldiers." I could see that this announcement was difficult for him, as he knew, in many ways, we were still children and we would be facing much more danger than before. Captain Grimm didn't say "Heil Hitler." I felt that what he wanted to say was, "Go with God," as he was a devout Catholic. I hoped that this kindly man would survive the war and become a priest, which was his true calling. That day was one of the most difficult and emotional days of my life. I had to say goodbye to my Russian friends. We had become close comrades, and I knew I would never see them again. Each one of these tough and hardened men had tears in their eyes when I told them the news. We wanted to hug each other but knew that we couldn't risk others seeing this token of our forbidden friendship. My heart filled with sorrow. I felt a deep spiritual connection with these men, and it was through them that I had experienced the beauty of the Russian soul.

The next day, all the 17-year-olds travelled to their hometowns by train. There were 12 of us returning to Herne. I was surrounded by Nazis again, and keenly aware of my vulnerability. I was shocked to see the devastation in the cities caused by the bombs. When I got home, my family was happy to see me, but were all saddened by the thought of me becoming a soldier. The next morning, I reported to the military station and was told that I was to report to the premilitary boot camp, Bredenscheid in Wuppertal Hills, in one week. This was 30 km south of Herne. For me, this meant it was party time again. I went out every night that week and didn't come home until I was very drunk. My friends who were home on furlough from the Russian front and I had the philosophy, "Eat, drink, and be merry, for tomorrow we may die." Some of the women at our parties were sadly already young widows from the war. They shared the same morbid philosophy as we did. After a few nights, my mother asked Papa to speak to me about my behaviour. I heard Papa say, "Leave the boy alone. Nobody knows what his future will be. Let him enjoy himself while he can." Mama was frustrated with my behaviour. "I'll be glad to see you go to boot camp, I can't take it anymore!" I didn't blame her. I was leading a wild life without a care as to how it might affect my health or that of others.

On September 15th, 1944, I reported to Bredenscheid. Right away, I sensed that this was going to be a completely different experience than my time with Captain Grimm. We were all separated by height into 12 platoons consisting of 12 men. The stone faces and the harsh words of the sergeants gave us a good indication of what to expect. We were treated like criminals and considered as good as scum. The commanding officer gave his talk, "From today onward, we will make men out of you. You will become soldiers of the Third Reich and made fit to fight for the final victory." The captain looked us over with contempt and asked, "Who is a cook?" No hands went up. "Who is a baker?" Again, no hands went up. "Any butchers?" Not a single hand went up. The army needs cooks, I thought. I'm good at that. I raised my hand. "I'm a candy maker, sir." A boy named Manfred also put up his hand and we were marched to the kitchen and given instructions. The instructions were brief, as there were only potatoes, cabbage, and the odd onion for us to work with.

We began working immediately to cook the evening meal for 144 soldiers. One day we prepared potatoes with cabbage, and the next day we prepared cabbage with potatoes. In the morning, the guards woke us up at 4:00 a.m. to work in the kitchen. We had to light the fire in the large military stove and boil the water to make coffee. In the evening, we cut up the bread rations, four slices to each man, a small piece of cheese, canned meat, and a tablespoon of butter. At 6:00 a.m., a high-pitched whistle blew, and everyone had to line up outside to go on a cross country run through bushes, up hills, and over creeks. Meanwhile, Manfred and I continued working in the kitchen. When they returned, they washed up, put on their drill uniforms, and lined up again to receive their daily rations. I quickly realized that I had made an error by volunteering for this job. I thought working in the kitchen would be easier than other duties, but it was much harder. I never finished my kitchen work until 11 pm, whereas the others finished work by 6 pm and had free time in the evening. I decided

I wanted to get out of the kitchen, and I asked to be transferred back to my unit to take part in the training.

My first job, after being placed back with the others, was to dig a bomb shelter. This was completed just in time, because at the end of September, we were heavily bombed. If we hadn't been in the bomb shelters at the time, we would likely have been killed. Everything was demolished, including the kitchen and the sleeping quarters. Each platoon of 12 men had completed their bomb shelter prior to the bombing, and there were no casualties as a result. The next day, we evacuated to Bredenscheid's schoolhouse and carried on with our training in the nearby woods and fields. We were learning to handle machine guns, storm rifles, explosives, and anti-tank bazookas. Old scrap tanks were used for us to practice on. Once, we had been a bunch of kids playing war games. Under Captain Grimm, it had been like a summer camp vacation for us. Now, we were starting to toughen up under the harshly strict ways of boot camp life. In mid-October, we were suddenly assembled and told we were discharged to report back to the military station of our hometowns. The commanding officer congratulated us on our achievements. "Now, you are real soldiers." I didn't want to be a real soldier. I wanted to survive this war and go home. An SS officer appeared and shouted, "Platoon one and two line up!" We were the tallest ones out of all the platoons. "You will be enrolled in the Waffen SS." I was aghast and panicked by this news. The Waffen SS were highly trained storm troopers who were known for their unmatched brutality. I immediately thought to myself, "How the hell do I get out of this?" They always chose the tallest and strongest young soldiers for the Waffen SS. Death was knocking at my door.

The others felt they had been given a great honour and were enthusiastically shaking hands with the SS officer. We had to sign up to become part of the Waffen SS. A line formed in front of the officer. My heart was pounding, and I was desperately trying to find a solution to escape this unwanted appointment. I heard the man in front of me say, "I am very regretful that I can't sign up, because I have already signed up for the paratroopers." The SS officer replied, "Okay. Next." I was thinking fast and realized I couldn't use that exact excuse, but it gave me an idea. I stepped up to him and with as much conviction as I could muster said, "I regret that I can't sign up because I have already committed myself to the Panzer Corps." He looked at me with his dark, penetrating eyes, assessing me. "Where and when?" My grand skills at bluffing that I had developed over the years came in handy. I looked him right in the eye and boldly lied, "At the military station in Herne, before I came here for this training." He was suspicious, but he reluctantly accepted it. My bluff had worked, and it had given me time to reach Herne and sign up for the Panzer Corp. Lady Luck was once again sitting on my shoulder.

We received our discharge papers and immediately left for our home towns. My parents and Oma were pleasantly surprised to see me back so soon. I was the first one at the military station in the morning to sign up for the Panzer Corp, which was the tank division. They told me to report within three days to the Panzer Kaserne in Iserlohn. I went by train and was received by the sergeant-at-arms in a friendly manner. It was soon clear to me that the military was running out of men. Now, they had only old men and children to fight the war. We were sent for special training to Lette, near Coesfeld. This was the toughest and most rigorous training I had experienced. Our sleeping quarters were in a barn. For the young guys it was fun, but for the older men it was a hardship. We did night training and made dugouts in the frozen ground. In early December, a supply train near our camp was bombed. The supplies had been evacuated from the Netherlands as the front was coming closer. There was tobacco, liquor, chocolates, blankets, and exotic spices from Indonesia. Our company was assigned to guard the train to prevent looting. When we saw all the goodies on that train, we were delighted, and we became the looters we were meant to fend off. We decided to take a barrel of cognac to the commandant to keep him happy. Our looting adventure was brief, as the SS arrived the next day. They loaded everything on to trucks and our precious contraband was gone.

We returned to the barn where we were stationed to carry on our training to become soldiers of the Third Reich. Every day was dangerous, as low flying Mosquito bombers were combing the countryside for military targets. One day we were out in the field and a Mosquito bomber came over us. The man next to me was hit. I was certain he wasn't long for this world, as he had been disembowelled and was bleeding profusely. Another man helped me, and we dragged him into the bushes for cover. He appeared to be already dead. He was just a boy, like me, like all of us. I never knew him, but he was my comrade in this surreal war. As I turned to leave, I noticed that he had a brand new cap. My cap was in bad shape. Without a thought, I reached down and took his cap and threw my old cap beside him. Later, I thought, "How heartless can you be?" But war had changed me. I had become a different person. Not the soft-hearted three-year-old Robert who cried when he found out the pretty little blonde girl was going to die. Not the compassionate six-year-old Robert who gave his wool sweater to his freezing, undernourished classmate. I had always been overly sensitive and altruistic. Now, I was just in survival mode and taking care of myself first. The medics came and took the boy away. The next day, I found out he had survived against all odds, and I was glad. In the hospital, he would have no need for his cap.

Our training moves became more and more dangerous, as the mosquito bombers were looming above continuously from morning to night. It seemed to us that our German air force no longer existed, and the Western allies air force controlled the sky. Our sergeant told us that most of the bomber pilots were Canadian. I've now lived in Canada for 62 years, a country that I love and respect. It is morbidly ironic to think of those Canadian pilots shooting at me so many years ago, trying to kill me.

Our morale was low, and Christmas, 1944, was upon us. We were miserable to be cut off from the rest of the world and away from our families. Train tracks had been bombed, vehicles were hunted down and destroyed, and no mail was getting through. There was a Catholic church in the nearby village of Lette. On Christmas Eve, I went with the other Catholics in my unit to midnight mass. It was a hazardous journey to the church. The Mosquitoes were still flying, looking for easy targets in the snow. We strategically decided to walk along a country road that had apple trees on either side. That way, we could take cover under the trees if we were attacked. Additionally, we had more camouflage if we walked 10 metres apart from each other. It was risky, but we made it safely to the church. The smell of incense and the chanting in Latin by the priest both touched me deeply. I felt a spiritual connection with my family, and fervently hoped we would all survive and be together again. The priest spoke of "Peace on earth." These words saddened me, but that sadness quickly transformed into rage. "What bullshit," I thought. "Mankind has never had peace. We will always make war on one another." We made it back safely to the barn and crawled onto our haystacks.

When we awoke on Christmas day, we had no food because the bombers had prevented any supplies from coming through. There were 120 hungry men thinking of their families with fond nostalgia and craving the traditional Christmas goose with all the trimmings. We were feeling pretty sorry for ourselves when the elderly farming couple appeared with baskets of Schaafsnasen apples. They are called "Red Delicious" in Canada and the U.S. We eagerly scrambled down and lined up to each receive an apple and warm Christmas wishes from our gracious landlords. Without exaggeration, I can say that apple was the best tasting apple of my life. Even today, decades later, I can still remember that apple's juicy taste and its robust aroma. We all thanked our benefactors and wished them,

"Froehliche weinachten," which is "Merry Christmas" in German. This act of kindness boosted our morale and we were able to embrace the Christmas spirit after all. We decided to entertain ourselves with skits, jokes, and songs. Johann, a handsome 17-year-old from Cologne, had a beautiful voice. He sang "Ave Maria" in Latin with a light, captivating sound. I thought of my mother, as this had always been her favourite song, and felt my eyes fill with tears. My fellow soldiers likewise found themselves with the warmth of involuntary tears. That evening, there was a powerful feeling of comradeship. At the end of the evening we sang "Stille Nacht." The touching lyrics of that most beautiful of Christmas songs floated gently on the night. It was sung by men whose only hope was to survive this terrible war and once again be home with their families.

The next day, our captain told us that there were no food supplies. He ordered me and another soldier to get in the back of the truck to go to the garrison of Muenster for supplies. Our sergeant drove the truck along the country roads the entire 50 km to our destination. We were alert to danger and kept our eyes toward the vast blue sky. Soon we heard a plane and immediately ran to throw ourselves in the ditch. We heard the truck being hammered by machine gun bullets as the plane raced by. Amazingly, the truck was still drivable, and we were able to continue on our journey. At the garrison, we loaded the truck with loaves of dark rye bread and canned meat, waiting for nightfall just to be safe. When we reached our unit, we were greeted like returning heroes. The day before New Year's Eve, a convoy with supplies reached us. They brought canned tomato paste from Italy, as well as bread and bottles of Schnapps. On New Year's Eve, we all got drunk. Our sergeant said, "Let's give a toast to Mussolini to thank him for the tomato paste!" We each slathered a piece of bread with the paste and our sergeant led us in a toast to Mussolini as we held up our metal mugs of Schnapps in one hand, and our bread in the other. At midnight, we were feeling no pain and wished each other a happy new year as we wobbled and fell onto our straw beds. The Schnapps had been a welcome distraction for us that night.

CHAPTER 8

In late January, our captain called an assembly. He named 12 of us and said we were to meet him in his office. My name was among the 12 called. "Pack up immediately. You will be transferred to a new location." We quickly packed up and were told to follow a sergeant to our new location a few kilometres away. The sergeant was a highly decorated soldier from the Russian front. He was tough, but I also felt that he was a fair leader. When we stopped, we were in a bush area. The sergeant told us, "You have been chosen to be special commandos. You will be trained in the destruction of tanks and explosives for demolition." I immediately panicked and was filled with dismay. I knew what special commandos did. It meant they sent you out on suicide missions. In order to blow up a tank, you also had to blow up yourself. My mind began racing while desperately thinking of ways to escape my fate. I was determined to survive this insane war. I even considered deserting, but I knew all roads had SS roadblocks and escape was hopeless.

I had cheated inevitable death once, and I planned to do it again. For the next few hours, we cut down trees, made dugouts for our sleeping quarters, and built a primitive outhouse. Heather has always entranced me with its scent, and we decided to lay heather at the bottom of our dugouts. Even in Hell, one can enjoy the scent of heather. I couldn't sleep, as my mind was filled with thoughts of escape. In the middle of the night, I finally got an idea that might save me. If I could develop pneumonia or a fever, I would surely be sent to the sick bay. The allied forces were already on German territory and advancing ever closer. It seemed as though the war would be over soon, and I just had to find a way to survive until then. I quietly stripped naked and went outside. I stood there for over an hour until I felt numb with cold. I went back to the dugout, got dressed and fell into a deep sleep. When I woke up in the morning, I felt like a million dollars. Not even a sniffle... I was disappointed but consoled myself with the thought that I was one tough guy. I have been able to look on the bright side of things all my life. I was about to be sent on a suicide mission, but laughably reassured myself that at least I was tough.

I still had to conceive a plan for getting out of this suicide unit. A desperate plan came to mind. Earlier, I had noticed a large boulder of about 50 kilos hanging at the side of the ditch. I decided that I would use it to smash my foot since my attempts to get sick had failed. My plan was to wait until dark, then tell the sergeant I needed to go to the outhouse. On the way there I would go into the ditch, dig out the rock, and drop it on my foot. If I succeeded, I would have many broken bones in my foot and be sent to the army hospital. This diversion would save my life. After my injury, I would scream for help and tell them I had accidentally slipped into the ditch. That night, I set my new plan into action. I dug the huge boulder out, held it up, and let it fall on my left foot. It hurt like hell but did not do the trick. I was still able to wiggle my toes. Not to be deterred, I picked up the boulder again. I hesitated for a moment. I knew what I had to do. I lifted the boulder as high as I could, and mustering as much force into the drop as possible, I smashed it again on my left foot. This time, I felt severe pain stabbing upward all the way to my belly button. As I collapsed in agony, I knew I had succeeded. I screamed for help with tears streaming down my face. The sergeant-at-arms came running and ordered two men to carry me back to the dugout. They took off my boot, which caused excruciating pain. I snuck a glance down at my foot. It was a horrendous swollen sight, but I was exuberant that I had found a way to survive. It was clear that my injury would take a long time to heal, and my participation in this war was finally at an end.

I couldn't sleep because of the pain, but I felt a great sense of peace knowing that I would live long enough to return home. The next morning, our sergeant came and questioned me. He believed my story and had a stretcher built to carry me to the sick bay in the village of Lette, located inside an old farmhouse. When we got there, I saw there was only one elderly medic. He examined my foot quickly. "It is only badly bruised. Keep it elevated and apply cold packs." I was certain he was wrong and that bones were broken, but I kept quiet and stayed there for the next two weeks. There were many soldiers there who had been wounded by the Mosquito bombers. A medical doctor came and examined me eventually. "Several bones are broken in your foot. You need to have an X-ray at Coesfeld Hospital. You can borrow the medic's bicycle to get there. It's only six km." I knew there were broken bones in my foot and was glad to be able to confirm that with an X-ray. It was a long and painful ride, but I managed to make it to the hospital, have my X-ray, and return to sick bay. It was quite the trip. Three days later, the results came that there were indeed four broken bones in my foot. The medic told me it was too late to use a cast, as the bones were already starting to knit. "Don't walk on it. I will give you crutches."

I began making friends with the other soldiers, and every day we would go out into the field, take cover under the trees, and enjoy the sunshine. Mother Nature has always been healing for me, and I revelled in the sights and sounds of our field sanctuary. We shared stories about our lives, told jokes, and soon we developed a true sense of camaraderie. I became especially close to three of the soldiers from Poland. Alfons was in his mid-twenties and had served in Russia. He was finished with war and, like me, was not a Nazi. There was a bullet wound in his leg that was healing. One day the medic told him, "In a couple of days, your leg will be healed, and you will be sent back to the front lines." He didn't want to go and begged me to help him. "Robert, please remove my bandages and open my leg wound. Put sugar in the wound and rewrap my leg. Tomorrow my leg will be infected, and the pus will run freely. Then, I will never have to return to the front." I immediately agreed to help him, scratched open the wound until it bled, and poured in sugar before wrapping it back up. Two days later, the medic came to check the wound. He was mortified to discover how badly infected it was. "You must have unclean blood!" he said with disgust. The Nazis believed they were the only ones with "clean" Aryan blood. Every night, I poured more sugar into his wound. The medic became truly puzzled as to why his wound was not healing in the slightest. Alfons and I became even closer friends as we were now bonded by a painful, but life-saving, secret pact. For the next few weeks, our trick kept Alfons safe from returning to the front.

Michael was another Polish soldier I befriended during this time. He had bleeding ulcers and was adept at feigning illness. Michael was able to convince the medic that he was in considerable pain and managed to prolong his stay in sick bay. He was in his 50s and not in line with the Nazi ideology. It was clear to him that Germany was losing the war and it would soon be over. Then there was Manfred. He was a 15-year-old farm boy who had a bullet wound in his posterior. I especially liked him, because he was a true innocent with a jovial attitude and great sense of humour. He didn't want to be a soldier. We formed a tight little group of anti-Nazis who shared stories and jokes and talked of going home soon. One day, I felt an itchy feeling on my chest and back. I started scratching and noticed the others were also furiously scratching. We quickly realized we were all infested with lice. The medic gave us disinfecting liquid soap to wash ourselves and our clothes. There was some relief for a few days, but in the end the lice won the battle. The soap just wasn't strong enough. The lice kept coming and we had to learn to live with them. We did everything we could, but it was hopeless.

On top of the lice problem, we ran out of food. We were starving and only had a few rotten potatoes to eat. It was a desperate situation and we could only hope that the allies would arrive soon. Leaflets were dropped from allied planes and we all went out into the field and picked them up. Of course, this was strictly forbidden, and we could be court marshalled for the offense. In

German, it stated that the U.S. tanks were rolling on the autobahn towards Frankfurt, and that the Red Army was closing in on Berlin. It also said, "KEEP THIS LEAFLET AS A PASS FOR MEETING THE ALLIED FORCES." This gave us all a great morale boost and increased our hope. On March 27th we heard wagons, trucks, and militia movement on the nearby country road. I was curious to see what was happening and hobbled over slowly on my crutches to see German soldiers in all different uniforms walking in a haphazard way along the road. One soldier shouted, "Run, the Tommies are only two km away!" My heart leapt for joy. I would have run back to tell my friends the good news had I been able, but I just had to crutch my way slowly back. I burst in when I arrived and told them the news.

They were rejoicing to find out the end was near and we all revelled in the news, crying and laughing at the same time. That evening, the medic rushed into the sick bay looking distressed. "There are orders from the head office. Everyone is to retreat and go to Duelmen to be regrouped." Then, in seconds, he had packed some things and disappeared. We could hear explosions coming closer and closer. Michael, the oldest and most experienced among us, knew what to do. "Get a white bed sheet and hang it out the window." Suddenly, there was a blanket of eerie silence outside. It was late now, and we decided to just go to bed. We slept like babies because we all knew we had survived this terrible war.

The next morning, Alfons woke me up. "Robert, look out the window. You won't believe it." I looked out and saw an English soldier wearing a red beret guarding the house across the street. He was holding a submachine gun and pacing back and forth. I could see movement inside the house and realized the British army had moved in during the night without a shot fired. Then, I saw another remarkable sight. The majority of the houses along the village street had white sheets hanging out the window, and the Catholic Church bell tower also had been draped with a white flag of surrender. At that moment, a profound feeling of relief came over me and I was filled with a deep sense of peace. This was the day I had been waiting for all through the war. Now I knew I was finally safe and my plan to live had worked. I looked forward to becoming a prisoner of war.

Michael said, "Robert, you speak English, so you should go and tell the British we want to surrender." I slowly crossed the street on my crutches and greeted the Tommy guard. "Good morning, sir." He answered, "Good morning" and walked away from me. He just kept patrolling, going back and forth on the sidewalk. I was a little taken aback by his behaviour. Here I was, trying to surrender, and this guy was just ignoring me. I saw a young fellow with a friendly face leaning out a window with a cigarette in his mouth. I slowly made my way over to him. "Good morning, sir. We are four German soldiers across the road in the army hospital. We would like to surrender." With typical British humour and a smile, he replied, "Jerry, for you the war is over." He came outside. "Let's go, Jerry." He was holding a handgun and had a big grin on his face. "I'm sorry I have to point the gun at you. It's just procedure. You go ahead of me and I'll follow." We went across the road and into the sick bay. My friends were waiting for us there.

"Everyone step outside. Leave your belongings and we'll retrieve them later."

We crossed the road and entered the house to find several soldiers having tea. The Tommy escorting us politely asked, "Will you join us for a spot of tea?" I thought I must be dreaming. We surrender and they ask us to join them for tea? I wasn't complaining. So, four Germans and six British soldiers sat down for tea. Our Tommy host said, "Would you like a cigarette?" and offered each of us a Woodbine. I looked at these young British soldiers and thought, "How can these gracious and generous gentlemen be our supposed enemies?" As we sipped tea together, I couldn't imagine them shooting at us. They seemed so kind and amicable. How was this possible? I was accustomed to harsh and unsparing German militarism. We learned that their unit was called "The Red Devils." They were paratroopers and a well-respected unit of elite soldiers. After landing at Arnheim, they made their way through Holland and ended up in the village of Lette across the road from our sick bay. The soldier I surrendered to began to chat with me. His name was Bill, and he told me he was a 19-year-old from Liverpool. He showed me pictures of his family and we talked happily of sports as if we were two normal teenagers. We were both soccer players and avid boxing enthusiasts. Bill was a friendly fellow and we could have become friends had the context been different.

Another Tommy came in. "Okay, Jerries, the jeep is here, come on." Bill said, "Good luck, Jerry" and I thanked him for the tea and the smokes. We climbed into an open jeep with two Tommies, the driver and a guard, and drove across the fields to a large farm. We noticed that concertina barbed wire had been rolled around the barn with just an opening and an exit. Both sides were flanked with two guards. They led us into the barn. On the left side were horses, and on the right side were cows. The space in between the two was ours. We were told to climb up to the loft and throw down bales of hay for our bedding. As soon as we did this, a British officer came in and interrogated each one of us separately. When my turn came, I noticed he had a Dutch accent. "Are you Dutch?" "Yes. "My Oma came from Holland." That made him feel a connection with me, and the interrogation became a bit of a sham after that. They knew the war was almost over, so it was just a formality. We were told to cover the entire floor with hay because there were more German POW's coming. Shortly after this, trucks arrived with over a hundred German soldiers from different units and a group of Italian POW's. The Dutch soldier came up to me and Alfons. "Do you want to help in the kitchen to make soup for all the men?" We were delighted to help. None of us had eaten a decent meal in weeks.

He took us into the farmer's house and showed us potatoes, carrots, cabbage, and turnips. They had taken them out of the farmer's cold cellar. To our delight, there was also a chunk of smoked ham. We finished making the soup, the men lined up, and Alfons and I scooped the hearty soup into their canteens. Once again, my interest in food and my culinary skills had come in handy. We were cleaning up the kitchen when a British medic came over to me. He had a kind face that I can still remember vividly today. "What happened to your foot?" He had observed that it was badly swollen with visible edema in the ankle. "There are several broken bones in my foot." He asked me to sit down so he could examine it more thoroughly. It was still very painful, and he could see it was in terrible shape. He offered to help me and sent me to the barn where he brought me a bucket of cold water and told me to keep my foot in there to ease the swelling. That reduced the swelling by a significant amount and my foot was less painful. When I hit the hay that night, I felt like a kid on Christmas Eve. My belly was full and there was peace in my heart. I fell into a deep sleep, one of the sweetest of my life.

The next morning, all the POW's received six army biscuits each and a can of corned beef to share among 12 men. There was an abundance of hot tea. As we sat together eating our biscuits and drinking our tea, we began to relax and feel safe. For us, the war really was over. I was sitting next to a soldier who had been on the Russian front and had several medals pinned to his uniform. One of the young British soldiers pointed to the Iron Cross on his lapel and asked, "How many cigarettes do you want for that?" The POW replied, "Ten cigarettes" and they finalized the deal. This triggered a brisk bartering business. We could smell the aroma of the British cigarettes, and our craving for nicotine was overwhelming. Any POW who had a medal was soon offering it to the British for cigarettes. Medals such as the Purple Heart, given to those who were wounded, and the Iron Cross, given for heroic actions, were quickly turned into cigarettes. I was surprised how little my fellow soldiers valued these medals of honour. The next day was Good Friday, and we were told we were to be transferred. Several hundred POW's started marching westward guarded by British soldiers with submachine guns. A German medic, another POW, gave me a bicycle. I sat on it and he pushed.

We passed through several villages and took a short break beside the road. An older POW came over to me. I think he felt sorry for me because he could see that I was obviously in pain. "Bubi, I have a present for you." He handed me a piece of dry German army bread. "Bubi" is a nickname for a young boy. I thanked him for his kindness. "I was one of the last rescued by plane from Stalingrad. Both of my sons died on the Russian front." He told me his name was Atze, and that he was a Berliner. A young German officer saw this act of kindness and came to Atze. "Comrade," he said, in a polite way, "do you have a piece of bread for me too?" Atze gave him a hard stare. "How strange, a few days ago you probably would have been giving me shit, and now you are so tame as to eat out of my hand." The soldiers all hated the officers who gave the orders. I could see the humiliation in the officer's face, and I couldn't help but feel sorry for him. Atze said, "Of course I can give you a piece of my bread." He handed him the bread and walked away. I felt a growing fondness for Atze in that moment and valued him as a potential friend.

Our next break was at the village of Gross Reeken. The villagers and liberated Russian POW's had just looted a nearby German supply depot and they shared their canned meat with us. It felt good to have our former enemies now generously sharing food with us. After about 30 km, we arrived at a big lumber yard.

Soon, trucks arrived to carry us to our next destination. We continued west, towards the Dutch border, and finally arrived at a large meadow near the village of Weeze, close to Kevelaar. I estimated that there were over a thousand POW's already there. Concertina barbed wire surrounded the meadow, and it was guarded by a multitude of British soldiers. There was an announcement that all prisoners would be deloused. We were ecstatic about this prospect and lined up and stripped. British soldiers then sprayed our bodies and our clothes with anti-lice powder. We got dressed and each received two army blankets.

We were exhausted after the march and lay down in the meadow to sleep. I woke in the middle of the night and felt a fine rain. Unfortunately, the rain became heavier, and in the morning the meadow had turned into a swamp. We couldn't sit down, so we stood and leaned on each other instead, hoping the rain would stop soon. It was Easter Sunday and we were a miserable lot. Morale had dropped. We were soaking wet and hungry. The next morning, we saw the other side of some of the British soldiers. Five of them came, with guns, and went down the rows stealing the prisoner's wrist watches. This was yet another blow to our morale. We remained two more days in the meadow-swamp. The rain never stopped, so conditions were deplorable. By this time, I was part of a support group consisting of Atze, Alfons, Michael, Manfred, and myself. We began to tell jokes in an attempt to raise our spirits. Atze had a sardonic sense of humour and told us tragic stories of Stalingrad. I was the most prolific jokester in the group and was able to make them all laugh with some typical teenage filthy jokes.

Even Atze had to laugh at times. Our laughter brought us closer together and made the conditions almost bearable.

After two days, the rain finally stopped. A German officer with a loud voice called everyone to attention. He shouted, "The British commanding officer has given me the authority to impose discipline and have you line up to march to the railway station at Goch. A freight train is waiting for you." When we got to the station, we were divided into 40 men for each box car. A container full of water was on one side, and on the opposite side was a can for shit. Each prisoner received a loaf of British army bread and a can of corned beef. "That is your supply for the next three days, so make it last." We were all extremely hungry. Some of the men ate their rations right away. Others wisely saved some for the trip. I decided to keep my rations for the next day, and then enjoy a meal fit for a king. This made me feel strong, and I was proud that I was able to discipline myself. The floor of our box car still had the remains of horse manure scattered on it, which gave off an offensive pungent odor. We started on our journey and could see through a small opening that we were crossing the Dutch border. Along the tracks we saw that the citizens had gathered rocks to throw at us: the hated and despised Germans. We heard the sound of rocks hitting our box cars. I felt a deep sense of sadness and again had that old feeling of being trapped. I laid down on the bare floor and put my bread and can of corned beef behind my head for safe keeping. As I fell asleep, I was dreaming of my royal meal that I would have in the morning. At daylight, I woke and found that my royal meal had disappeared. I felt a pain in my soul that one of my comrades would stoop so low as to steal my food ration. I glanced around and wondered, "Which one was it?" It was a low point for me in my journey. For three days I had nothing to eat and I turned bitter at this act of greed committed by one of my fellow Germans. War makes criminals of us all and we lose our humanity.

I could see through the peephole that we were now in Tillburg. There were many people gathered to greet our train. Again, a hail of rocks hit our box car. An older soldier commented angrily, "They're letting their anger out on us. This is thanks to the Nazis!" I couldn't blame the Dutch for hating us. They had been treated with brutality by the Nazis during the occupation. I felt that I personally didn't deserve their hatred, because I was also a victim of this war, but I accepted it. I didn't expect them to know all the differences and nuances of who was willingly involved in the crimes committed against them. Later that day, we crossed the border into Belgium. Now we were given the pleasure of experiencing the intense hatred of the Belgians. They gathered along our route and pelted our box cars with rocks, just as the Dutch had done. At one point, I looked out the peephole and made eye contact with a woman who ran her hand across her throat with eyes full of venom. Insults were being hurled at us constantly, but we couldn't understand what they were saying. We knew, however, what they meant. It was a relief when night fell and it was finally quiet in the box car. Early in the morning we came to a stop in the town of Wevelgem. Belgian soldiers, speaking Flemish, were opening each box car. I could hear them ordering the German prisoners out. As the Germans scrambled out, I could hear their screams and cries. The soldiers were beating them with heavy sticks and assaulting them with their fists as they exited.

Our door opened and my comrades were beaten as they jumped out. I moved to the back of the box car and waited until everyone was out. I limped to the door and told them in Flemish, "Ick can nit loope" and pointed to my injured foot. One soldier showed compassion by helping me out of the box car. An officer came and gave orders in German for us to line up and we began marching. As soon as they noticed that I could not keep up, an army jeep drove up with two older amputee POW's inside and I was told to join them. The approximately 600 able-bodied POW's were ordered to run at double speed. As they ran, the Belgian soldiers hit them with their rifle butts to get them to run faster. The ferocity of it all was alarming. As we went through Wevelgem, the citizens were lined up to give us their now familiar welcome. We all ducked and tried to shield ourselves from the projectiles coming our way. I noticed an elderly woman sitting in front of her house. She called out, "arme jungens, arme jungens." She was looking at us with compassion and saying, "poor boys, poor boys." I felt relieved in the face of this brutality by hearing these compassionate words. She reminded me of my kind-hearted Oma.

After running several kilometres, some of the POW's collapsed. As punishment, they were kicked and hit with rifle butts and commanded to get back up. After a while, I saw watchtowers and barracks and we all entered through a large gate into a compound. It was April 1st, which was sadly funny. A day for fools. At that point, British soldiers took over, and I immediately felt some optimism that we would now be treated in a more humane manner. We were told to line up in groups of 50 men, and each group was assigned a barrack. I had become separated from my friends during this process. I was exhausted and beyond hunger, as it had now been three days since I had eaten. I immediately fell asleep on the concrete floor. In the morning, two POW's entered our barrack carrying a huge vat of steaming porridge. That porridge tasted like a warm, happy feeling, and was the best porridge of my life. It comforted me and reminded me of home. I went outside to be in the sun and look for my friends. For several hours, I chatted with other POW's and then I spotted Atze, the humorous Berliner. We were overjoyed and hugged each other like long lost brothers. "Have you seen the others?" I asked. "Yes, I'm in the same barrack with them. I'll take you to them." When we entered their barrack, my friends surrounded me to express their happiness to see me again. I wanted to move into their barracks, but my name was registered in the other barrack. Of course, we were all dying to enjoy smoke together. I had already found out that the inside of the camp was run by British soldiers and the outside of the camp was guarded by Belgian soldiers. High fences and barbed wire surrounded the camp. "I'll try to get some smokes."

I didn't see a British soldier once I was outside, so I walked to the barbed wire fence where I saw a Belgian soldier patrolling on the other side, carrying a rifle. I asked him politely in Flemish if he could spare a smoke. "Do you have anything to trade?" I didn't have anything. "A gold ring or wrist watch would get you

142

some smokes." I told him I'd be right back and went as fast as I could with my bum foot back into the barrack. "Has anyone got a ring or watch to trade for smokes?" Two men came up to me. Each man had a gold ring in his hand. One ring had a ruby, and the other had several opals. Both of them said they would trade their rings for a pack of cigarettes. Then, a third man came up to me and showed me his medal from the Eastern front. This was a highly valued medal from the battle of Demjansk, Russia. It was given for acts of exceptional heroism. "Try to get whatever you can for it. I don't want it anymore." This whole interaction had a profound effect on me. Suddenly, I felt energized and strong. Trading and bartering, wheeling and dealing; these were some of my best skills. It was in my blood from my Oma and Mama. Also, I was the son of an Ashkenazi Jew, who was the master wheeler dealer of them all. He was the best businessman I had ever known. I could use my skills to help my friends.

I returned to the Belgian guard to make a deal. "I want two packs for each ring and one pack for the medal." He gave me an appraising look. "Let me see one ring first. You can trust me." I had no choice but to trust him, so I threw one of the rings over the fence. He picked it up, and after examining it closely, he threw two packs of Players Navy Cut cigarettes over the fence. I threw the second ring over and he sent back two more packs in exchange. Next, I threw the medal for heroism over. "I'll give you ten cigarettes for it." I shook my head. "No, this is a valuable medal, I want a whole pack." He reluctantly agreed, and I walked away with five packs of smokes. I gave one pack to each of the ring

time there was no horse manure, and we had benches to sit on. We were worried about our destination. I felt trapped again. Where the hell were we going now? There was an ominous silence in our passenger car. It almost felt as though we were going to a funeral; our funeral.

The train travelled east across Belgium for several hours and stopped between two big slag hills. We got out, crossed the tracks, and went single-file along a country trail to a barbed-wire POW camp. At the entrance to the camp we saw several hundred Belgian citizens waiting for us. They had bats, iron bars, and rocks in their hands and began shouting, "Deutsche schweine," while making gestures of slitting our throats and lynching us. It was terrifying. I wanted to tell them, "I am not a Nazi, I am innocent of Nazi war crimes." But I couldn't, I just had to keep marching. Our British soldiers tried to form a protective shield for us. They pointed their rifles at the Belgians and I heard them shouting, "Fuck off!" They saved us. The Belgians backed off and we marched into the camp. I felt like I had come to the Siberian Gulag and that this was the end of the line for me. I had arrived in 106-109 Mining Company. We were lined up and addressed by Oberfeldwebel Kurt Eckardt. "I welcome you. I have been a prisoner since the Battle of Caen, Normandy. If you have any questions, I'm happy to meet with you in my office. This is an organized camp. There is a German doctor for you. Tomorrow, you will be interviewed by the Commission from the Berringen Coal Mine, and you will start work." Porridge soup was served for dinner and we were assigned barracks. There were 24 men to a barrack, and we were each given two blankets. It felt like heaven to sleep on a wooden floor, but I felt that ominous sense of being trapped once again. Why did I impulsively agree to this?

Roll call next morning was 8 am. We were addressed by the commanding officer of the camp, Captain Metcalfe. He talked to us like a grandfather, and our German commandant, Oberfeldwebel Eckardt, translated. Metcalfe welcomed us, but also reminded us to keep discipline, as we were still in the military. We received our food ration for the day and were registered by the Germans and the Mining Company. When I was asked how long I had been a coal miner, I lied and said, "one year." I was given a beginner's job as a schlepper, the lowest job of them all. There were three shifts, and I had the afternoon shift from 2 to 10 pm. We were placed in barracks according to our work shifts. They gave me a badge with my number, 7290. It was an exciting time, as we had been living in rags, and now we received clothes for the mine. These clothes consisted of British army drill clothes and lovely army boots. However, the question that was in every prisoner's mind was, "How long will it be before we will be free again?"

An older prisoner made a comment which struck fear into our hearts. "We will be slaves until all reparations are paid by Germany for what we did to the other European countries." As soon as I heard this, I began to think about escape. The completion of such reparations, if even possible, seemed like an eternity away. We began work in the mine the very next day. My foot was still swollen and painful, but I managed all the same. The route took us on a catwalk across the railroad tracks to the mine. We changed into our work clothes and I faced my first experience of going underground. A double-decker cage appeared to transport us down the shaft. Before we got on, we passed a checkpoint where we gave our badges and received an underground headlamp. An experienced miner gave me advice once we got into the cage. "Keep your mouth open to prevent pain in your eardrums from the pressure change." The others were calm, which helped me to stay calm. I felt exhilarated as we plunged 800 meters into the depths of the earth. As I descended, I began to plan my escape.

We got out and I saw many coal cars on tracks waiting to take us into different areas of the mine. I climbed into a coal car and we went to an area called 70 north. Herman, the shift boss, spoke to each of us about our jobs and sent us off to the coal seams. I asked him in Flemish if I could have lighter duties due to the current injured state of my foot. "Take a shovel and go up and down both sides of the conveyer belt to clean up the spill." I was alone in this task and felt like I had some autonomy, despite being a prisoner. I met some Belgian coal miners during my shift and began to get to know them by chatting while we worked. They were completely the opposite of what I had experienced on the surface. I was pleasantly surprised to find them to be so friendly. Perhaps it was the camaraderie of the coal miners I felt. At the end of the shift, we went back up the shaft to the surface. It took about 15 minutes to ascend. All of us were completely blackened with soot except for the whites of our eyes. At the checkpoint, we turned in our headlamp and received our badge. We showered, dressed, and lined up to get counted by the guards. Afterward, we marched back to camp. They conducted another count at the gate to make sure no one had escaped. I was thoroughly exhausted and hungry, but there was only water. I had worked eight hours without food. My hungry stomach would just have to wait until morning.

The next morning, we saw an announcement on the bulletin board from Dr. Goebbels, the Minister of Propaganda, Education, and Culture. It stated that any German soldier who surrendered to the enemy would never be allowed to enter German territory again. We paid no mind to threats from this Nazi clown. Unfortunately, the Ruhr valley had still not fallen to the British forces. This increased our worries, as we knew our families were still in danger. The camp was well equipped with running water, toilets, and an outside swimming pool. I wondered who had built this efficient camp and asked one of the German sergeants. "This camp used to be a Russian POW camp built by German engineers. It is absolutely escape-proof." Could he read my mind? Looking around and closely assessing the area, I saw that he was likely right. There were four watch towers equipped with search lights, each with a guard holding a submachine gun. I felt as though an iron door had dropped on my plan and I was truly imprisoned. My mind raced with frantic thoughts and my heartrate elevated. I quickly became obsessed with contemplating different impossible ways to escape.

Sunday was our day off. Several commissioners from the mine came and praised us for our hard work. They told us production was up and asked us if we had any requests. Several older POW's asked for better food rations, sleeping quarters, and opportunities for recreational activities. They replied that bunk beds were already ordered and told us they would do their best to fulfill the other requests. Our bunk beds arrived a few days later. It was now the end of April and the Ruhr Valley was occupied by allied forces. On May 2nd, we heard that Hitler had shot himself on April 30th in his Berlin bunker. He was gone at last, that evil manipulator of the German nation. Many of us were uncontainably jubilant at this news. The coal miners were mainly communists and socialists who hated Hitler with a passion. The sun was shining, and it reminded me of my hiking days back in Herne. I decided to report as sick and use this beautiful day to finalize my escape plan. They told me that I had to see the doctor the next morning, and if he thought I was lying about being ill, I would have to do a double shift as penalty. I took the risk, as I knew I needed this day to make my plans. George, another miner, also reported sick.

After everyone left, we sat together on a bench in the sunshine and introduced ourselves. He told me that he was a 19-year-old paratrooper from Silesia. "I escaped the American POW camp in Normandy last year. I stole an American truck and drove through the German front and got shot by my own countrymen." He showed me the bullet wound in his chest and back and then whispered to me, "How can we get out of here?" I knew I had been right to book off work today, as now I had found a companion to escape with, and he appeared to be a tough and fearless fellow. It was only later that I discovered he was a fanatical Nazi and lacking in general intelligence. We began to talk about how the escape could be done. It was obvious that there was no hope of escape from the camp itself. The only possibility would be during the march back from the mine after our shifts were over. Darkness would aid us in our endeavour. We decided our best chance was when we crossed the lumber yard outside the mine. It was full of piled up timber, which provided us some cover. Together, we had finally come up with an escape plan. It seemed safer to make our individual escapes separately, then meeting behind a large bush at the end of the trail that went to the railway track. We looked into each other's eyes and made a pact: tomorrow, we would be free. Our first task was to make two berets from my army blanket. My plan was to wear khaki drill pants, my British boots, and a sweater to hide my German uniform. I made sure that nothing would visibly give me away. Foolishly, I assumed that George would know well enough to do the same. I couldn't sleep that night due to all the escape plan scenarios constantly buzzing around in my head.

CHAPTER 9

In the morning, we both saw the British army doctor and told him we were feeling better. He didn't believe we had been ill, and we received the promised penalty of a double shift for the weekend. Neither of us cared, because we knew we would be far away by then. Marching to the mine that afternoon, I felt exhilaration overcome my senses. My eyes thoroughly scanned the lumber yard for areas where I might be able to take cover. My shift seemed to last for an eternity, and all I could think about was my impending escape attempt. Finally, the shift ended. The procedure for crossing the lumber yard after the shift was for a guard with a flashlight to lead the way. Then, a group of ten prisoners followed him one at a time, with another guard following behind them with a flashlight. It was a serpentine labyrinth to navigate around the lumber piles. Every time the line turned a corner, there was my chance to jump between the lumber piles and fall to the ground. I found the perfect spot and jumped. My heart beat louder than a drum as I felt my blood rushing to my face. I lay flat on the ground, not breathing, as the others passed by. It helped that I was so skinny and able to fit in tight places. When I saw the last British guard go by, I got up and silently stalked behind with the finesse of a cat. I kept 20 metres behind him and was guided by his flashlight. I felt confident that I was going to escape. It was May 3rd, 1945, and I was going home.

Once they reached the lit trail to the catwalk, I dropped back into the shadows. I moved quickly to the big bush that George and I had agreed upon to be our point of rendezvous. He wasn't there yet, so I waited a few minutes until he arrived. We felt triumphant and felt as though we had conquered the world. In the distance, we could see the prisoners entering the large gate and being counted. I thought, "Oh, oh, now they'll know we're missing!" We quickly scuttled across the railway tracks on all fours and began running east towards Holland. The full moon lit the way on our journey. We ran several kilometres until we were too exhausted to take another step. I felt free as a bird and couldn't contain my overwhelming sense of excitement. Tall trees now surrounded the trail and made it harder to navigate in the darkness. After several hours, we reached a high hill and could see that down below there was farmland. To the far right, we saw a large construction of four watch towers, barbed wire, and search lights. My heart sank and filled with doom. "It looks like our camp..." George replied, "It is our camp!" We had literally been running around in circles. I was reluctant to admit it, but there it was, our own POW camp. We were just two arrogant idiots running in circles like chickens with their heads cut off.

We began running as fast as we could in the direction we thought would lead us towards home. Every farmhouse we came to had dogs that barked at us, causing us to make a plethora of detours to avoid them. As daylight came, we knew we had to find a hiding place fast. There was a meadow nearby with a strip of bushes and we hid underneath them. We both passed out immediately, and woke up to find a redheaded, freckled boy of about ten, holding a cow on a rope and staring at us. He said, in Flemish, "What are you doing there?" I quickly answered back, also in Flemish, "We are English soldiers." I heard a woman's voice calling from the door of the nearby farmhouse. "What did you find?" The boy replied, jokingly, "Mama, get out the rifle. I found a couple of Germans here." She laughed. "That's all right, I'm not afraid of Germans." "No, I'm just joking, Mama, they're English." George and I heaved a sigh of relief. "Invite them into the house." Because George only spoke German, I whispered strict instructions to him, "Don't speak at all, just keep nodding." We followed the boy into the farmhouse, which was little more than a tumbledown shack. There was a wooden table, two benches, an old grandmother in a dark dress, and a sweet little girl with long blonde braids inside.

The mother gave us a friendly smile. "Are you hungry?" I was starving, but I knew I couldn't admit that. The British soldiers had an abundance of food, so we had to pretend to be well fed. "No, but we're thirsty." She gave us water and we sat at the table and chatted. I silently thanked my Oma for teaching me the Dutch language, which is quite similar to Flemish. George just kept nodding. I purposefully planted some English words throughout the conversation to maintain our deception. By this time, I had come up with a plan to explain why we were there. "We are part of a British combat unit and have just come back from Germany. Our unit dropped us off here, and your meadow has been chosen for our unit to camp here for the next two weeks. We will have our jeeps and supplies stored here during that time, and you will be compensated handsomely for it with cigarettes, tea, and coffee." The whole family cheered at this news. Then, both the mother and the grandmother asked, "Do you have any cigarettes?" I had only four left, so I gave them each one and we joined together in a friendly smoke. The mother asked us to join them in a bowl of buttermilk soup with homemade noodles. It was quite generous of her to offer, because I could see how poor they were. I was getting a headache from keeping up this charade and I felt terrible to be deceiving these kind Belgians. It had been all too easy to fool them. If her husband returned, we were done for. No Belgian man would believe that we were British soldiers.

"We have to go now, as our unit will be coming at any time. Thank you for your kindness. We will see you tomorrow." We left, walked until we were out of sight, and then began running like scared rabbits. The sky was our navigator and we followed the railway tracks going east. Around midnight, we saw an open box car loaded with coal. The locomotive was facing east and we couldn't believe our dumb luck. Both of us climbed in and immersed ourselves into the coal so that only our blackened faces stuck out. We heard the signal for the train to leave and saw a man coming with a flashlight. The train started and I just lay in the coal looking up at the stars as we headed towards home. I was totally relaxed in that coal pile, glad for the rest, and making plans as to how we could cross the border into Holland. The train was gaining speed before I realized, in horror, that it had turned south. I knew I couldn't jump off a speeding train with my injured foot. My spirits sank once more. George and I decided to wait until the train slowed down enough to jump off. It was almost dawn when I looked up and saw the faces of the train traffic controllers in the windows of the section house. They

Germany and had worked there during the war. "Did you go there voluntarily?" He replied quietly, "Yes, I have a large family to feed." The policeman hit the Belgian in the face with a punch that broke his jaw and knocked him unconscious. I felt the violence of that blow as if I had received it myself. The policeman kicked this unconscious man several times with his boots and shouted, "You're a collaborator!" Then, they handcuffed the unconscious man and dragged him away. I felt sorry for this older man who was just trying to feed his family in desperation. If that is how they treat a fellow Belgian, how will they treat us, two German soldiers, once they get the chance? A jeep arrived with two armed guards and we were told to get in. The MP officer handed a sheet of paper to the driver. I could just barely read over his shoulder the words, "KEEP THESE TWO GERMAN POW'S UNTIL FURTHER NOTICE." We were taken to the local jail and put in a large cell. The Belgian policeman showed the American guard the cell and asked him, "Is this okay?" The reply uttered by the American is still burned into my brain. "It's good enough for these German pigs."

Here I was, trapped again. George and I looked at each other mournfully. I was sorry that he had been beaten and was suffering, but I was also pissed off at him for being so stupid as to wear his German paratrooper pants. What an idiot he was, and what an idiot I was to have him as my partner. Now I realized, much too late, that I had made my escape with a man who had lots of guts, but little to no brains. I passed out in a deep sleep and woke to loud screams of terror. A prisoner was being beaten in the hallway. The cell door opened, and two Belgian police threw a man into our cell. His face was covered in blood and he was obviously severely injured. He lay down next to me on the wooden bench, moaning and crying. I asked him, in French, "What happened?" I saw that he had German military boots on. "I was in the French SS division, Charlemagne, and fought on the Russian front." This explained why he had been beaten by the Belgians. To them, he was a collaborator, a traitor, a man who was even worse than a German. He was lucky they hadn't killed him. We heard more screams and beatings, and soon, one by one, four more men in civilian clothes were thrown into our cell. I'll never forget their faces, which had been furiously beaten to a pulp. My heart was heavy with sorrow to be witness to such brutality and suffering. Damn Hitler. I told them we were escaped German POW's and shared our story. One of them was a young man dressed like a wealthy gentleman in suit and tie. "I was a clerk in Berlin as a member of the Belgian Leon de Grelle Party and was in charge of the administration of a Belgian labour camp in Germany." I remembered them. They wore black shirts and were enthusiastic Hitler supporters. He wept as he shared his story, knowing he would soon be executed for his associated war crimes.

As the night went by, the other three men told me their stories. One was a member of the Dutch SS division Nederland, and the other two had belonged to a Flemish SS unit. All four of them were from the Russian front, and all four of them were SS members. The former clerk whispered to me, "When you get home to Germany, tell everyone how we were mistreated here by the Belgian police." I looked at him sadly. My spirit was crushed by this point, and I had lost all hope of any future. "I don't think I will ever see Germany again." He looked me in the eye and said kindly, "No, you will be sent back to Germany eventually, while there is no chance of going home for us. We're finished." I felt a surge of hope at his words. How morbidly funny, I thought, that at my lowest point I would feel lifted up by the words of a Nazi. The cell door opened, and two Belgian policemen came in with long wooden batons. One said brusquely, "Get up! Get up and make a circle." We did as we were ordered. He told us to start running, and they began to beat our head and shoulders with the batons. I instinctively covered my head with my hands, so they battered me on my back and sides instead. It was like a game of "ring around the rosy" with a diabolical twist. As we ran, they told us to shout in French, "Hitler est casse", which meant, "Hitler is dead." Then, they ordered us to crawl on the concrete floor on our knees and elbows as they continued to beat us. They seemed to be quite experienced in the art of torture.

I was completely exhausted and ready to collapse. The young clerk did collapse, and they beat him even more ferociously while he lay there. I figured this must be how a wild animal must feel as it is captured and killed for sport. I was crawling through blood on the floor and felt the ragged pain from the soiled open wounds on my knees and elbows. We were completely at their mercy. I was being punished for the sins of the Nazis. Our tormenters finally became satiated in their hunger for vengeance and left us crumpled in a downtrodden heap. I felt that this was the end of the road for me, and I had little hope of surviving this ruthless trap. I looked down at the clerk who lay seemingly lifeless at my feet. Several hours later, the cell door was opened by a police officer. I noticed that our door was marked "SS" in white chalk. Two civilians were let into our cell, crying bitterly over and over, "Dachau! Dachau! Dachau!" I knew instantly that they were liberated concentration camp survivors brought in to show us what atrocities had been done to them. They were senseless with grief. I could feel their pain emanating through me; almost palpable in the air. I looked at them pleadingly and said, "I am a German POW, not a Nazi." The policeman standing at the cell door struck me hard across my face with his baton. The pain jolted through my body like an electric shock. The police took the Dachau survivors out of the cell and closed the door.

I lay on the wooden bench, feeling more dead than alive, and spent the night listening to my companions weeping and moaning. The inequity of the situation reverberated through my mind on repeat. All my life I hated the Nazis and what they stood for, yet now I had been labelled a Nazi, a member of the murderous SS. I no longer felt hungry, as my extreme thirst overpowered the hunger. Although it was daylight now, all I could see was darkness. I felt the life slowly seeping out of me. None of us dared ask for water, as we feared we would be beaten for simply uttering the query. In the morning, three young American soldiers entered our cell. One was a photographer and took photos of us as we lay there tortured and bleeding. He took multiple photos of me and I thought to myself, "Now I will be labelled a Nazi, an SS bastard, in some magazine in the United States." One of the Americans spoke perfect

German, and I had a feeling that he was also Jewish. "Which SS unit did you serve in?" I replied with tearful desperation, "I am a 17-year-old German soldier escaped from a POW camp. I just want to go home." "Were you a member of the Hitler Youth?" "It was mandatory, from age 10. But I-" I was about to tell him that I had a Jewish father, but he grabbed me by my hair and smashed my head against the wall with such force that he broke my jaw. "Nazi swine!" he spat. I kept seeing the bulb flashes as the photographer took pictures of this attack. Then, having obtained what they came for, they left. I lay on the bench in agonizing pain and thought, "How can I get something sharp enough to cut my wrists?" This was the first time in my life that I ever wanted to end my own life. I looked around for anything that might work. Alas, there was nothing. I felt totally hopeless. There was no escape, not even by suicide.

My jaw was swelling and became more painful as time went on. That night, the cell door opened, and there was a different guard standing there. A thought came to me to speak German to him so that it would be clear that I was not a collaborator. Up until now I had spoken only French which may have led them to believe me to be a collaborator. He had a friendly face that gave me a sliver of hope. "My friend and I are German POWs. Why are we with the SS?" He replied in fluent German, "How did you end up in here?" I told him that I deserted, surrendered to the British, was sent to a Belgian Coal Mining camp, and escaped with George because we wanted to go home. I spoke slowly and carefully, as I knew this was the most important story I would ever tell. Our lives depended on it. The guard listened with what appeared to be compassion. "I have no hard feelings against you. I was a POW myself and escaped. However, these men who collaborated with the Nazis are traitors and deserve the worst."

It seemed I now had an ally. "Are you hungry?" I replied, "I am beyond hunger, but I am dying for a drink of water." A second policeman entered the cell and my merciful guard told him to get a jug of water. George and I drank thirstily of the water and he refilled the jug for the night. As he handed me the jug he said firmly, "Do not give a single drop of water to these pigs. I can see what you are doing through the spy hole." He left, and I knew he meant what he said. I felt hope rising within me like a flame. Perhaps George and I would get out of here and make it home after all. I put the jug of water beside my head where I slept. The others began whispering and begging, "Water...water...please" I didn't want to be caught handing it to them, but I whispered to them to help themselves when I pretended to fall asleep. I sensed the jug was moving from man to man, and when it returned, I was surprised to see that there was still some left. I respected their integrity that they would leave some for me. This compassionate act felt beyond past crimes, beyond hate, beyond politics, beyond war.

In the morning, the cell door opened and two armed American MP's stood there. One of them read out, "George Heinrich and Robert Schulte-Middelmann, come with us." They escorted us outside to a covered transport vehicle. We stumbled along, half dead, apathetic as to where we were going. With great effort, we climbed in the back with the armed MP's, and the driver took off to drive through Liege. There were

encounter with an American Jew had resulted in the current horrific state of my jaw, so I hoped this encounter would go better than the last one. He asked me to show him on the map where the POW Coal Mining camp was where we had been held. I showed him and he asked, "When did you escape?" "May 3rd." After a few more questions, he seemed to believe us and told the MP's to take us back to our POW camp. We got in a jeep with them and had a guided tour across Belgium back to Berringen. The MP's turned us over to the British and they greeted us with much laughter. The sergeant said, "Go to the far side of the barrack and sit down." They seemed to be amused by our escapade and treated us as though we were a couple of clowns. As I sat there, I felt such gratitude that I was now in safe hands again. From my personal experience, the British were never unnecessarily brutal or hateful to the prisoners. "Could I please have a drink of water?" I asked the sergeant. "Would you care for a cup of tea?" He brought us tea, and as he handed it to me, I saw the kindness in his face and in his big grin. The message I read was, "Nice try, kids, but have you learned your lesson?" It felt good to be home from our nightmarish escape attempt.

I sat on the floor drinking my tea and reflecting on our failed escape. "You schmuck, why did you take George along? You would have made it if it weren't for him and his damn paratrooper pants." I realized how unprepared I had been for the escape. No food, no maps, no money, and no real plan. We were about as prepared as immature and impulsive teenagers running away from a boarding school. I decided that my next escape would be planned significantly better. Just then, a Belgian police officer came in and told the sergeant, "We have seven escaped POW's to return to you." Two armed British soldiers went out and came back with the POW's. To my surprise, I recognized them all as fellow prisoners. They sat down by us and I asked Ernst, the one nearest to me, "What happened?" He looked at me with mixed disappointment and astonishment. "We thought you and George were already in Germany. Your escape gave us hope that we could make it, too. Bernie stole wire cutters from the mine, and we cut through the wire and escaped two nights ago." I was surprised to find that George and I had inspired their escape. "How far did you get?" "About ten kilometres. We got thirsty and stopped at a farmhouse to ask for a drink of water." I didn't feel quite so stupid anymore. These guys surely won that contest. I asked, "What language did you use when you asked for water?" "German," he replied. "None of us speak Flemish." I could see that all seven of them were in their German uniforms. It was unbelievable to me that not one of them thought to disguise themselves in the slightest. "They gave us water and we kept walking down the country road afterward, but we were soon stopped by the Belgian police who ordered us, in German, to put up our hands or they would shoot us dead." In German that is, "Haende hoch ich schiess Dich kaput!" Definitely an order you want to take seriously. "We were handcuffed and a police vehicle came to bring us back to the police station for interrogation. We told them about our escape, and they promptly brought us back here." All of them looked disappointed to see us, their inspiration, back in camp.

The nine of us were taken by guards to Captain Metcalfe's office. I could see that he was seething with anger. He shouted at the top of his lungs, "Why did you do this to me?" I replied, "I just want to go home." "So do I, so do I!" His whole body was shaking with frustration. "I sentence all of you to 28 days detention." We had really pissed off our kind-hearted Captain Metcalfe. As I was the only one who spoke English, he asked me to translate his message to the others. He gave orders to the guards to take us then added, "Get out of here... just get the hell out of here!" I felt like the disobedient son who had just greatly disappointed his father. We were taken by army truck to a Belgian military garrison in nearby Waterscheid to serve our detention. A Belgian officer told us, "You will be treated fairly and humanely by our boys. They are honest, decent soldiers." I believed him to be a good man and trusted him with our safety.

CHAPTER 10

We were placed three to a small cell and given two blankets to sleep on the concrete floor. The next morning, they shaved our heads. Our daily ration was water and a small piece of bread. Every third day, we were provided a bowl of thin soup. Once a day, we were taken out into the yard for 20 minutes. We remained handcuffed and tied together with a big rope during this recreational time. If one man ran, he would have to drag the other eight along with him. We stumbled around in a circle, getting weaker by the day. My jaw was swollen and painful, and I was still unable to chew my food. After 14 days, I was too weak to get up for the exercise walk at all. I was lying in my cell feeling helpless when my door opened and there were two Belgian guards standing there. One of them told me in Flemish, "Here, eat this." He handed me a plate with a slice of bread with butter and jam and a canteen of tea.

This act of kindness lifted my spirits and gave me faith in humanity again. The teachings of my Oma came to me then. "There are good and bad people in every nation. The devil has no nationality." After thinking of my beloved Oma, I began to feel stronger. The next day, much to our surprise, we were driven back to our camp. Captain Metcalfe received us. "I will let you serve the remaining time here at the camp." I sensed that he truly felt sympathy for us despite our previous insubordinance. He likely heard of my weakened condition and wanted to help me. He had always been rather fond of me. I thought, "He is like a grandpa to us, and, like us, he just wants to go home." We were placed in a barrack right by the barbed wire fence. The kitchen was next door, and I heard Captain Metcalfe tell the cook, "Give them a good meal." That meal was as delightful and fulfilling as if it were a grand holiday feast. We were given corned beef, potatoes, cauliflower, and delicious Dutch gravy. I have yet to forget the smell and taste of that feast. Unfortunately, I had to eat it with excruciating slowness due to the current state of my jaw, essentially just gumming this fabulous feast. We all felt blessed by Captain Metcalfe's act of generosity. For the rest of our detention, we had generous portions of food and enjoyed the luxury of sleeping on a wooden floor.

We had plenty of room in the barrack and lots of time to inspect it thoroughly. The walls were covered with beautiful paintings from the former tenants, Russian POW's. One scene was of the famous Caucasus Mountains with the peak of the Caspek. Another one, which covered a large part of the wall, was the face of a beautiful woman. There was also a ping pong table, much to our surprise. The floor was covered in 4 x 8 pieces of plywood that were nailed down. I noticed that one plywood piece was loose, so I lifted it up to discover a 4 metre deep shaft with a ladder leaning against the earthen wall. Immediately, I climbed down and found several empty tin buckets and rusted up kitchen utensils. I climbed back and showed my discovery to the others. "I know what this is, it's a Russian cooler to store food," said Ernst. Right away, I had an idea. "We're only a few metres away from freedom. We have to dig a tunnel." Most of them enthusiastically agreed to give this a try, so we began planning. George did not join in, as he had sunk into a deep depression and had become mute from his trauma. This time, I decided we would do it right. The barracks were all one metre above ground with a skirted crawl space below. We made a plan to dig into the wall of the Russian cooler and make a tunnel under the barbed wire to freedom. The dirt would have to be disposed of so as not to arouse suspicion, of course. We decided to hide the dirt in the skirted crawl space. We constructed meticulous escape plans, measuring everything and figuring out how to get food, water, and a map of Belgium for the journey. I couldn't help but feel bad for poor Captain Metcalfe. He feels sorry for us, brings us back, gives us generous portions of food, and we repay him by immediately planning another escape even grander than the one before.

We began working right away on our tunnel. It was tedious and tiring work. We only had two buckets, a kitchen ladle, and a few tin cans to use as tools. George just laid curled up in a fetal position in the corner, a broken man. It pained me to see him that way. We needed a rope to pull up the buckets of dirt, so we took a long canvas off the top of the ping pong table for this purpose. We made a knife from one of the kitchen utensils and cut off a piece about 6 inches wide all around the canvas. That way, the British wouldn't notice it missing. We twisted this into a strong rope to use in order to pull up the buckets. German ingenuity was at work! Werner, a tough paratrooper, made an important discovery that night. He came across a loose piece of skirting which could easily be taken out, meaning that we would have free access to the camp and its needed supplies. This also meant that we could continue working on our tunnel after we returned to our regular

171

barracks, saving us precious time. We endlessly debated the best way to plan our return to Germany. At one point I said firmly, "When we get out, I want to go alone. I don't want to travel with anyone." I knew I had a better chance on my own because I was fluent in several languages, while the others could only speak German.

We finished our plans and then focused on digging the tunnel and locating necessary supplies. All work and no play makes for a dull time, so sometimes we would lie on the ground and peek out through a hole in the skirting. One day I saw Achim, a man I had befriended previously. I trusted him, so I called his name softly. He came over, watching to make sure he wasn't observed. "Next week, we're getting out," I whispered to him. He nodded.

A kitchen helper, who was an older man, came over one day and I struck up a conversation with him at the locked window. I told him to meet me at the peephole. We met there, and after I established that he was an ally, I asked him, "Can you do me a favour? Can you lend me a shovel? I'll give it back to you later." "I'll try," he replied. The next morning, there was a shovel in the crawl space and the skirting was back in place. The shovel made our tunneling much faster. Now, we could dig two metres of tunnel a day. However, we stopped digging when one of the professional coal miners told us, "You have to timber this tunnel, or else it will cave in and suffocate you all." It was good that at least one of us had some sense. We stopped and had a debate about where to get the lumber. We had to wait until we were out of detention to have access to timber. My strength was coming back with the generous food portions, and my jaw was progressively becoming less painful. I was energized by the thought of the escape and my return home.

On June 12th, we came out of detention to find that the entire camp had assembled to welcome us like homecoming heroes. They sang a rousing rendition of, "In der Heimat in der Heimat da gibts ein Wiedersehn." In English this translates to, "At home, at home, we all will meet again." This song has a special significance to Germans, as it is often sung by soldiers who are thinking of home and hoping to see their loved ones again. One of the prisoners accompanied them on his violin. The deep and penetrating sound of the violin permeated through my heart and I felt a warm flood of emotion and strength rise within me. Even the British guards in the watch towers were smiling and clapping to the beat of the music. In that moment, I thought of the tunnel and said to myself, "I am halfway home already." We were then assigned to our barracks. I was overjoyed to see that the barracks now had double bunk beds with straw mattresses. This was the first time since I left home that I would be sleeping in a real bed again.

We managed to meet secretly to discuss our plans, even though we were on different shifts at the mine. To our great delight, we had already realized we could remove two boards from under our mattresses for the lumber for our tunnel. Then we could space the remaining six boards so that no one would notice them missing. We planned to steal two boards from every bed in the camp and would accomplish this by stealing from the beds of prisoners whose barracks were empty during their mine shifts. My new job was now a real coal miner's job, breaking the coal with a jack hammer. It was a tough job. I could only work on my knees, as the space was just four feet high. I was 6'2" and this was painful, backbreaking work. This made me even more determined to finish our tunnel as soon as possible. Whenever I was off duty, I would be busy snitching boards to shore up the tunnel. My left foot was healed enough that I could at least walk again without significant pain. My broken jaw still ached something terrible, but the pain was no longer unbearable. Whatever spare time we had was spent digging and shoring the tunnel. Our progress would have been faster, had we not already been working 8-hour shifts in the mine and subsisting off of very minimal food rations.

My good friend, Achim, had already joined our group. I also trusted two friends from my hometown, Heinz and Leo, and invited them to join us. They were excited about our plans and eager to join. Now, our escape group totalled 11 men. We all believed that we would be free by September. I had made an amicable relationship with Franek, the Belgian janitor in charge of the shower room at the coal mine and shared our escape plans with him. He offered to help us in any way he could. One day, he gave me a much-needed flashlight and a map of Belgium. Since the escapes, the British had tightened up their security. They didn't want any more wire cutters to disappear. The guards frisked every man returning to the camp, so I had to figure out how to smuggle out the flashlight and map. I came up with an ingenious plan which worked out beautifully. Each prisoner was given a tin container for tea. It had a felt cover around the tin and a cork plug in the top. I chiselled out the bottom of the tin can and put the felt cover back on, successfully creating a safe passage for the contraband. Bless the British and their love for tea! When they frisked me, I just put up my hands, with my soap and towel in one hand, and my tea tin in the other. It never occurred to them that I might have anything in my tea tin. How would I get anything in that little hole at the top? Sadly, this also meant I was never able to enjoy the delicious British tea on my shift. Thankfully, Heinz worked close to me and was quite happy to share. Now we had a flashlight to work by and a map of Belgium to memorize.

July 10th was my 18th birthday. Kurt Eckhardt, the German commandant of the camp, had made a gentleman's agreement with the British that each prisoner could get the day off work on their birthday. The agreement also included that the birthday boy would get a double portion of soup as a much welcomed gift. On my special day, I went to the kitchen to get my extra soup ration. The cook in charge was of an unfriendly sort. When I asked him for my birthday soup, he said brusquely, "Can you prove this is your birthday?" I thought, "His belly is full while I'm starving, and he is already looking for reasons to turn me away. How selfish and unnecessarily callous of him!" I felt sorry for him that he was such a cantankerous creature. To his surprise, I showed him my German military ID with my birth date. I could tell he was not happy about having to give me my birthday soup. On my way out, an older prisoner, who had silicosis from working in the mine, called me over to him. He was a kind-hearted kitchen helper. He leaned forward and whispered, "Happy birthday," and quickly placed a loaf of British white bread under my jacket. "Eat it in the shithouse so no one can see, or else they will all want a piece!" I felt blissfully grateful for this small act of kindness, and went right to the shithouse to enjoy my birthday meal alone. As I sat there slowly eating my soup and bread, I felt like the richest man in the world. I savored every precious slurp and every bite, taking my time. I had the whole day off to celebrate my birthday and could take all the time I wanted.

When I got back to my barrack, there was an unforgettable surprise waiting for me. On my bunk was a tin can with a beautiful flowering thistle in it. There was also a home rolled cigar accompanied by a poem written by my bunk mates. "Now that you are 18 and have become a man, you're entitled to smoke a cigar. If you don't, you are sentenced to crawl naked through the bunk house from one side to another." In German, this poem rhymes and sounded quite clever. All my friends wished me a happy birthday with big grins on their faces. At 18, I was the youngest one in the barrack. They were all like big brothers to me. I was touched by this show of brotherly love and thanked them for their generosity. I knew how precious tobacco was, and that each one had sacrificed some to make the birthday cigar. "How did you get the thistle?" Heinz replied proudly, "It was growing in the forbidden zone between the barbed wire and the warning wire, and we wanted to get it for you." They knew I loved plants, and this would be a special gift for me. The guards had permission to shoot anyone who entered that area. "How did you manage to get it?" I asked. "We told the guards it was your 18th birthday and negotiated with them to go in and retrieve the thistle." I lit the precious cigar and shared it with others. Seven or so decades later, this remains the most unforgettable birthday of my life. I relive that day every year on my birthday, and relish in the selfless kindness of my friends who made it the best birthday of my life.

Unfortunately, at the end of July, our benevolent British unit was replaced by a Belgian unit. They were Walloons, French speaking soldiers from Southern Belgium. What a disagreeable lot of young punks they were, and so filled with malice. They took their hatred out on us whenever they saw fit. On our way to work we were insulted, kicked, and hit with the butts of their rifles. We immediately reported this abuse to our commandant, Kurt Eckhardt. Without delay, he called a strike for all three shifts. The Belgians responded to our strike by cutting off our food supply. After three long days, they came to an agreement. No more physical abuse, and we would go back to work. Two weeks later, the Walloons were replaced by a Flemish unit who were the complete opposite in demeanor. They treated us with respect and fairness, and were almost as kind as the British. I made a positive acquaintance with Leon, one of the sergeants. He told me he had been in the resistance, the "White Brigade," and had blown up railway junctions, bridges, and a control tower at the Beverloo Airport. We were both happy the war was over and became good buddies. Meanwhile, our escape group continued to work hard on the tunnel, hoping to be out by September.

In mid-August, something quite unexpected happened. Commandant Kurt Eckhardt called me into his office. He was calm, and looked at me with penetrating eyes and a diplomatic smile. "Robert, I know you are going to pull another escape." My stomach turned over and I made every effort to put on a visage of innocence. "No, no, no," I protested. He paused and gave me a long look. "I know everything. I even know where the tunnel is located, but don't look so upset just yet, Robert. I can make you a deal you can't refuse." I felt my body relax a bit. We were caught, but perhaps some good could come out of this. "I have negotiated with the mine that all prisoners will get better rations and be paid five Belgian francs a day in tokens. You will also get recreation equipment and a canteen where you can buy cigarettes and toiletries." He paused, and then continued in a stern voice. "But if you boys attempt this escape, all my negotiations will be in vain and the entire camp will suffer for your actions." I felt the immense weight of guilt flow over me when I heard this news. What he said next sweetened the deal, however. "If you give up the tunnel, I can get you and your escape group home within a couple of months at the latest." It sounded far too good to be true. "Why should I believe you?" He gave me an appraising look. "We have almost 60 men unfit to work underground who have to be replaced by healthy men from the main camp. If you give me the names of your escape group, I will put all their names on the exchange list. You will be transferred to the main camp and registered for release to go back home." Up until this point, he had been a fair and honest commandant who always made decisions in our best interest. I decided to trust he was telling the truth. "I agree, and I will let the others know." We shook hands on our deal, and I went to tell my fellow escapees what had happened. I knew it wouldn't be easy.

The first one I run into was Achim. I told him the whole story. When I was done, he looked at me and shouted, "Du Blindgaenger!" That translates to, "You total dummy!" Then he added, "Now we'll all end up in a maximum security camp." No matter what I said, I couldn't convince him that it would be alright. I saw Heinz next and told him. "I hope you're right, Robert," he said, with resignation in his voice. The word spread to the others, and we were able to meet the next day, which was Sunday. I found out that the group was split between those who accepted my decision, and those who were totally pissed off with me for falling for what they saw as a trap. We discussed it at length, and finally made the decision to stop work on the tunnel. I was optimistic that Kurt Eckhardt would keep his promise, and that my peers would regain their faith in me. The next Sunday, several truck loads of POW's came into the camp. The prisoners were assembled. Commandant Eckhardt called out over 60 names to come forward. Everyone from our escape group was on that list, just as promised. I was elated and knew I had been right to trust him. Achim was nearby, so I walked up to him and asked, with great satisfaction, "Do you still believe you are going to a maximum security camp?" Within 20 minutes, we were on those trucks, with British guards, driving across Belgium. I asked a guard what our destination was, and the replied, "Camp 2228, near Antwerp." I felt immense gratitude to Commandant Eckhardt for saving our skins and sending us home. A profound feeling of safety and hope came over me. I was going to make it home. Oma was waiting for me, my safe nest, my beloved Oma. Later that day, however, we arrived at the camp and experienced a rude awakening when I realized that this was a tough military camp run by Germans. The guards were Flemish, and the officers were British. There were over 30,000 men in 30 marked areas called compounds. We were housed 12 men each to a teepee style tent. The camp was patrolled by capos and POW sergeants. There was not a single smiling face among these men, and I knew I was in for another rough time.

I ended up with total strangers in my tent. That night, I became friends with Josef, the guy sleeping next to me. He appeared to be another soldier like myself, but he later confessed to me that he had been a lieutenant. He disguised himself in a soldier's uniform because he knew officers would be detained longer than soldiers. Officers were to be screened and "denazified." The next morning, we assembled in typical German military order. We were told the rules, and I immediately knew I would have trouble obeying one in particular; there could be no talking to the guards. That meant there would be no trading and bartering. I simply decided that rule didn't apply to me, and later on, when I was sure I wouldn't be seen, I struck up a conversation through the high barbed wire fence with a friendly looking Flemish guard. "We have orders not to associate with you," he said quietly. "I know, but I have a brand new woolen blanket. Would you trade it for a pack of tobacco?" He looked around nervously. "Come to this spot again at 2 a.m. and we'll do the deal. Roll the blanket tight." We quickly moved away from each other so as not to arouse suspicion. I had thought of a way to still keep warm without my blanket and told Josef about my plan. "We each have two blankets, so we'll trade one for smokes, and then we can still keep warm if we share the remaining three blankets." He agreed right away. Just before 2 a.m., I rolled up the blanket as tight as I could, tied it with a string, and put it under my jacket. It helped that I was extremely skinny. I waited at the rendezvous spot for the guard. When he came, I threw the blanket over the fence. Immediately, two capos arrested me. I realized I had been set up. Now I had lost the blanket, had no smokes, and was under arrest.

I was taken to a pen surrounded by barbed wire, 4 metres across, with a wooden pole in the centre. They threw me in there. "In the morning the commandant will see you." After roll call, I was taken to the commandant's office. He sat there looking like an overly fed Pasha, with puffy cheeks and a look of disdain on his face. "I will give you a choice. You can be tied to that pole in the dog pen for 24 hours without any water or food, or you can burn shit for 14 days." As he spoke, he blew smoke from his cigarette directly in my face. I thought wryly, "I guess that's the only smoke I'll be getting out of this escapade." I pondered my choices. Twenty four hours tied to a pole is a long time with no water or food. It seemed like yet another torture session to me. "I'll take the shit." The capos immediately took me to the other side of the camp where there was a huge fire pit. I could see the smoke rising from the pit as we got closer and smell the excrement burning. Stanis, a POW in charge of the shit pit, immediately put me to work with Tomas, an older POW. I went with him and he showed me the ropes of the new job, explaining that the British brought used oil to get the fire going. Our enormous feces furnace covered the waste for 1,000 men. Each shit shift consisted of eight men. Everyone there was being punished for up to 28 days. The only exception was the shit boss, Stanis, who was in charge. I wondered why he would take that job voluntarily and found out later that he received double food rations and smokes for doing the job. It was a job no one wanted, but Stanis seemed to enjoy himself. He was a seasoned lance corporal, who made all of us laugh with his good-natured dark humour. Stanis made our misery easier to carry.

Tomas asked, "Comrade, where are you from?" "Herne." He looked at me in surprise and said, "My mother lives in Herne on Muehlenstrasse!" I couldn't believe it. "That's the street where I was born and raised. What's her name?" "Kucsnierek." "Frau Kucsnierek lives three doors from us!" It felt like a good omen. For the rest of my time at the shit pit, Tomas and I exchanged stories of Herne. He soon told me he was there for stealing a loaf of bread. The shit burners slept in a large tent near the pit. The 14 days at the shit pit were only made tolerable by Stanis's jokes and my friendship with Tomas. Cleanliness had always been of upmost importance to me, so I anxiously counted the days until I could escape the shit. At the end of my punishment, I was covered in shit and smelled like an outhouse. I threw all my clothes into the fire, and Stanis gave me some old clothes he had in his tent.

I can still see Stanis' friendly face and remember his jokes to this day. I had an emotional farewell with Tomas and went back to my tent, all too happy to leave the shit pit. Josef told me that interrogations had already begun to assess the POW's. The next morning, after roll call, the entire camp stood in line for hours waiting to be called. When it was my turn, I was interrogated by a British officer who had a POW acting as an interpreter. I had to give all the details of my background and also my parent's background. The officer asked, "Have you ever been a member of the NSDAP?" He was referring to the Nazi party. "No, never!" The initials stand for "Nationalist Socialist German Labour Party." The officer pointed to a large map on the wall. "Germany has been divided into four occupation zones. The Ruhr valley is in the British zone. Tomorrow, those of you in the British zone will be transferred to a camp where you will get your discharge papers and prepare to go home." I had come to appreciate the British humour and this officer didn't disappoint me. He added, in a jovial manner, "And then you all will become British subjects."

On October 4th, all men in the British zone were transported in open trucks to a transit camp near Ville Woorde, north of Brussels. The camp was run by the British, but the outside guards were Belgians. This was a huge camp. We were housed in a large tent and given two Royal Air Force woolen blankets each. As we settled in, Heinz looked at me with sudden alarm. "Robert, you are jaundiced! Your face and eyes are yellow. Don't let the British see this, or you will be sent to a hospital, and only God knows when you'll get home then!" I immediately realized that I had got jaundice from working at the shit pit, and I had to come up with a way to hide this from the British. I was with my close friends, Heinz, Achim, and Leo. We were all dying for a smoke. Leo proposed, "the British quarter master supply tent is in the middle of the camp. Let's steal a blanket and sell it to the Belgian guards for cigarettes." We discussed this at length until I came up with a feasible plan that the others accepted. "Leo and Heinz can go inside and distract the quarter master by talking about his favourite topic, soccer. Achim and I will be outside and lift the canvas in order to slowly inch out the bottom blanket. If one of you guys inside leans against the tall blanket pile, it won't fall over when we pull the bottom one out." We were all excited about this plan and anxiously looking forward to enjoying our smokes. The plan worked beautifully without a hitch, and we managed to get two blankets in the end. As I was experienced in bartering, and the only one who spoke Flemish, I was the obvious candidate for making the deal. I truly hoped, for the sake of my sanity and the health of my liver, that this deal would go better than the last one.

Soon I befriended another of the Belgian guards and arranged to meet him at midnight where there was a blind spot from which our meeting could not be observed. He said to bring both blankets, and he would give me two 50 gram packs of Belgian tobacco. Just before midnight, I rolled and tied up the blankets and took them to our meeting spot. I threw them over the fence to the guard and he threw the packs of tobacco to me in exchange. We celebrated our good fortune in our tent that night by smoking and sharing some of our tobacco with others. There was a sense of joy in the air, as we knew we were almost home. The next morning, Leo took one look at my face and furrowed his brow. "You're even more yellow today than before. You need to go to the last row during roll call, close your eyes, and look down so they don't see that you have jaundice." I did what Leo suggested, and no one noticed my yellowed face. I wanted to get home first and foremost and would find a way to see a doctor from there. On October 6th, we received our discharge papers and 40 German Reichsmarks. They lined us up and marched us about 5 km to the train station in Ville Woorde. There was only one British guard for 200 men, and 1,000 men were going home in total. We were all filled with intense excitement that we could hardly contain. With money in my pocket and my freedom on the horizon, I felt like a tourist travelling economy class. Adding to our happiness was the sight of the Belgian civilians who were waving to us and wishing us luck. I felt a deep sense of peace that I was no longer an object of hatred in their eyes.

We got on the train, 20 to a boxcar, and toured Belgium and Holland. At daybreak we crossed into Germany near Wesel, and we were overjoyed to see the Rhine River. The train stopped there for a few minutes, so I jumped out and kissed the ground. I felt as though I had a new lease on life. My mind kept reiterating the same refreshing thought, "Now nothing can hurt me. I've survived and I'm really going home." An air of supreme confidence flooded through me. We arrived in Muenster around noon. They unloaded us from the trains and marched us into an old garrison which had been partially damaged by a bomb. We were allowed to leave the garrison until 7 pm, so Heinz and I went on a stroll. We passed a garage where a woman and child were living instead of their house, as it had been reduced to rubble.

She told me her husband was a POW in Russia and offered to share her potato and carrot stew with us. Stew never tasted so good! It tasted like a gourmet meal in a five star hotel compared to the thin gruel we had been eating previously. More importantly, it felt like home, as though Oma had made it for me. We thanked her for her generosity and continued our stroll.

Nearby, we came to a house with a large garden. At least twenty of the POW's were in the garden pulling all the carrots out. The woman of the house begged, "Please, please, take some, but leave some for me!" I felt sorry for her, but could also understand these men. Hunger can make you put your conscience on the shelf. We returned to the garrison, and the British served vegetable soup with a loaf of bread to be shared between four men. After dinner, they separated all of us into our regions. My region was Arnsberg. In the morning, everyone got tea, the shared loaf, and a piece of sausage that we nicknamed, "The Churchill Sausage" in honour of Winston. Our group of 20 was taken by truck to a meadow in Arnsberg and given our discharge papers. Then, one of the funniest moments of my war experience took place. The British sergeant in charge, a jolly man with a robust belly, made repeated motions with his arms as though he were chasing chickens. "Shoo, shoo, shoo," he said, with a big grin. "Shoo, shoo, shoo!" "I'm really free," I thought. "Finally, I'm free. This chicken is coming home to roost!"

CHAPTER 11

Heinz, Leo, and I went to the train station and took a train to Dortmund, then to Herne. I had been on such a high since our release, but on the train ride I had time to decompress and reflect. "What will I find when I get home? Will my family be alive? Oma is old. Will she be there to hug me?" I saw that the others were also thinking such thoughts. We got off at Herne and I ran into Amos, an old school friend. "Are my parents and Oma alive?" I asked, fearing the answer. "Are they alive? Yes! And their business is booming." My fear subsided and my high came back tenfold. "Come home with me," I said happily to Leo and Heinz. "I'm inviting you for supper." Ten minutes later, we arrived at my family's home. It was Sunday, October 9th, 1945. My hand was shaking as I rang the bell. Through the glass, I could see a figure coming slowly towards the door. Oma opened the door warily and looked at me with no recognition. My appearance had changed drastically since our last encounter. I had lost over 70 pounds, had a shaved head, and a yellow face. I was a bald, jaundiced skeleton with skin stretched taut across my bones as if it were struggling to keep them from falling apart. I hardly resembled her beloved Robert. Still, I thought my Oma would surely recognize me. "Oh Oma, it's Robert. I'm home." Her eyes opened wide as she pulled me into her arms me and starting sobbing.

It was a sweet and unforgettable moment. Oma and I held each other up so that neither of us would fall. We held each other for a long time until Mama came to see what was going on. "Oh, my God, oh, my God!" she screamed and broke into tears. She embraced me and we had a long hug. When she gathered herself, she said, "Come in, come in!" We all tromped into the house while Mama made tea, fried ham, eggs, and, to top it all off, a glass of cognac and English cigarettes. A feast fit for the three kings. "Papa is on his nightly walk and will be home soon," Mama told me. Unfortunately, I could not partake in the feast. My stomach wouldn't accept the food as I was simply too ill. Leo and Heinz thanked my mother and we said goodnight, wishing each other luck and promising to meet soon. "Papa goes every night around 8 pm to the train station to watch for you, as the POW's have been arriving daily from east and west," Mama told me. I was touched to know that my Papa was doing this. I knew he loved me deeply.

I always loved to tease Oma, so I told her, "The Dutch were so mean and threw rocks at us. I wonder if they could have been some of our own relatives." She replied indignantly, "The Germans had no right to invade Holland in the first place." Then, Papa came into the kitchen. He had heard that I was home. He hugged me, kissed me, and began to weep intensely. I had never seen him quite so emotional. He left the room and came back, saying proudly, "I have saved this box of Sumatra cigars for you Robert. However, you must go to Dr. Pole for an examination first thing in the morning!" My family was horrified to see how ill I was and how much I had changed. I left as a healthy and strong 16-year-old, and returned as an 18-year-old, emaciated, yellow-skinned man. For the rest of the night, until 3 am, when we almost dropped from fatigue, we shared stories of what had happened to each of us since I left. Papa told

188

me that the Americans had occupied the Ruhr Valley in May and were replaced by the British when the zones were set. I told them about my first escape, my attempted second escape, and how lucky I was to have been sent home so early.

Mama said that the Rosenberg children, Irene and her two younger brothers, had survived the concentration camps but their mother had died. "Irene was in Riga and the boys were in Bergen-Belson. Irene is married, but her husband lives near the Czech border to be in a more advantageous location for smuggling goods." I was glad that some of the family we had helped had survived. Mama showed me my bed, which she had prepared special just for me. It had the best mattress in the house and the softest feather quilt on top. I went to bed, but I couldn't sleep. Eventually, I got up with the quilt and lay on the floor instead. I felt more at home on the floor, and quickly fell into a deep sleep. My last thought before drifting off was, "I'm home. I'm safe. This is heaven."

When I finally woke up, I looked around in amazement. It wasn't just a dream. I was really home. I had made it. I survived. Then, I smelled Oma's coffee, so I quickly went to join her. Oma was sitting alone and waiting for me. We hugged for a long time and wept together again. Mama and Papa were out working in the factory. Oma put out a spread of Dutch cheese, Italian salami, Westphalian smoked ham, and German rye bread. Then, she fried me some eggs, sunny-side-up. To my great disappointment, I found that my stomach had shrunk so much that I could only eat a small portion of each delicious item. After breakfast, I went to the hospital to see Dr. Pole. He examined me and found that my liver was swollen and inflamed, explaining the source of the jaundice. "For the next six weeks, you must adhere to a strict fat-free diet without anything fried or roasted. All you can have is porridge, puddings, noodles, and boiled potatoes. Alcohol is strictly prohibited in the meantime. See me in two weeks. You are seriously ill, Robert, you must do as I say if you want to get better." I went home and began my diet. After four days, I began to feel better. "To hell with the diet!" I cooked up a big plate of ham and eggs, followed by pork chops and steak. To make sure I had a nutritious diet, I added some vegetables on the side.

After the two weeks had passed, I went back to see Dr. Pole. "You are healing well, Robert. I am glad you followed my instructions. You may now have a boiled egg in the morning and a lightly buttered toast." I thanked him, and intentionally neglected to tell him what I had actually been eating. I didn't want to upset this kind doctor. The next day, I went to visit Irene and her brothers. They invited me for dinner and told me that their mother survived the liberation of Riga by the Red Army but had sadly died a few days later from typhoid. Irene had also contracted typhoid but recovered in the hospital. The boys were recovering from starvation and illness. Their father was an officer in the British army, and they were expecting him to return soon. Together, we all exchanged horror stories of the war. It was an emotional reunion for all of us. Irene still looked entrancing to me and I couldn't help but admire her beauty, despite her recent illness. She told me about her husband. "I was starving in Riga and extremely ill. Paul was in the men's camp, saw me through the barbed wire fence, and fell in love with me. He had access to extra food through the black market and threw it to me over the fence. That is the only thing kept me alive. He saved my life. As soon as we were liberated, we married." She smiled sadly, and I knew that this was a marriage made out of gratitude, and not for love.

The next day, I went to town and ran into Heinz. I asked him, "How is your family?" He had tears in his eyes and struggled to reply. "My brother was killed in Holland, and my father was killed on the Italian front." I felt so sad for him that he returned home to such devastating news. We chatted, and he invited me to come and meet his sister, Mary, and her husband Eric. They were humorous and friendly people, and soon we were planning a party. Sorrow can sometimes be held at bay by celebrating life with friends. I offered to bring the food, drinks, and smokes. Mama had turned half of our house into a supply warehouse for their black marketeering. I told my parents I was going to a party with some friends from the camp and that I would come home in the morning. They were happy to see me enjoying myself after my time in the war. Heinz told me, "Robert, you also have to bring some girls with you." I was confident that I could do that. Every corner pub had live music and dancing in the evening. Germany was coming back to life in the wake of its dark times. That night, I walked into the closest pub and checked for girls that might want to come to our party. I was turned down twice, but the third time was a charm. I saw two attractive girls sitting together and chatting. I walked over to them. "Would you like to come to a nice party? It's right around the corner." They looked at each other and smiled. "Sure!" I escorted them to the party, one to accompany Heinz, and one to accompany me. We all got drunk and enjoyed a raucous night. We had survived this terrible and tragic war, and now we just wanted to live for today. It was party time.

Late one night, in early December, I heard someone knocking at the window. It was Sergio, a man I had met when I was 13, and had assumed to be dead. Sergio was an Italian man who was a high position in Mussolini's fascist party, the Black Shirts. In 1940, tens of thousands of Italian workers were sent to Germany to build bomb shelters. Sergio was in charge of the supplies for the workers. He was also a thief who sold stolen Italian wine to the Germans. That is how I ended up running into him. I saw him as an opportunity for my parents in their black market work and brought him home. He took a liking to me because I spoke Italian. Papa bought wine by the truckload from Sergio and sold it for double the cost. Sergio became a close family friend and spent a lot of time in our home for the next three years until he was sent to Yugoslavia. We had heard at the time that he had been executed in Yugoslavia by the partisans.

I opened the door and found that Sergio was very much still alive. He looked worse than I did when I had returned home from the POW camp. Sergio was filthy, emaciated, and smelled absolutely rancid. I took him to the bath, gave him some of my clothes, and put him to bed in the living room. He had a wife and two children in Italy, but I knew he could never go back or he would be executed. In the morning, my family was surprised to see him alive. Papa asked him what happened. "My brother and I were sentenced to death by the partisans. A guard helped me to escape, but my brother was shot down." Sergio told us how he had walked and hitchhiked from Yugoslavia, through Austria, to come to Herne to see us. Papa took Sergio in and treated him like a member of the family. Mama nourished him back to life with healthy soups and nutritious tidbits. Little did I know that Sergio would end up betraying my father and me by eventually serving as the final death knell of my parent's marriage.

I was healing from the many traumas of my war experience and feeling positive about my future. Christmas, 1945, was a special celebration for our family. Mama and Oma prepared our feast of baked goose, potatoes, cauliflower, carrots, cabbage, wild berries, and Oma's rich Dutch gravy. For dessert, Mama had baked a cherry torte and Rodon cake served with whipped cream. To top it all off, she made Dr. Oetker's chocolate pudding with vanilla sauce, which had always been my favourite. Sergio had been drinking excessive amounts of wine since he arrived, but he didn't touch a drop on Christmas day. He announced, rather pompously, "This day is sacred to me." I had been noticing something that puzzled me. Mama seemed to be favouring Sergio. She started saying, "Robert, leave some food for Sergio." She began serving him almost like a wife might serve her husband. I also noticed the discreet glances they were giving each other when they thought no one was looking. Papa didn't seem to notice anything. I tried to put it out of my mind, but it came to bother me more and more. Papa gave Sergio a job working in the factory, but Sergio had other ideas of how to make money. After the war, the black market was flourishing. The government struggled to find ways to feed a defeated and desperate population. They issued ration books to each citizen with coupons you could exchange for food and other items considered essential. Each person was allotted 50 grams of meat, 25 grams of butter, and 500 grams of bread per week. They also received a coupon for two cigarettes a day and one bottle of Schnapps a month. The food was not enough to really live on, which greatly aided in helping the black market flourish.

Sergio decided to get into the black market business in partnership with Mama. They bought barrels of ground up horse meat and Mama knew a trick to increase their revenue. At night, she would pour a jug of cold water into each barrel. By morning, the dry horse meat would have soaked up the water and be heavier by about five pounds. Everything was rationed, so what they were doing was completely illegal. Mama was a gentle and clever outlaw. She was a successful smuggler and black marketeer. Mama knew how to make a buck, legally or illegally. We were not emotionally close, but I admired her intelligence and determination. She was a survivor of the slums of Herne. At the age of two, her father died, and her mother struggled to raise four children during desperate times. I think this early time of poverty and struggle had hardened Mama. She had a heart of gold and helped many people, but she was as tough as nails and had nerves of steel. In many ways, she was a renaissance woman. Mama was clever and courageous. She was a lover of history and music, a gourmet cook and baker, a talented trickster, a brilliant problem solver, and a fearless anti-fascist. I will never forget when she saved the young communist from the Nazis by hiding him in my bed. She did this at the risk of her own life, but nothing fazed her. Nothing could make her lose her cool, except me. From early childhood, I managed to drive her crazy and irritate the hell out of her. Only now do I realize how much I must have frustrated and tormented her with my reckless antics and escapades.

It wasn't long before I also joined them in the business. The black market was a long family tradition and something at which I was quite adept; wheeling and dealing. One day Sergio brought over his friend, Amanda, who owned a trucking company with her husband. Mama and Sergio needed trucks to carry their black market goods. By now they were buying and selling silk, cotton, butter, wine, liquor, sugar, pork and, of course, horse meat. Mama and Amanda bonded as friends and went into business together. Amanda knew how to bribe the police to avoid getting busted while carrying the contraband. A couple of weeks later, it was Amanda's birthday, and she invited Mama to her house to celebrate. I dropped in that evening to congratulate Amanda. Sergio was already drunk and being obnoxious. While I was there, I accidentally glimpsed Mama and Sergio kissing in the hallway. I was taken aback. Mama saw me and looked ashamed. She came over to me, her face flushed. "What a guy, he tried to make a pass at me!" I thought, "Nice try Mama, don't bullshit the bullshitter." It was obvious that Mama had been kissing Sergio as passionately as he had been kissing her. I was deeply distressed by their actions and Mama's lies. I had been suspecting something was going on with them for some time now, but now I knew for certain.

Mama was betraying Papa. I loved Papa and felt angry at Mama for being unfaithful. Later, I was able to be more understanding when I recalled how many times Papa had assaulted Mama when he went into his rages, and how often I saw her weeping. Additionally, I knew theirs was a loveless marriage. I had never observed one moment of tenderness and love between them. Since the age of four, I knew that Papa wasn't my biological father, but I loved him just the same. He spent time with me, took me for walks, was concerned about my education, and he loved me as his son. I also knew how much Mama hated him, though with good reason. Papa loved her but treated her like shit most of the time. Then he tried to buy her love with expensive fur coats and jewellery. Of course, Mama would never accept his gifts. I had come to realize that Papa was a sick man who had a rage problem that he couldn't control. Who could love someone like that? But I did love him. He was my father. I could forgive my mother, but I couldn't forgive Sergio for betraying the trust of Papa, when Papa had shown such kindness by taking him into his home and giving him a job. Now, there was yet another family secret I had to keep. What a mess. I couldn't wait for the day when I left this all behind and escaped to another country. However, as long as my beloved Oma was alive, my heart would not allow me to leave her.

In early 1946 I met Fritz, a well known fox in the black market. Fritz offered me a partnership to bootleg Schnapps to Canadian military units in Oldenburg, North Germany. With my usual luck I happened to meet Adam, who had a distillery in his basement. He made straight vodka and blended in various flavours so he could pass it off as genuine Jamaican rum, English gin, and Scottish rye whiskey. Adam had counterfeit labels that passed for genuine. He offered me a batch of 40 bottles for a reasonable price. I immediately agreed, and bought a batch from Adam every week. Fritz and I took them to Oldenburg and traded with the Canadian soldiers. We paid 100 marks a bottle and traded it for five packs of smokes. We then sold the cigarettes to small businesses for 500 marks.

Fritz and I went every week to visit the thirsty Canadians and made a killing until our luck eventually ran out. We were busted by the Canadian military police, and we were searched as we got off the train. Our boozy bonanza was confiscated, and that was the end of our Oldenburg escapade. That particular venture may have been foiled, but I was just beginning my career as a busy black marketeer. It was a third generation family business now, going back over 50 years. Every day I would go to town and make the necessary connections and affiliates needed for things to continue running smoothly. One day I met Kurt, a watchmaker, who bought broken watches to repair and sell. He offered me a partnership. My job was to obtain these watches for him. Soon, I was buying watches for a few cigarettes and selling them to Kurt at a profit. I had heard of a Canadian military base in Northern Germany, called Bad Zwischenahnen, and suggested to Kurt that it would be a good place to sell first class Swiss watches. He agreed and decided to add Leica cameras to our wares. We had an attaché case which we filled with 50 or so watches and several cameras. Then, we took the train to trade with Canada.

We found out where the soldiers met with the local black marketeers: a spot on a country road. When we arrived, there were about a dozen soldiers and some civilians doing business. We immediately began showing our watches and cameras to the interested soldiers. Suddenly, we heard police sirens coming from both directions. We were trapped. Kurt quickly grabbed the attaché case and threw it over the barbed wire fence into the meadow. He lifted the barbed wire up and I went under it. I did the same for him. Within seconds we were running for our lives across the meadow. We moved fast as we were both quite lean. Sometimes it pays to be super skinny, I suppose. We heard the police shouting, "Halt oder wir schiessen!" That means "Stop, or we'll shoot!" Both of us knew that the German police were not armed, so we just kept high-tailing it across the meadow while making an effort to not spook the horses. We glanced back and saw a couple of heavy police officers trying to get through the barbed wire and getting caught. There was a farmhouse some distance away, so we headed for it. The door was unlocked and we ran inside without a second thought. There, we found a woman with two young children having lunch. Kurt was more experienced in this line of work than I, so he said, "Quick, hide this, the police are chasing us, we'll pay you later!" She quickly took the attaché case to another room and hid it. "Pretend we are visitors having lunch with you," Kurt told her.

We all sat around the table partaking of the newly baked bread and homemade jam. There was a loud knock at the door. The farm woman quickly went to the door. "Have you seen two men?" "No, what's going on?" "We're chasing two men who were last seen running across your field." Without missing a beat, she replied, "I haven't seen them. I'm just having lunch with friends." Fortunately, they believed her and didn't even come in the house. I peeked out the window and saw eight policemen fanning out to search for us. She was very calm and collected, but Kurt and I were still panicked. "Now, you can have your lunch, relax, and wait until dark. I will show you a trail to go safely back to town." We stayed until dark and we each gave a pack of our own cigarettes to thank her, which was the new currency in Germany. She was delighted, and Kurt and I felt we had been lucky again. We retrieved the attaché case and took the trail. When we got to town, we hopped on the first available train home. We had already decided to give up on this particular stunt due to our close run-in with the law.

On the train, Kurt devised a new plan. "We'll go to the American zone and try our luck there instead." The next day, we made our plans. We decided to go to Frankfurt and check things out. You needed a permit and an inter-zonal pass to travel long distances. You could buy almost anything with a pack of cigarettes those days, so we easily purchased the necessary documents. Kurt proudly showed me his large, round, metal container which had a false bottom. He placed all the watches and cameras in the false bottom while we mixed water and strawberry flavoring from our candy factory to pour into the top of the container. It had a screw top, which made it look like an innocuous container to anyone who might be suspicious. There was a handle on each side and we carried it onto the train with us. We got to Frankfurt safely and went to the trading post at Taunusstrasse, in the centre of town. Before we knew it, we had sold all our wares and received payment in cigarettes. We packed these into the false bottom of our container and made our way home. Our profit was now 20 fold! Even Mama couldn't have done better.

While in Frankfurt, I learned that Giessen was the largest American military supply depot in Germany. I also learned that there was a large demand from the soldiers for German Schnapps, which is similar to vodka. I went to see Adam, my friend with the distillery, and made a deal with him for 40 bottles. Kurt and I headed for Giessen with an abundance of Schnapps, the Leicas, and the Swiss watches. We decided to take a chance and just put everything in suitcases this time. When we arrived, I saw an American soldier smoking nearby. "Do you know anyone who would be interested in buying Schnapps?" I knew I was taking a risk by asking, as he could arrest me. Luck was on my side once again. "How many bottles do you have?" "Forty." The soldier raised his eyebrows in interest. "I'm Jim Saunders," he said, holding out his right hand. We introduced ourselves, and Jim took us to an apartment building where we could sleep on a sofa for a pack of cigarettes each. Jim pointed at his elegant brown leather shoes. "One pair for one bottle. Tomorrow, I'll bring 40 pairs and I'll meet you here at noon."

I tried to contain my excitement. Those shoes were worth at least 1,000 marks, and there was a real shortage of such well-made shoes in Germany at that time. I paid 100 marks for each bottle of Schnapps, so we would be making a tenfold profit. At noon the next day, Jim arrived and we made the deal. We sold our watches and cameras for American dollars and arranged to return in a week to repeat the deal. Kurt and I were thrilled with our profit and managed to squeeze the forty pairs of shoes into our four suitcases. We got home safely, treasure and all. My parents and Oma couldn't believe it. I felt proud. They knew I had gone to make a deal in Giessen, but were amazed to see what a good deal I had made. "I prayed for you, Robert," Oma said. Mama and Papa congratulated me, and I told them the whole story of my risky adventure. Later on, I noticed that Papa was admiring the shoes. "Papa, find a pair that fits, and they're yours!" It made me happy to see Papa trying out his new pair of elegant shoes. Our home was essentially now an underground corner store for the black market. People came every five minutes or so to purchase coffee, cigarettes, Schnapps, horse meat, clothes, and other supplies that weren't available in the stores. Word spread quickly about the shoes, and within one day I was sold out and split the profit with Kurt. After a few more trips to Giessen, Jim began to trust me and shared how he was able to steal the shoes. "I have a connection in the supply camp. Many soldiers are lifting stuff from the supply camp. No one seems to notice."

Kurt and I continued our weekly trips to Giessen for several months. One day in early July, we were in Giessen having coffee with our landlady, Frau Kaltenbach, when two American MP's raided the place. She was running an illegal brothel there and it was off limits for American military. They asked for our ID, and when they found out we were from the British zone, we were arrested. They were quite friendly, but turned us over to the German police who took us to jail. The next day, Frau Kaltenback bailed us out. She knew the police officer in charge and bribed him with cigarettes for our release. He warned us, "You have to leave town immediately, and don't let me see you here again." We thanked her for rescuing us. When we got back to her place, we were happy to find out that she had all our contraband, 40 pairs of new shoes. We gave her four pairs to thank her and went home to Herne. This was the end of our Giessen adventure.

On July 10th, 1946, I turned 19. Life was good. My health had been restored and I spent a lot of time at the Herne swimming pool. My friends and I went on bicycle trips to Haltern Lake and had picnics. Often, we would camp at this beautiful lake and stay up late drinking and singing raunchy songs. Every week I would meet a different girl and have casual and exciting sex. I was making up for the years I lost in the war, I suppose. On my birthday, I had a somber tea party with my family. Sergio was still living with us, and I tried my best to turn a blind eye to what was happening between him and Mama. I made efforts to convince myself that Mama should have a chance at happiness, but it still galled me. Papa seemed totally unaware of what was happening in his own house. Then again, he always went out in the evening to meet his rich widow and prostitutes. The tension in the house was unbearable, and I was home as little as possible to avoid it. After the tea party, I was relieved to go to Kurt's house for the real birthday bash with all my friends.

I have always enjoyed swimming. On July 23rd I went to the pool to watch the provincial women's high diving finals. I saw a slim young woman with dark hair climbing the tower to do a 10 metre dive. I was immediately attracted to her well-endowed breasts and fine figure in addition to her athletic skill. Breasts have always been my downfall when it comes to attraction. If the breasts are gorgeous, I'm a goner. She made a perfect double salto into the pool that resulted in thunderous applause. At the end of the competition the announcer said, "The gold medal goes to Alma Schreiner from Herne!" It was her! As she was leaving the stage, I realized I better get over there fast before someone else approached her. "Congratulations, you were wonderful." She gave me a charming look with her dark, seductive eyes. "May I invite you out for a nice evening?" She looked up at me from beneath her long lashes and replied softly, "Yes." After she changed, we walked along the promenade followed by a night out of dancing. We soon ended up at Kurt's home where we spent the night making love. Alma taught me a lot that night. She could have won a gold medal in lovemaking to add to her collection, in my opinion. By morning, I had decided that this was my woman and was practically ready to ask her for her hand in marriage. Keep in mind that I had just turned 19, and my knowledge of love and life was still in its developing stages.

We spent the next day together sharing our life stories with each other. Alma told me her mother was Duchess Marizza, who was famous as the most beautiful and sought after prostitute in Herne. For years I had heard Mama and her friends talking about the Duchess with admiration. They said she had real class and only the best clientele. I recalled that I had met Duchess Marizza once when I was four years old. My cousin, Elsbeth, who was eight, had taken me to her home to play with her and Alma, strangely enough. I shared this with Alma and we realized with amazement that we had played together several times at her home during our childhood. I vividly remembered playing with her dolls and her elegant little general store with an abundant supply of pots and pans (much better than my own.) As a result of being an only child surrounded by female cousins as my playmates, I often enjoyed playing with what society would have labelled as "girl's toys." I have always had strong feminine tendencies as I love to cook, clean, and shop. Also, I have often been told that I am nurturing, with a sensitive, tender nature and a soft heart.

I shared with Alma that I had a memory of going to her mother's funeral when I was eight years old. Mama had told me that the Duchess died of syphilis. She had been ill for a long time, and the syphilis had gone to her brain. Knowing that the disease caused erratic and "crazy" behavior in these later stages, I knew it must have been hard on Alma. "I saw you walking sadly behind your mother's coffin and it touched my heart. I have never forgotten that. You were wearing a long dark coat and weeping." She looked at me, her eyes full of tears. "That day, my life changed forever. My father remarried shortly afterwards, and I went from being a princess to Cinderella, the scullery maid." I felt sorry for her. She lost her mother so young, and then was mistreated by her stepmother. I knew in that moment that I would take care of this woman in any way that I was able, and that one day she would become my wife. It seemed that damsels in distress were my speciality.

When I went home that night, I told Mama about Alma, the daughter of Duchess Marizza. "I'm in love with her, Mama." Mama looked at me with great concern. "She's a beautiful girl, but remember other mothers have beautiful daughters too." Mama was probably horrified by my news, but perhaps a bit relieved that I had found one woman I was serious about. She knew I was going after any apron in town that enticed me, so perhaps this was safer. For the next two weeks, Alma and I spent every spare moment together. We went to the canal to swim, and in the evening we made love in the meadow near the canal or at Kurt's place. I found out that Alma worked as a waitress. She showed me where she lived. It was a small rented room in an old house that was next to the hospital morgue and had an eerie feeling about it. There was just a bed and a chair, nothing else. I felt sad for her having to live in such poor conditions. Ever the impulsive one, I decided I would ask Mama if Alma could move into our house. Sergio was sleeping on the sofa in the living room. I didn't allow myself to think that he also might be sharing my parent's bed when Papa was not there. Mama had a big heart, and when I told her of Alma's meagre existence, she said, "Yes, she can come here and help Oma with the cooking and housework." Mama was busy doing her black market work in partnership with Sergio, so it would be helpful to have Alma there to do the chores. Alma moved in and slept on the sofa, while Sergio went to the extra bed in my room.

In order for Alma and I to have privacy, we went to Kurt's place for a few hours each night. At first, I thought I had won the sexual jackpot. Alma was my love goddess. We would have eight or more orgasms each night. However, Alma was never satisfied. She always wanted more. She wanted sex all the time. After a while, I became totally exhausted by her demands. The sexual jackpot had now become a sexual nightmare. By the middle of August, I was in excruciating pain with my testicles being swollen so much from the excessive sex that I could hardly walk. I went to the doctor, and he was rather astonished at their size. "Robert, you have badly inflamed testicles. You have to lie down and ice them for several days. And for God's sake, lay off the ladies for awhile." I went home and told Mama, "I'm in trouble. The doctor says my testicles need to be iced for several days." Mama gave me a long, hard look. "Well, I hope you've learned your lesson."

I lay down on the couch, and Mama regularly brought me ice packs to ice my balls. The pain felt unbearable, but I had survived actual torture before, so I figured I could survive this. On the second day, my friend, Manfred, came for a visit. I told him about my predicament, and he found it most amusing. By now, everyone was making fun of me. I became the butt of many jokes and everyone was greatly entertained, with me being an exception. Mama had to go out, so Manfred became the Ice Man, laughing the whole time. After three days, my balls were almost back to normal, and I could walk normally again. Alma was very happy to have me back, and we returned to our marathon of nightly love-making. By September, I was losing so much weight that my friends and family became concerned about my health. I felt trapped by Alma's sexual demands and began to search for ways to avoid her just to get some rest. But no matter where I hid, Alma would search me out and find me. One time, she found me walking through a side street. I just wanted to be left alone and not have to perform sexually. Alma had other ideas for me in mind. She guided me into an entrance way of a Catholic kindergarten, unbuttoned my pants, fondled my genitals and I was done for. My black market business was going well, and my only relief was when I went out of town overnight to make my deals. I had always loved sex, but I began to think I had met my sexual Waterloo. I wondered how I could make my escape before Alma finished me off for good.

Robert during Blackmarket times 1946

CHAPTER 12

Alma was helpful in the house, but she remained quiet and reserved. She didn't talk with Mama or Oma much except when it was absolutely necessary. One day Mama said, "I can't get close to her at all. She makes me uncomfortable." I thought, "She also makes me uncomfortable, Mama, just in a different way." I was doing well in the black market and I showered Alma with gifts of clothing and jewellery. It made me happy to do this for her. One day, I was in town to pay off Bernard, the cop on Main Street who always looked the other way regarding my black market work. I supplied him with cigarettes on a regular basis. Bernard took one look at me and said, "Robert, you look terrible. Lay off the screwing for a couple of weeks and put some meat on your bones!" Even the cop on the beat was giving me relationship advice. I didn't know how to get out of the situation. Alma needed to be taken care of, and my hope was that her sexual demands would lessen over time. On New Year's Eve,1946, Alma and I went over to Kurt and Margaret's home to celebrate. Little did I realize that this would be my first and last New Year's Eve with Alma.

On January 6th, we were having our afternoon tea when three police detectives arrived. The one in charge, Lieutenant Koch, announced, "We know you bought a large load of stolen cigarettes two days ago." Papa and I looked at each other. Koch was right, we had just made the deal. I tried to bluff my way out. "You must be mistaken," I said politely. Papa put on an innocent face and told them we didn't know what they were talking about. Koch gave us a dirty look. "We have the thieves,

Erwin and Gunter, in custody and they have already confessed." Now I knew they had squealed. I was pissed off, but I knew we were caught. "Okay, we did buy the cigarettes, but we didn't know they were stolen." Koch replied, "Who did you sell them to?" I didn't want to betray my hotel owner customers who bought them, so I said, "I sold them to two strangers from out of town." Koch gave me a look of disgust. "Oh, the great unknown, I've heard that one before."

Papa and I knew we were in trouble. "Okay," Koch said. "Let's see what we can find." He showed us a search warrant and they immediately started searching every nook and cranny. Papa was turning pale at the thought of what they might find as Mama, Papa, and Sergio were involved in dealing many illegal goods. They searched the house and the factory and found one thousand kilos of illegal sugar under the factory, contraband liquor, American cigarettes, Dutch cigars, and bales of silk. That was bad enough, but then they found a hunting rifle and a box of 50 bullets under my bed. This was a serious offence. On January 1st, 1946, the British military occupation government had announced an amnesty for 30 days for Germans to turn in their firearms. As of February 1st, the penalty for possession of a firearm would be two to ten years in prison. At that time, Papa and I discussed it, and decided to keep the rifle since it was a collector's item and valuable. Not the best decision, as it turned out. The detectives handcuffed Papa and me. Koch phoned the station and told them to send five policemen and a truck to come and pick up all the contraband.

Koch held up the rifle and pronounced sternly, "If I turn this in to the Brits, you could get up to ten years in prison, so you better tell me where the cigarettes are that you bought." Koch pressured me to tell him, but I prided myself on never being a snitch. When they were taking us to the police station, I managed to whisper to Papa, "I will take the blame for the rifle, Papa." Papa shook his head vigorously. "Do you want to spend the next ten years of your life in jail? No, I will take the blame." When we reached the station, we were put in separate cells. Koch took me to his office for interrogation. The rifle that I had hidden under my bed was standing right beside his desk to remind me of the ten year sentence looming above me. "Do you now recall the names of the men who bought the cigarettes off you?" "If I see them again, I might recognize them." Koch gave me an angry look. "I don't believe you. You're lying. Now I will give the rifle to the British, and you and your father will have to face the consequences."

I was taken back to my cell and was interrogated by an officer from the British Military Police the following day. I had made up my mind to take the blame. Papa was old, and a long prison sentence would be too hard on him. "It was my rifle, and Papa didn't know anything about it." I was locked up, then called for another interrogation by the same officer about an hour later. He gave me an appraising look. "We have talked to your father, and he said it is his rifle that was supposedly completely unknown to you, so clearly one of you must be lying." The next day, Papa and I had to go before a British Military judge in Herne. When Papa was asked about the rifle he stated in a firm voice, "I am totally responsible. My son knew nothing about the rifle." Then it was my turn to speak. "The rifle belongs to me, my father knew nothing about it." The judge looked irritated and shook his head. "Only one person can be held responsible for illegal possession of this firearm. One of you is lying. So, now, tell me the truth." Papa and I both repeated what we had said. The judge became more frustrated with us. "In my court I can only give up to a one year sentence so this case will have to be transferred to the British Military Court in Iserlohn. You will both remain in custody until that time."

We were returned to our cells, and the following day Mama came to the station and   brought food, cigarettes, coffee, and chocolate. She generously shared these treasures with the two guards. To show their appreciation, they let me go to the office to visit with her. I chatted to one of the guards and found out the two cigarette thieves had been transferred to the Central Prison in Bochum. Papa and I were taken there the next day. The prison held 2,000 men, 1,000 women, and was maximum security. I had to undress while my body and clothes were searched. I was taken to cell 51, on floor 5, and placed in solitary confinement. For the first few days, my spirit was almost broken. I felt a deep sense of suffocating hopelessness. The food ration was even worse than the POW camp in Belgium. No talking or sound of any kind was allowed. If you broke the rules, you were put in the dark room for up to 14 days at a time. Once a day, the prisoners were alotted a 20 minute exercise walk in the yard, with 10 metres distance from man to man. I resolved to face this, as there was no escape. Instead, I found another way to escape by using my imagination. I recalled all the happy events in my life and my many adventures. It was a meditative state I would enter, where I could spend hours in nature and build a fantasy world. I repeated Oma's wise and amusing sayings over and over endlessly. Often, I would translate sentences into Morse code and recite the French, Latin, and English alphabets. Sometimes I would count to a thousand in Russian, French, English, and Italian. I would make up jokes to amuse myself and devise daring escapes. By living in my imagination, I was able to keep my sanity. Many men lost their minds while in solitary confinement and were completely broken by it. I was determined to survive with my mind and soul intact, and I did.

Mama hired the best lawyers, one for each of us. When they took me to meet Mr. Abel, my lawyer, he advised me, "Let your father take the blame for the rifle. Your father is 60 and he will get a much lighter sentence than you." I knew Papa was stubborn like a mule and would never change his mind, so I realized it made the most sense to comply with the lawyer's advice. With a heavy heart, I reluctantly agreed. Mr. Abel informed me of the legal procedure. "You will go to the German court first, in regard to the stolen cigarettes. The British court will come later. I like your story about selling the cigarettes to two strangers from out of town." He grinned. "We'll stick with that story. I'll try my best to keep your sentence to under six months, as this is your first offence. Your mother and Oma are just fine. They send their love, and your mother will do all she can to get you out." Mr. Abel then gave me two liverwurst sandwiches made by Mama, a package of tobacco, matches, and rolling papers. "Do not get caught with any of this. I have not given you anything. Remember that." I was taken back to my cell, and knew I was now in an advantageous position to bribe someone in order to find out where Papa was being held.

Kilian, a long-time prisoner and trustee, came sniffing around to find out what had happened. I thought he might eventually serve useful, so I gave him some tobacco to get on his good side. "Can you do me a favour and find out where my father is?" The next day, Kilian told me that Papa was on level eight. "Here is some tobacco for you, and please give the rest to my Papa." On Sunday, all prisoners went to chapel. All week I had been planning how to connect with Papa. There was a blind spot that I could use where I was out of the sight of the guards. I waited until Papa came by and jumped right behind him in line so I could sit with him at chapel. While all the others were singing hymns, Papa and I were whispering to each other and making plans for court. We did this every Sunday for three months before we were called to court. "Don't fall for any of the tricks from the police, Robert. Stick with the story about the two strangers," Papa advised. We knew that Erwin and Gunter, who stole the cigarettes and sold them to us, had already confessed. Also, the police had traced Papa's check for 40,000 marks for the payment.

Prison was boring, but every cell had a bible, so at least I had some reading material. I was surprised to find out how racy the Old Testament was and how much corruption existed at that time. One day my cell door opened, and an unknown guard asked me, "What is your name, and what are you in for? Show me your cell card."

Then he whispered to me, "Your friend Kurt sent this to you." He opened his coat and gave me a big pouch of tobacco, matches, and rolling papers. "Only smoke at night after lockup." Then he quickly disappeared. I didn't feel as alone anymore, knowing that my friend hadn't forgotten me. His gift made the time there significantly more bearable because I knew I could look forward to a smoke each night. In chapel, I shared my precious gifts with Papa. After three months, we both went to the German court in Bochum. Gunter and Erwin each got one year for breaking and entering. Our lawyers were clever, and as a result, Papa and I only got a three month sentence for breaking the law against the consumer rule. Also, our time in prison was credited, so the judge said, "You have served your time." Unfortunately, this was not the end of this particular nightmare. We still had to return to prison because we had to face the British military court for our charge regarding the rifle.

One month later, we were taken to the military court in Iserlohn. Papa and I were waiting in the hall before court when two Polish men came out. They had been sentenced to five years for possession of two handguns. I thought, "Oh my God, the rifle is bigger than the handgun so Papa will end up with ten years!" I was horrified. Papa was old, he wouldn't last that long behind bars. Just then, Captain Scott of the British Salvation Army came down the hallway. "I've come as a character witness for you, Otto, as I know you are a good man." Last Christmas, Papa had donated 100 kg of our best caramel candies to the orphan refugee children. I felt a ray of hope for Papa just then. When we got into the court room, I had the impression that the judge was a compassionate man. I saw Mama and Sergio sitting in the court, side by side, and I felt a pang in my heart. Captain Scott was called as a witness, and he spoke about Papa's kindness and generosity to the orphans. He praised Papa for his community spirit.

The judge had our rifle in front of him. "Who owns this rifle?" Papa jumped up and said, "I do, my son knew nothing about it, and is just trying to protect me by saying otherwise." The judge turned to me. "Robert, you have to tell the truth now. Is this rifle yours?" I replied "No." This statement broke my heart, as I felt I was betraying my dear Papa. "All right, Robert, you are free to go." I joined the spectators, and felt terrible that Papa was this lonely, little old man sitting there and taking all the blame. The judge looked kindly at Papa. "You appear to be a good man who helps others in need, but the law is the law. I will give you the minimum sentence of two years, but the sentence will be suspended. You can also get up and go home." Papa began to weep by this unexpected wonderful news. We were free! Mama had brought coffee and sandwiches, so we had a family celebration together. Nevertheless, I knew there was a viper in our midst, and that viper was soon to strike and tear our family apart. Papa and I were taken back to prison. I signed my release papers and could leave, but Papa had to stay until the next morning to be released.

On May 5th, 1947, after four months, I was finally going home. I was happy that I would see Alma again. I had missed Oma and couldn't wait to hug her. A man offered me a ride to Herne. "No, no, thank you, I prefer to walk." I wanted to feel the sun on my skin, the wind in my face, and the joy of the freedom to simply walk. I was only two blocks from home when I ran into Sergio. "Welcome, Robert," he said as we greeted each other. I asked him how things were at home. "Everything is fine for the most part, but your girlfriend is something else." There was a funny feeling rising in the pit of my stomach. "What do you mean…?" He replied with terrible news, news that changed my life. "Alma came with me to deliver some contraband to Dortmund. On the train back to Herne, we were the only ones in the compartment. She came right up to me and grabbed my balls. She got me going and we had sex right there." He seemed delighted to tell me this news.

I felt my body go rigid. I was thunderstruck. Alma had betrayed me, and with my own mother's lover at that. Immediately, I knew I never wanted to see her again. I had to go home and get her out of our house and out of my life. Sergio left, so I walked home, filled with absolute rage. Oma and Mama grabbed me and gave me long hugs. Alma was standing behind them, with a loving smile. She came up to me to hug and kiss me. "Come outside with me," I told her. When we got outside, I pushed her roughly away. "I heard about your train trip from Dortmund to Herne. Pack up your things right now and I'll take you to your brother." Alma began weeping. "I knew it was a bad thing to do, but I had a weak moment and lost my way." At least she didn't try to deny it. "It was Sergio's fault too, he made the first move!" I looked at her with disgust. She was dead to me. Alma looked at me beseechingly, "What about your Mama? She had sex with Sergio all the time your Papa was in jail." It made me even angrier that Alma

217

somehow thought this justified her betrayal. "Get packed." We went inside and I told Mama and Oma what had happened. "Alma betrayed me with Sergio, I can't stand to be with her. I'm taking Alma to her brother's place." Both of them just sat there, stunned by this news.

On the way to her brother's place, Alma kept sobbing and repeating, "I'll kill myself, I don't want to live anymore. Please forgive me, Robert, I love you." I didn't answer. When we got there I told her brother, "Please take care of her. She will explain everything to you," and I returned home. My heart was stone. My only consolation was that I knew now what kind of woman Alma really was, and ended the relationship before I foolishly married her. When I got home, Mama said, "I can't believe it. She seemed such a nice, quiet girl." She didn't say a word about Sergio, and I felt sad for my Papa who had been cuckolded by the man he had kindly taken into his home. Mama had betrayed Papa, but now I felt she had also betrayed me. The next day, Papa was released from prison. News spread quickly that we were both home. To show their appreciation that we hadn't informed the police about their involvement, the hotel owners we had sold the cigarettes to sent over their best wine. We decided to have a party to celebrate our freedom and safe return. A dozen or so friends came to celebrate with us.

Later on, Uncle Willy arrived. He was already drunk, and went straight to Papa. "While you were in prison, Sergio was screwing your wife." Papa's face flushed with rage. He grabbed Sergio, who was sitting at the kitchen table drinking, threw him to the ground, and began beating him senseless. Jan, a friend of Otto's, got in between. "You'll kill him, you'll kill him!" He held Papa back so that Sergio was able to escape. He ran out of the house, afraid for his life. Papa glared at Mama. "You whore, get out of my sight and don't come back!" Mama, who could always keep her cool, replied quietly, "Don't listen to Willy, he's drunk." Otto went into my room and threw all of Sergio's belongings out the window. I was fearful that Papa would attack Mama, but he came back and he seemed to have calmed down. The guests all left. That was certainly one party they'll never forget. I said goodbye to them, only to turn and see Papa with a knife in his hand and murder in his eyes. He was heading straight for Mama. I knew he meant to kill her. I wrestled him to the ground and wrenched the knife from his hand. Mama then took advantage of the situation by grabbing a one kilo weight stone from the nearby scale. She raised her hand to bring down the stone to bash Papa's brains out. In a split second, I let Papa go and grabbed her hand to stop her. Papa saw his chance and grabbed another weight stone with which he smashed Mama in the face repeatedly. Mama was bleeding heavily and had lost several teeth. I jumped on Papa to hold him down, and Mama ran out of the house screaming.

My poor Oma saw everything and was sobbing piteously. I let Papa up. He was as white as a sheet. I tried to calm him down to no avail. "Why do you protect that whore? Your Mother is nothing but a whore!" An hour later, Mama returned with two policemen. Her face was bandaged. They handcuffed Papa and he went with them without protest. Papa was a broken man. The police took him away. It tore at my heart to see this small, defeated figure between the two tall policemen. The next morning, a police officer came with documents that said we had to come to court the following day about the charge of assault Mama had laid against Papa. I was to go as a witness, which was a terrible feeling. My parents had just tried to murder each other. I was confused and conflicted. I blamed Papa for his years of abuse to Mama, and I blamed Mama for betraying Papa with Sergio. Sergio had betrayed all of us. He betrayed Papa, who had taken him into his home when he needed help. He betrayed Mama and I both by having sex with my girlfriend. My soul ached in a shroud of sadness. I had my freedom now, but I had no home and no peace of mind. The emotional distance between Mama and me had now grown too great to ever bridge. All I had left was my beloved Oma. My heart went out to Papa, his untreated sickness, his uncontrollable violence, his defeat. He had just been released from jail, and now he would be there again. While he may not have been a role model on how to treat a woman, he had been a good Papa to me all these years, and I loved him dearly.

On May 10th, Mama and I went to the police court. Papa was there, and all of us made a statement of what had happened. The doctor who treated Mama had given a written statement regarding her injuries. It stated that she had a broken nose, several smashed teeth, a split upper lip, and other facial injuries. I spoke as a witness to the assault. In that moment, I felt as though I was the adult, while my parents were the immature and reckless children. I was disgusted with both of them. "My parents tried to kill each other. My father found out his wife was having an affair, and he lost it. He came running at my mother with a knife in his hand. Meanwhile, Mama was busy weighing some merchandise on our scale. I grabbed Papa, wrestled him to the floor, and took his knife. Then, I saw Mama taking a one kg weight stone and bringing it down to smash Papa's head. I let go of Papa to stop her, and pushed her down to make her drop the stone. As I did so, Papa moved quickly and grabbed another weight. Before I could stop him, he smashed Mama's face several times. I grabbed Papa while Mama ran away, bleeding profusely."

Papa spoke next. "My wife betrayed me. I took a man, who was a political refugee, into my home. My wife had an affair with him. They both betrayed me. When I found out, I lost it, and I couldn't help myself. I want her to leave, and I will buy her out of the house. I gave her a good life. She came from poverty and I built a rich life for her." I was full of sorrow that my parents were accusing each other, and their marriage had come to such a violent and tragic ending. Mama spoke last. My clever Mama, always the innocent one. With a demure look, she said, "I have been abused by my husband all our married life. I can prove that with witnesses. He has been physically and verbally abusive to me. Now, he has tried to kill me. What he says is simply not true. I've been falsely accused of having an affair. He has no proof. I fear for my life, and I ask your honour to please put a restraining order on my husband for my protection." Mama wiped her tears away with her handkerchief. I suspected they may have been exaggerated in order to gain more sympathy. In my heart, I knew that she was lying, and she had indeed been sleeping with Sergio. At the same time, there was another part of me that couldn't conceive the idea of my mother having sex at all. After all, she was almost 50. It was beyond my teenage imagination to think that a woman her age would still want to have sex. At 19, I really didn't have a clue.

I had seen my mother abused by Papa all these years and knew how much she hated him. I also knew that now she had the power to get her revenge. In 1930, in order to protect himself in case of bankruptcy, Papa had signed over the factory to Mama. The house had been Oma's, so it was now also in Mama's name. Mama owned everything on paper. Papa had no legal rights to their assets at all. The judge's decision came quickly. "Otto Schulte-Middelmann, you are sentenced to three months in jail for assault. However, this is a suspended sentence." The judge went on to explain Papa would be on probation for three years, and if he got into any trouble, he would have to serve the three months jail time. "You are under a life-long restraining order to not go within 100 metres of your wife or her home." I looked at Papa and Mama. She had an enigmatic smile on her face, but Papa looked like he wanted to try to kill her again. I wondered who I should go with when we all parted. Mama was strong and would be all right, but Papa was a broken man. He needed me. I went with him to a business friend who was willing to take him in and give him a room. When we got there, Papa started crying. "It was all meant for you, Robert, that you would have the business and a good career. Now that whore has destroyed everything." He was consumed by his anger. "I won't let her get away with it. I'll hire the best lawyer and fight her. I made the money, I worked the business, she just helped. I can prove it." I couldn't take any more. My heart was heavy with grief. "I'll see you tomorrow, Papa. Get a good night's sleep."

When I got home, Mama was all smiles and looked happier than I had ever seen her. She had cleaned the house until you could almost eat off the floor. I knew that this was for Sergio. "I feel that my new life is starting, a life without fear. I am protected by the law. He can't hurt me anymore." She was glowing, her cheeks rosy, her eyes dancing. "Robert, I invited Sergio to come tomorrow for dinner." What could I say in response, especially after her testimony? "All right, Mama." That was the end of my family life as I had known it, and there was nothing I could do about it. Mama had chosen Sergio over me and Papa. Sergio came the next day, and in the evening, went into my parent's bedroom to sleep with Mama. The following day, Mama filed for divorce. Sergio not only replaced Papa in the bedroom, but also in the factory. Papa had taught him how to make candies, and now he began working with Mama in the business. My whole world felt shattered.

I needed to talk to a friend about all that had happened, so I went to see Kurt. I shared with Kurt and his wife, Margaret, about what had happened. Kurt gave me support, but Margaret was visibly upset. "Alma is very upset about the breakup and loves you so much, Robert. She doesn't want to live anymore and took rat poison to end her life." I didn't respond. "She went to the hospital, and they saved her by pumping out her stomach. She is going home tomorrow." I just turned away and started talking black market business with Kurt. Margaret was angry with me and left. She was Alma's friend, and I suppose she wanted me to feel sorry for Alma, but I didn't. She had brought this on herself and I wasn't obligated to forgive her. A week later, I went to the cinema with a woman I had met at a dance. The usher who guided us to our seats was Alma. I felt a moment of pain, but then thought, "At least she has a better job." Alma looked up at me with a penetrating look that reminded me how incredibly beautiful she was. "The doctor who saved my life said that the man I tried to kill myself for isn't worth it, because he never even came to see me in the hospital." I just brushed past Alma and sat down with my date. She was nothing to me. I just had to block her out of my consciousness. Margaret bumped into me a few months later. She told me that Alma had left town and had a job as a chamber maid on the island of Sylt. I knew that was a posh resort island for wealthy tourists. "Your photo is on her night table." Her remark missed my heart again. I didn't care. If someone betrays me, they are dead to me forever.

My beloved Oma had seen too much on that terrible night. She had seen the marriage she had arranged for her daughter to better their lives come to a murderous end. Oma no longer wanted to live. Every night, she cried and prayed to God, "Please, father, take me away from this world." It broke my heart to hear her say such things. I decided that as soon as Oma died, I would leave Germany. I didn't care where, I just wanted to get out of Germany and find some peace. Papa was now out on the streets, but one of his wealthy business associates gave him a room. I went to visit him, and he began weeping piteously. "It was all for you, my son. Now she has it all. Why would you ever bring Sergio into our home? This whole mess is your fault." He got angry and berated me over and over. I felt Papa was being unfair, and I left feeling distressed and despondent.

At home, I tried to avoid Sergio and get on with my life. He was an alcoholic and drinking heavily. Mama would stay up for hours waiting for him to come home, just to make him coffee and fry him a steak in the middle of the night. Some nights, he brought others home with him; lawyers, businessmen, and Italian consulate officials. All of them were Italian fascists. How ironic, I thought, that now our home was now filled with fascists? Mama was essentially a servile maid to Sergio and his fascist friends. I continued to visit Papa but was filled with dread at the thought of these visits. He told me he was planning to take Mama to court to get the factory and house back. It filled him with rage that Sergio had taken his place both in the bedroom and in the factory. Papa wanted Mama and Sergio out of the house, and he planned to buy her half out from under her. I tried to talk him out of this plan that was doomed to fail, but he wouldn't listen to reason. With every visit, I became more depressed.

It was no longer bearable at home, so I spent most of my time with friends or out of town. The German mark was of virtually no value. The American dollar was worth 200 marks in 1947. To give you a better idea, an average laborer's monthly wage was 200 marks. I threw myself back into the black market business. The family tradition continued. I made business partners with Heidelberg tobacco farmers and was able to increase my profit by tenfold. At the end of June I was at a cafe and met Fritz, a master smuggler. He was 45, and always broke because he was a compulsive gambler. Fritz took a liking to me and soon offered me a partnership with him in his smuggling business. He needed me to front the money for a venture to France in order to sell surgical pins that were not available for purchase in France. These were made in Kiel by Professor Kuenschner, and used in surgery for hips, arms, and legs. I fronted the money for the pins, and we took the train to Kaiserslautern to illegally cross the border into France. We crossed the border at Bruchmuehlbach to enter the Saarland, a German territory that had been annexed to France in 1945. It was a 15 km walk through the bush at night. In Saarbruecken, we went to a medical supply store and sold the two sets of surgical pins for 100,000 francs.

We didn't make much profit on the pins, but our goal was to get French currency to purchase goods that weren't available in Germany, then take them back to sell for a good profit there. We spent 50,000 francs on bottles of Chanel #5 and nylon stockings. These were highly valued luxury items in Germany. The rest of our money was saved for the next trip. We each had a packsack of about 50 lbs and headed back to cross the border. Our return was uneventful. The next day, we went to several beauty parlors and sold all the Chanel #5. The nylons we were able to sell to a fancy lingerie store. It was a profitable partnership. Fritz had been in the smuggling business for years and knew what was in demand. For instance, the French wanted utility bicycles, while the Germans wanted cigarette papers, perfume, and nylons. The best profit was in cigarette papers and nylons, especially with their ease of transport. Fritz always gambled his profit away, while I spent my profit on wine and women. On July 10th, 1947, I turned 20. I was well known now as one of the top black marketeers. Everyone came to me. I was "the middleman" and living the high life, trying to make up for the time I lost in the war.

CHAPTER 13

On a sunny day in August, my life took yet another turn. I looked out the window and saw two lovely, young, and fair-haired women. They appeared to be lost, so I went outside to ask them if I could help. One of them said, "we heard there is a woman on this street who sells groceries. We were hoping to buy a pound of butter." I laughed. "Well, you're talking to the right man, that woman is my mother. May I show you in?" They looked relieved and followed me into the house. "Mama, these ladies want to buy a pound of butter." She took them to the storage room, weighed the butter, and charged them 200 marks. Both women were beautiful, but one was especially stunning. She had a perfect face and figure that accompanied a sweet and gentle voice. Her copper hair, blue eyes, and delicate fair skin were enchanting. She told me her name was Emilie. I had an elegant suit from America among my wares that would fit her perfectly. The colour was called "Mars Gold" in Germany. Mama called it our "Marilyn Monroe" suit.

"May I show you something?" Emilie came with me to our textile room, and I showed her the expensive suit. She tried it on and it fit like a golden glove. I decided to impress her by offering it for my cost price, which was 800 marks. It was quite a steal at that price. She looked downcast. "All my sister and I have is 200 marks for the butter." I took a look at this beauty with the sweet face and gentle voice. "Why don't you keep it, and pay me when you can?" She didn't know what to say. I could see that she was ashamed that she couldn't pay for the suit. Then, Mama came in and invited them for tea. We all sat and chatted, and I learned that Emilie was the older sister at 22, while Helma was 20. I couldn't stop looking at Emilie. She looked absolutely spellbinding in the gold suit. It had a graceful flared skirt that was made for dancing. Impulsively, I said to her, "I am inviting you to come dancing at the Central Cafe tonight, and I can invite a friend for Helma." The sisters looked at each other and agreed to come.

My friend, Gunter, was keen to join us, and it resulted in an evening of romance that one might compare to a summer night in Venice. The orchestra, led by Kurt Edelhagen, played swing, boogie woogie, and Latin American music. It was when we danced the Argentinean tango that I officially lost my heart to Emilie. Gunter and I walked the sisters home and I landed a kiss on Emilie's cheek. "Do you like swimming? Shall we have a picnic at the Rhine Herne canal?" Emilie nodded, and I walked home slowly, wondering if she liked mc and was as excited about tomorrow as I was. The next morning, I made a horse meatloaf and packed bread, an excellent wine, cigarettes, and the succulent meatloaf in a picnic basket. I picked Emilie up and saw that she was wearing a light blouse and skirt over a black bikini. My heart skipped a couple of beats. We walked five kilometres to the canal, had a swim, and sat on our beach towels to enjoy our picnic. Emilie told me about her family, and I realized I had once known her cousin, Marlene.

Marlene and I met during an air raid in a bomb shelter. We were able to leave the shelter about 5 am that morning, and she invited me to her house. We had breakfast, went for a walk in the park, and spent the rest of the day talking. She told me she was 23 and married to an anti-aircraft soldier stationed in Norway. She was a beautiful red head and quite flirtatious. When I left to go home, she invited me to come back that evening for a glass of wine. After the second glass of wine that evening, we had a kiss. Then, she took my hand and led me into the bedroom. She undressed and slipped into bed, beckoning for me to join her. I saw the photo of her husband sitting on the nightstand beside the bed. He was a tall and handsome man dressed in his uniform, smiling rakishly at the camera. I knew she wanted me to replace him for the night, but I just couldn't do it. It wasn't right. "I'm sorry, I can't do this. When your husband returns, how will you face him?" She looked at me with a coquettish look. "You are turning down something that you would love." I left and went home. A year after the war, I ran into her and she stopped me to talk. "I want to thank you, Robert, for being a decent fellow. My husband returned, and we are very happy. You saved me from ruining our marriage." I felt good that I had been mature enough at 15 to make the moral decision not to succumb to her seductive charms.

Emilie and I went dancing every night at the Central Cafe. She introduced me to her parents and Ilse, her older sister. It was obvious they were very poor, so I decided to help them. I brought Ida, Emilie's mother, gifts of coffee, tea, horse meat, and chocolate regularly. I began to feel that this was a different relationship than the one night stands I'd been having. Six weeks later, we went camping to Halterner Lake for the weekend. The full moon bathed the lake in her silvery light, and we made love. The next day, we made a plan that after our dancing at the Central Café, I would sneak into her bedroom nightly to continue our love making. I was busy on the black market, and in September 1947, we heard that the German mark was to be devalued and would be completely worthless. Everyone tried to invest in precious gems, gold, salt, and other goods. Salt was not rationed, so people bought it by the ton. I met a young man named Gunter, and he offered me jewellery and gold. We made a deal and I bought diamonds, gold, amethyst, rubies and lapis lazuli from him for 45,000 marks. I walked out of his home with all my goods in an attaché case, but I only made it a block before two undercover policemen stopped me. They opened the case and saw it all. "How much did you pay Gunter for this?" I was stunned. I had just spent almost all my capital and was immediately busted.

They arrested me and took me to the police station in Herne. After a few hours, I was interrogated by Sergeant Koch, the same officer who arrested Papa and me in January. I saw Gunter being interrogated in the next room. "There's no point in lying, Robert, this time we have the evidence right here. The jewellery has all been stolen by Gunter. He is being charged with 42 breaking and entering charges. There's no way out for you this time." The next morning the judge said, "You could be released until your trial, but you need 20,000 marks for bail." I gave him Papa's name and phone number and returned to my cell. In less than two hours, Papa came, paid the bail, and got me out of jail. He was furious. "Will you ever learn, Robert? How many times have I told you not to deal with anyone that you don't know and trust?" I had lost all my money by trusting the wrong person. Papa was right. I was too naïve. I had to be wiser and more cautious with these dealings. Never one to dwell on negative happenings, I immediately began to make plans on how to recoup my loss.

I contacted Fritz, and we were crossing the border into France within a few days. Fritz was as broke as I was due to his gambling. Neither of us had money, so we borrowed 20,000 marks from Papa to purchase surgical pins that were still in high demand in France. Fritz had a close business connection with two brothers, Werner and Bernard. Werner lived on the German side, while Bernard lived on the French side. They both did short-distance trucking. Werner drove us to Bruchmuehlbach, right by the French border. He let us out, and we walked 6 km in the bush to the French side. Bernard was there to pick us up, and he dropped us off at Sulzbach. We sold the surgical pins to the medical supply store there. The next day, we bought 10,000 books of cigarette papers, which cost us 2,800 francs. We returned to Germany safely and sold the papers for a tenfold profit. We then paid Papa back and began making weekly smuggling trips to France.

At the end of October, I went to court to face the charge of buying stolen goods. The judge sentenced me to 10 months, but I was free until the notice came to serve my sentence. Of course, I went back to smuggling the very next day. My finances were improving, but my relationship with Emilie was not going well. She was extremely dependent on me and full of anxiety. I began to understand that it would be hard to build a future life with her. It seemed clear that she wouldn't be an equal partner. For me, life was a grand adventure, but for

Emilie, it was a fearful journey. Ria had been a strong and independent woman, but Emilie needed to be taken care of very delicately, and I didn't want that kind of relationship. I wanted to travel and see the world, while Emilie wanted everything to stay the same. Ria and I had the same values, political beliefs, and fearless spirit. We could talk endlessly about our dreams of making the world a better place and the adventures we would have when we would meet again after the war. Emilie, on the other hand, didn't want to hear me speak of such ideas, and we never talked about anything on a metaphysical level. When Papa met her, he made a remark that made me think harder on the longevity of our relationship. "Robert, you will never reach a green branch with her."

I had now started to realize he was right. I didn't want to hurt Emilie, but I also didn't want to be with someone who would always hold me back from my dreams. By mid-December, I had made the difficult decision to break up with Emilie. I went to her house to tell her. It would be hard, but I knew it was the right thing to do. I would never have the kind of life I wanted if I stayed with her. I tried to break the news to her as gently as possible. "I love you, Emilie, but I can't see a successful future for us." Emilie started sobbing, and Ilse told me angrily, "Robert, Emilie is pregnant!" It was a shock, but I immediately knew that I couldn't leave Emilie to face the shame of having a baby without a husband. Powerful emotions suddenly rushed over me as the truth set in. I had always wanted to be a father... and now I was going to become one. Emilie was still weeping, so I hugged her tight to my chest until the heavy lurching sobs began to lose their rhythm. "I'm sorry that I hurt you, Emilie. I love you, and we'll get married as soon as possible to make this right." She nodded her head and stifled her tears as I held her in my arms.

I went home to tell Mama and Oma the news. Oma was delighted that a baby was coming. She had always told me, "If a woman is good enough for you to sleep with, then she's good enough to marry." Mama, however, was stunned by the news. She knew from the start that we were not a good match. "Robert, you have ruined your life, but now you must face the music." Mama was always practical, so she came up with a plan. "The upstairs is boarded off because of the bombing, but you could rebuild it and make it liveable for you and your family. You can live rent free as long as you can pay the cost of the renovation and repair." It was a generous offer from my mother, even though she was not at all pleased by my news. The next day, I went to tell Papa. I knew he would not be happy with the situation. He was disappointed with me and became angry. "I could see it coming, Robert, and now you're in for it. You've made your bed, now you'll have to sleep in it." Right away, I hired four tradesmen to build the upstairs loft for me and my family. I paid them in black market goods, coffee, cigarettes, and schnapps.

Fritz and I continued our profitable smuggling operation. Now that I was going to become a father and a husband, I had to make sure I made enough to support my family. Oma said with a big smile, "Kinder, betet, der Vater geht stehlen." That translates to, "Children pray, your father is out stealing." She meant that I would now have a child that would pray for my protection when I was out stealing. That line became the title of my first memoir, that was published in Germany in 2016. I don't live my life with regrets, so I just got on with it. One day Fritz said to me, "Robert, let's go across the border on Christmas Eve, no border patrol will be on duty that night. I bet we could get a ton of gold across that night." He was right, and we made a killing. We repeated the same plan on New Year's Eve when everyone was celebrating. That night, we shared a bottle of cognac on the way back and got royally drunk. At the train station in Kaiserslaughten, we got on a French military train, despite the sign that clearly stated that civilian passengers were prohibited. I got out a bottle of cognac, and loudly and drunkenly wished them all, "Bonne heureuse annee!" I then I offered to share my cognac. They happily passed the bottle around, and it wasn't long before Fritz, myself, and the French soldiers were all passed out. At Koblenz, the French military garrison, one of the soldiers woke us up and we jumped off to catch the regional train to Bohum. We boisterously bade farewell to our amiable military escort.

I finally had enough money to both pay the tradesmen and purchase the material for building the upstairs. In early January 1948, I got the notice from the court to serve my ten months in jail. I had to report within eight days. Dr. Hoppe had helped me in similar situations before, so I took a pound of Lyons Tea and paid him a visit. I told him that I had a ten month sentence and a court order for jail, but that I was about to be a new father. I asked him if he could help me delay the sentence so that I could provide for my child. He told me he would write me a doctor's note stating that I had a kidney infection and not fit to go to jail at this time. I thanked him graciously and gave him the British tea that he loved in exchange. This gave me time to make a few more smuggling trips to have money for my family before going to jail. In February, the new German government announced an amnesty for everyone who had received a jail sentence of less than one year. My affair with Lady Luck had not yet ended, it would seem. I no longer had to go to jail.

Fritz and I continued our weekly trips across the border. My home situation was a nightmare. Sergio was always drunk, and insisted my mother serve him and his drunken fascist friends like a maid. He was having parties all the time, would turn up in the middle of the night with his friends, wake Mama up, and tell her to cook some steaks for them. My strong Mama was completely subservient to him, which really pissed me off. Ironically, she seemed happier than I had ever seen her. I resented Sergio and the demeaning way he treated her. The divorce was dragging on from court to court. Mama and Papa couldn't agree, and the lawyers got rich from their divorce. I felt so sorry for my Papa during the whole ordeal. He was an angry and bitter man who just couldn't accept reality. He kept insisting that the house and the factory were all his because, "I earned it. I did all the work!" He couldn't grasp the fact that he had signed it all over to Mama legally, and that he no longer had any rights to it. The bank account, on the contrary, was in his name, so he had quite of bit of money to waste on lawyers fighting a lost cause. Both Papa and Oma had been spiritually broken by what had happened. I was filled with sorrow to see Oma as a shell of her former vital and witty self. She just kept weeping and praying for God to take her away.

Emilie was halfway through her pregnancy when a letter came for me from Bitburg Eifel, Germany. It was from Ria. With trembling hands, I opened the letter. She wrote, "I am alive and well, and hope to connect with you. If you still love me, and want to see me, write to me at this address. I was arrested in 1944 in France by the Vichy French police and given over to the German police. Since I was a Czech national, I was considered stateless, and extradited to Czechoslovakia. There, I was arrested and put in a labour camp. The Red Army liberated us in May 1945. I wanted to live free and escape the Iron Curtain, so I managed to cross the border into Austria and then to Germany. I still love you and I'm waiting for you, Robert. I hope this letter reaches you and you have survived the war. Love, Your Ria." I was ecstatic to find that Ria was alive. She had been my first true love and I had dreamed endlessly of spending my life with her. I realized that I was facing the biggest decision of my life while considering how to react to the letter. In my heart, I was yearning for Ria, and I was filled with joy to find out she still loved me. At the same time, Emilie was pregnant, and I knew that was where my responsibility lay. Why couldn't Ria's letter have come a year ago? Alas, it didn't. Now, letter or no letter, I was going to become a father. If I replied to Ria, it would just inflame my heartache and make it harder to give her up. After hours of impossible contemplation, I made the terrible and painful decision that I would not reply. I knew it was best to try to simply forget Ria. It broke my heart, but I felt I had no choice. I put my beloved's letter away in a drawer. Later, on the day I married Emilie, I burned Ria's letter.

The renovations on the upstairs were costly and kept me in a cycle of being completely broke. I had to keep smuggling weekly and crossing into France with Fritz just to cover the expense of the materials and pay the tradesmen. In April, we were returning with our contraband and had four large duffel bags filled with cigarette papers. We boarded the train from Kaiserslautern and were sitting cosily in a compartment chatting away when the door opened and two custom officers came in to conduct a random search for contraband. One of them announced, "Please open your suitcases one at a time." Fritz and I looked at each other, trying to keep calm. The officers checked a few suitcases and then came to us. "Where is your luggage?" Our four duffel bags were above us on the rack. They pulled one down, opened it, and there were the cartons of cigarette papers in all their incriminating glory. "Are these yours?" I tried to bluff. "No, they were there before we got on the train." They didn't believe me. "You are both under arrest for possession of contraband." At Koblenz, we got off and were taken to the custom headquarters where we were interrogated together.

"Where did you go?" the officer asked. "We went to Kaiserslaughen to see that beautiful historic city." Fritz nodded, leaving the bluffing to me. "We are both disabled. Fritz has silicosis from working in the coal mines, and I am still unable to work because of my liver dysfunction as a result of my time in a prisoner of war camp. We travel to old cities in Germany, as we are both keenly interested in historical places." The custom officer looked at us with some incredulous amazement. "Either you're both hard-boiled criminals, or two of the most innocent guys I have ever run into." He shrugged and handed us our ID cards. "You are free to go." I knew he didn't believe us, but he couldn't prove that the duffel bags were ours. "Gute Reise." he said, with a big grin. I thought it was nice of him to wish us a good journey. I was enormously relieved that we weren't going to be charged, however, we returned home totally broke from the whole ordeal. I had to stop the renovations for now and go to Papa in order to borrow money to survive on until Fritz and I figured out what our next plan of action was going to be.

Fritz had many connections in his social network. One of them was Heinrich, who worked as an engineer on the train from Saarbruecken to Koblenz. Fritz offered him 10,000 marks per trip if he would hide the duffel bags for us on the train. Heinrich was pleased with the deal, and said he would hide them under the coal where they would never be found. This worked like a charm. The next two trips went off without a hitch, and I hired the men again for the renovations. I concentrated on the local black market, because I knew now that the trips to France were a real gamble. My goods were mainly alcohol, cigarettes, clothing, and horse meat. I was visiting Emilie every day and taking them coffee, food, and cigarettes. Then, on June 29th, 1948, everything changed. The government announced they were devaluing the existing German mark and replacing it with the Deutsche mark.

They informed the population of West Germany that on June 30th, 8:00 a.m., that everyone was to come to city hall to receive their 40 Deutsche marks. This was to be done alphabetically. Our money was worthless, and we might as well burn it at this point. Forty Deutsche marks was equivalent to the weekly pay of a labourer. Suddenly, the stores were filled with goods that hadn't been available since the beginning of the war. This new supply influx meant that I was out of the smuggling business. The people who were employed would be getting their weekly wages, but I was up the creek without a paddle. I knew that no company would be hiring ex-black marketeers. Things were looking bleak for me. In a month I would become a father, so I was under immense pressure to figure something out. Fritz came up with a plan. In Germany, a booklet of cigarette papers was now selling for 65 pfennig, but we could buy them in France for three pfennig. So, off we went to the French Saarland to buy cigarette papers. We sold them to a German wholesaler at tenfold the profit.

The legal age for marriage at the time was 21. This meant we had to wait until I turned 21 on July 10[th,] and the baby was due in early August. I applied in April to the court to be exempted because my fiancée was pregnant. The judge said, "Due to your criminal record, we have to turn you down. I wish you good luck. You are turning 21 soon, so I hope the baby can wait until then." I had become more fond of Emilie with time and I was growing to love her. She was carrying my child, and I knew she was a good woman that would never betray me. I had great compassion for Emilie and felt protective of her. It was clear that I would always have to take care of her, but would we be able to build a life together? The day I turned 21, I went immediately to city hall to set a date for a civic wedding. This was considered scandalous, as Catholics would always marry in the Church, but we had to marry quickly because the baby was about to arrive. Also, I had lost my faith, and didn't have any desire or feelings of obligation to get married in the church.

I was given the date of July 30th, at 9:00 a.m., for our wedding. The night before was my stag party. I met with several of my friends for drinks, got totally drunk, and arrived home at 6:00 a.m. to crash. The next thing I knew Mama was shaking me. "Robert, get up!" she shouted. "What for?" I mumbled. "You're getting married in an hour, get up right now!" "Don't worry, Mama, they can't do it without me." I quickly got dressed in my suit and tie and tried my best to sober up. As I began walking, I saw a friend driving by and stopped him. "Can you give me a ride to city hall?" He took one look at me and said, "Go home, Robert, you're drunk." "No, no, I'm getting married." He reluctantly drove me to city hall, shaking his head at my condition, and shocked that his bachelor buddy was getting married.

We arrived at 9:10 a.m. and I saw Emilie and the two witnesses, her brother and his wife, standing outside. They began shaking their fists at me and yelling. When I got to Emilie she took one look at me and said with disgust, "You are impossible." She was fuming and I couldn't blame her. I was late for my own wedding. We had lost our spot to another couple, so we waited until they were done. Emilie looked lovely in a ruby red maternity dress. She wouldn't speak to me, and the witnesses kept giving me dirty looks. The justice of the peace pronounced us man and wife, and we walked to her mother's place. I provided the food and drinks for a brunch with her family, then we all did a procession through town to my home. Mama had prepared a wedding feast of sausages, breads, cheeses and a Rodon French cake, which was one of her specialties. Fritz, Uncle Willy, and my cousin Elsbeth were all there to greet us. My nemesis, Sergio, was also there, lording over my mother and bossing her around. Oma hugged me. "I never believed I would live to see the day that Robert got married." Later I walked Emilie home. As I returned to my house that night, I felt such a great sense of relief that my child would not be born illegitimate. I was ecstatic at the thought of being a father. I had been terribly lonely as an only child and had always wanted to have eight children. In my wisdom, I sensed this was not the time to mention that to Emilie.

There was no money to finish the renovations for my family to move into the upstairs. It was necessary to do another smuggling trip to France. Fritz and I arranged to meet at Emilie's at 9 a.m. on August 5th. At 2 am, the phone rang. It was Mrs. Rozanski, who owned the corner store near Emilie's home. "Emilie is in labour, get the midwife." I called Frau Glas. She had delivered me 21 years ago. When I got to Emilie's, Frau Glas was already there. She was an excellent midwife and I was confident all would go well. "Boil a big pot of water, Robert." Emilie's mother went into her bedroom and prayed with her rosary for a safe delivery. Frau Glas and I were with Emilie, one on each side of the bed. The contractions were getting stronger, but Frau Glas became concerned there was a problem. About 4 a.m. she said, "Robert, get

Dr. Veuhoff." I ran two km to his home, rang the emergency bell, and told him we needed him urgently at 101 Shamrock Street. As I walked quickly back, Dr. Veuhoff rode by me on his bicycle. I was amazed that he had got dressed so quickly. When I arrived, I saw that both of them were working on Emilie. "Wash your hands, Robert, and come here," he ordered brusquely. The three of us worked as a team to help Emilie birth the baby. Emilie's foot was against my shoulder and the other foot against Frau Glas's shoulder. Dr. Veuhoff said firmly, "Emilie, if this baby isn't born soon, you will have to go to the hospital. Take a deep breath and give a big push."

With that big push, our baby was born. It was 6 am and I was officially a father. We had a beautiful baby girl, the most beautiful sight I had ever seen. She had dark hair, olive skin, and a powerful voice. All the women, except Frau Glas, were crying. Emilie held the baby for a few minutes, and then handed her to me. I saw her sweet face and kissed her, tears coursing down my face. "What shall we call her?" Emilie was exhausted. "You pick a name." I looked down at my daughter. "What about Marie Louise?" Emilie agreed. Maria was my mother's name, and it went well with Louise. At 7 a.m., Fritz arrived early for the smuggling trip. He was disappointed about the cancellation of the trip, but happy about the baby. I saw he had come on his bicycle. "May I borrow your bike to go to City Hall to register my daughter?" "Of course." So, off I went. I wanted to be the first one to register a baby that day. It was a proud day for me when I filled in those forms! I returned the bike to Fritz and went home to tell Mama she was a grandmother and Oma that she was a Great Oma. They were happy that the birth had gone well. I went to Papa's next to deliver the news. He was not too happy, but he accepted it. "You have a tough life ahead of you now." I knew he meant my life with Emilie would not be easy. "I wish you good luck, Robert. You are no longer the playboy, but a mature man, husband, and father." As I walked home, I felt like a different person. Papa was right. Now I had to become responsible. I was a husband and a father. For me, family came first above everything else. I felt I had matured overnight, and I took on the responsibility of this new life with determination. I would make it work. All would be well.

The next day, Fritz and I crossed the border to buy cigarette papers. The profit from what we brought back was worth two months of wages in the coal mine. Fritz told me on the way that this was his last trip. He was a pensioned-off coal miner with silicosis of the lungs and his condition was getting worse. My smuggling partner was retiring. I visited Emilie and Marie every day. My daughter grew prettier each time I saw her. Her eyes were like two black Bing cherries, and her hair was thick and dark, just like mine. Emilie and I took her for walks. I would push the baby carriage, and traffic almost stopped on Main Street to see a man pushing a carriage. This was shocking to people at the time, but I didn't care. I was a proud father, and this was my daughter. The upstairs was finally renovated and liveable. I purchased furniture and we moved in at the beginning of September. I even bought a Blaupunkt radio, with which we were able to get any station in the world. We would listen to classical, Latin American, and jazz. Friends started visiting us, and soon we were having parties again. My dreams of a life with Ria were gone, as were my dreams of travelling. However, with the death of old dreams gave birth to the new. My new dream was to be a good husband and father with all my being.

Emilie 1943

CHAPTER 14

Emilie's mother, Ida, was a devout Catholic, and she began pressuring us to have Marie baptized. It was also important to Emilie, who was deeply religious. My mother could have cared less, but after awhile, we gave into Ida's constant lamenting. We made a date at the St. Bonifatius Catholic Church for the baptism and asked Hans, Emilie's older brother, to be the godfather. We all went to the church to arrange the event with Father Decker. We were not welcomed when we arrived. "I am sorry, but I cannot baptize this baby since the parents are not even married." I reached in my pocket and handed him our marriage license. He glanced at it with disapproval. "You are not married in the eyes of God." Thankfully, Hans saved the day. "I am the godfather, and a good friend of Father Duvell at Sacred Heart Church in Herne." Father Duvell was Father Decker's superior. Suddenly, he changed his tune after hearing this. "I will baptize the baby, but I expect you to get married in Holy Mother, the church." I was not planning to do that, but I reluctantly agreed. Finally, Father Decker, who was overdue for retirement, baptized our baby. It is the custom in Germany to have a big baptism party. All our relatives and friends came to celebrate the occasion with us. Mama baked her famous Rodon cake and cherry tarts, which she served with a generous portion of whipped cream. I brought the schnapps, wine, and beer, while Emilie made potato salad topped with knackwurst. It was certainly a feast fit for a baptism celebration of our first child.

Fritz had been my mentor and had taught me all he knew from his 20 years of smuggling. I looked for a new partner to replace him, resulting in my meeting of Franz, a man 15 years my senior. He was a smart businessman who personally knew several tobacco wholesalers. This connection meant we could make the sale for the cigarette papers before we even went to France. He was also quite the jokester. When we first met, he remarked, "Robert, tonight I'm going to a gay party and I want you to come. You have to be gay tonight and be my sweetheart. When we get there, just keep your arm around me and don't talk much." I was intrigued by this invitation as I knew gays had a hard time in Germany. It was illegal, and if you were charged, you went to jail for six months. I got a little drunk and played my part as his sweetheart. I didn't stay long, as they were all older businessmen and I found them boring. Franz and I made several successful trips over the next two months. Things were getting more dangerous at the border, however, because both sides started using German Shepherds to track smugglers. Many were caught. We decided to travel through the worst terrain possible, dense bush and a creek, so that the dogs would have trouble tracking us.

I began to have an ominous feeling that our luck couldn't hold much longer and we would soon be caught. In late November, I decided that I was going to quit smuggling for good but would do just one more trip. After the last trip, Emilie had found a French silk scarf scented with Chanel #5 in my suitcase. She kept it until my friends came over for a visit, and then brought it out and waved it around angrily with an accusing look in her eye. "Look at this! He even brought a souvenir home from France. I want to find out what's really going on! I've decided to go along on the next trip to find out the truth." I was surprised by this, as I had not been with any other woman, and I didn't know how the scarf got into my suitcase. I suspected that Franz did it for a lark, as he liked to stir things up with his jokes. "Emilie, I have no idea how this scarf got in my suitcase. I'm not seeing any women, I'm way too busy smuggling." The women got involved and stirred the pot. "You go with him Emilie, and find out what's going on over on the French side." In protest, I said, "You're still breast feeding, Emilie." "Marie can have the bottle. I'm going." Uncle Willy then added to my problems. "If this is going to be your last trip, take Elsbeth with you." She was his daughter and my older cousin. "She needs to make some money for Christmas," he said. My heart sank. Now I was stuck with two women who lacked experience in smuggling.

Two days later, all four of us went across the border for the last smuggling trip. We purchased the cigarette paper and made it back to Germany. The truck was waiting, and Franz and the women got on, but there was no room for me. I was the fittest, so I said I would walk and get the regional train to meet them in Kaiserslautern. We already had a room reserved there. When I got to Kaiserslautern, however, they weren't there. They should have arrived long before me. I had a bad feeling in my stomach and called the trucking company to investigate their whereabouts. A woman answered told me the bad news. "They all got busted by the German border patrol and are in jail in Landstuhl." I felt guilty that I had taken my wife and my cousin on this trip, and now they were in trouble. Emilie had stubbornly insisted on going, and I had tried my hardest to talk her out of it, but I still felt responsible. Should I go to Landstuhl and risk getting arrested too? I didn't have any money left for bribes. I knew Emilie would be anxious and scared. I had to go to her. When I got to the jail, I learned they were being transferred the next day to the women's prison in Zweibruecken, where I would need to apply to visit them. The next day, I took the train to the prison in Zweibruecken. The desk clerk was friendly, and I gave her their names to request visitation. "You can apply now for a visit in a week. I can give your wife a message that you were here, and that you are coming to visit." I was pleased to at least see how pleasant the guards were and felt relieved that my wife and cousin wouldn't be mistreated.

I'd lost most of my money, but I had a bit of reserve cash. I knew I had enough to support Marie and Emilie's sister, Helma, who was taking care of her. I told Uncle Willy what had happened, and he immediately came up with a plan. "Don't worry, Robert, you and I will do a smuggling trip to France next week, and we'll visit the women on the way back." I was happy that Uncle Willy had offered to do this, as I needed to make money and he had many years of smuggling experience. A week later we crossed into France, purchased the cigarette papers, unloaded them in Kaiserslautem, and then took the train to visit Emilie and Elsbeth. The guard brought them to a conference room for us to have some privacy. They came in crying piteously. I tried to comfort my wife, but she just kept on crying. I served them the tea and snacks I had brought, which soon calmed them down. They told us the guards had been very kind to them and made their jail life as easy as possible. "The guards know we are not criminals," Emilie said. "We were interrogated by a customs officer, and told him that we were not involved in the smuggling of the contraband. We blamed it all on you, Robert." I was glad they had put the blame on me, as they were more likely to get off lightly now. Elsbeth had purchased quite a lot of contraband in France, but Emilie had not bought any contraband. She had just come along because of that damn French silk scarf with the scent of Chanel #5. We had to catch the train, so our visit had to come to an end. As I left, I handed an envelope with 100 marks in it to the two guards. "Thank you for your kindness. Have a nice dinner with this." Uncle Willy and I made it safely home with our contraband.

There was a letter for me from the Staatsanwaltschaft, which is similar to the office of the District Attorney in Canada. They gave me ten days to come to the court in Zweibruecken, and assured me that I would not be arrested, but remain free until my court date. I was determined to go and face the consequences, but I figured that Uncle Willy and I could do one more trip beforehand. It went well, thankfully. Uncle Willy then accompanied me to court. The clerk was friendly to me. "The contraband was mine, and I admit I illegally crossed the border both ways and smuggled foreign goods into Germany." I signed the document. "You will be notified when your court case comes up." We then went to visit the women. I took a good picnic lunch for all of us, and some money for the guards. "Emilie, I'm visiting the baby every day and I take her out for a walk in the baby buggy. Mama bought her a teething ring with a silver elephant attached to it to bring her luck. She is really pretty and getting so big." Emilie was pleased to hear that Marie was doing well. I also told her I had signed the document to take all the blame. The women were relieved to hear that, hoping they would get out soon. The guards had told them not to worry, as their punishment would now be light.

On the way home, Uncle Willy came up with the idea of doing a trip to France on Christmas Eve. "The whole world is celebrating that night, including the border guards. We can go safely through the Holy Night as smugglers." Ah, my beloved Uncle Willy. He was even more foolish and impulsive than me, and yet I trusted his guidance. There was a big snow fall on Christmas Eve, and the snow covered our tracks. Thankfully, we had another successful trip. On the way back, we stopped to see the women, and gave them and the guards some Christmas goodies. Since the Holy Night smuggling trip had gone so well, Uncle Willy and I decided to test our luck again on New Year's Eve. There was not a soul in sight as we made our trip. I was able to start off 1949 with enough money to support my family. About a week later, the notice came for me, Emilie, and Elsbeth to appear at the court in Landstuhl. The charge against me was "illegal border crossing and importing illegal foreign goods." The women were charged with "illegally crossing the border and assisting in the importation of illegal foreign goods." The court date was in early February. Emilie was filled with anxiety, and I reassured her that everything would be fine. We were all to face a tribunal of judges. Before entering court, the head judge walked by and stopped to speak to the women. He appeared to be a kind elderly gentleman. "Don't worry, both of you will be going home today." All of us felt as though a heavy weight had been lifted from our shoulders. Marie would have her mother back.

The prosecutors presented the charges. Franz got a six months jail sentence, I got four months, and the women each got two months. The judge told Emilie and Elsbeth that they were free to go, as they had already spent three months in jail waiting for their trial. Franz got a longer sentence because he was older, and the police saw him as the ringleader. The judge gave me some good news. "You will be notified about your sentence, and you can serve it in your hometown." When we got home, we went to pick up Marie, and Emilie was pleased to see how healthy and happy she looked. We took Marie home in the kinder wagon and were happy to be together as a family again. A month later, the court notice arrived stating that I was to appear at the Herne jail within ten days. Right away I went to my tea drinking saviour, Dr. Hoppe, with a good supply of Lyons Tea. I explained that I had a new baby and asked if he could delay my jail time. He was happy to oblige, and wrote me a medical note stating, "Robert Middelmann is temporarily unfit to serve jail time and is undergoing treatment for three months for his kidney problem." The court kindly granted me an extension.

I knew I had to quit my smuggling business, but at this point I had practically become addicted to the adrenaline high I felt when successfully crossing the border. There was also the rush I felt when I outsmarted the French and German officials. Uncle Willy was quite ill with respiratory problems from his silicosis, so I decided to go on one last trip on my own before quitting. In April, I went across the border, purchased my cigarette papers, and tried to cross the border with two duffel bags on my shoulders. I came to the large, white, painted rock that marked the border. It had been my habit to touch it for luck. I was putting down my duffel bags to do my ritual, when suddenly two French border guards jumped from behind the rock and pointed their guns at me. I froze on sight like a deer in headlights. For a moment, I couldn't speak and just began shivering. "Let's make a deal. You take one bag and let me go with the other." They had serious looks on their faces. "No, you're under arrest." They marched me to the station. I was still carrying the heavy duffel bags the whole way there. They locked me up in a small cell where I began to berate myself. "You're such an idiot! Why did you have to do one more trip?"

In the morning, a young and handsome French officer searched me for ID. He found the thank you letter in my wallet that I had received from Abel Cerilot, the French prisoner of war that I had helped escape in 1943. He read the letter with great interest. "It seems you were very good to my people during the war. I'll try my best to help you. I won't mention the contraband in my report. Instead, I will say that you crossed the border to find a job, and, being unsuccessful, you tried to return home and were caught at the border." I felt overwhelmed with relief by this man's act of kindness. My good deed had come back to pay it forward and help me out of this mess. The next day, I faced the local judge who sentenced me to 14 days in jail for illegal border crossing. If I had been charged with smuggling, I would have gone to jail for up to a year. That thank you letter had given credence to the concept of karma and saved me from a lot of trouble.

When I got to prison, they asked if I would like to be a kitchen helper. I was delighted by the thought. Food has always been sacred to me and I love cooking for others. I shared a cell with two other inmates, and our door was only locked at night. One of my roommates was the head cook, and the other the maintenance man. All other cells were locked. I knew I was in good company. After becoming acquainted and chatting for a bit, I discovered that my roomies, Albert and George, were both sentenced for six weeks for living together by common law. Their wives were in the adjoining prison. At night, it was like a scene from a romantic Hollywood movie. The wives would serenade the men with passionate love songs. The two weeks went by quickly. My biggest concern was that I had no way to let Emilie know what had happened, and I knew she would be in a great state of anxiety worrying about my whereabouts.

At the end of my jail term, two French policemen picked me up, took me to the train station, bought me a ticket, and waited with me until I left. The train took me across the border to Kaiserslautern. I had no money, so I went to the Catholic Mission by the train station. "Could I borrow 5 marks so that I can send a wire to my father for money?" The worker looked me up and down and decided I was a worthless person. "It's your own fault you got into this situation, so I can't help you." So much for Christian charity… Next, I went to the Protestant Mission. "I'm not a Protestant, but I need help." The worker had a kind face. "I don't care what religion you are. How can I help you?" This Christian man had a good heart. "I need five marks to wire my father for money. I will repay you and I will leave you my ID as collateral." He chuckled. "I have a drawer full of those, I don't need any more." I wondered how I could convince him. "I know my father will send money. I just want to get home to my wife and baby. I will give you the money back, I promise." He looked at me for a long time, carefully assessing me. "Okay, you've talked me into it."

I thanked him profusely, then sent a telegram to Papa asking for 25 marks. Papa sent me 50. I went to the Good Samaritan and gave him the five marks back. He was pleasantly surprised. "And here, here's another five marks for the next stranded person." That brought a smile to his face. When I got home, I found Emilie, Marie, Mama, and Oma in the kitchen. They all burst into tears, except for the baby. Oma said, "I prayed every night for God to bring you home again." I hugged Emilie tight because she couldn't stop crying. I hugged Oma and Mama. Oma wouldn't let me go. "Don't ever leave again, Robert, please don't ever leave again." She looked so old and so sad. They had all been so worried about me, and I felt a bit ashamed. I knew my smuggling days were over. "I won't go smuggling again," I reassured them. "Tomorrow, I will look for work in the coal mine." I had already made that decision on the train. It hung heavy on my heart to go underground, but I felt I had no choice. They were all relieved to hear me say that. The next day, I went to Papa to thank him for bailing me out and let him know I would pay him as soon as possible. "Forget it," he said, "just don't take any more risks like that. You have a family to take care of now."

Two days later, the divorce of my parents was finalized. Mama could keep the house and factory, while Papa could have the machinery. They both seemed to be accepting of this division of assets. That same day, I got a job in the mine called Julia. Jobs were scarce, and no one was hiring ex-black marketeers, so I was happy to be hired. It was hard work, like the mine in Belgium where I worked as a POW, but at least I was getting paid for it this time. I could make enough to support my family, and that was all that really mattered to me. After work, I went to visit Papa. He had been quite depressed as of late, and I was concerned about him. He was in a state of great excitement when I arrived. "Robert, I have found a partner and plan to build a candy factory on his farmland! He is providing the land and the money needed to build the factory. My contribution will be the machinery, my knowledge, and years of experience. I am sure I can get you involved later and help you in your future." I knew he was completely broke because of the long and drawn out divorce. All his money had gone to lawyers and court costs because his pride outweighed logic. This seemed like a good opportunity for him to pick up the pieces of his life. A few days later he moved to the farm, where he had his own suite in the house. A week later, Mama was informed that a truck was coming to pick up Papa's machinery. Just before they were to arrive, Mama took me aside. "Robert, go to the processing machine, open the transmission, and take out the drive shaft." I was appalled by what she was asking me to do. Doing this would make the machinery completely useless, and the shaft piece could not be replaced. Spare parts for this machine were now only being made in East Germany, where they would be impossible for Papa to obtain.

As I looked in her face, I could see it was filled with hatred. I knew she wanted to sabotage Papa's chances of rebuilding his business. She still wanted revenge. I was filled with disgust and loathing for my mother at the thought. How could she ask me to do this? I loved Papa and she wanted to destroy him. "No, Mama, I won't do that. Let Papa have his machinery so he can make a new life." Mama's face went red with rage. "I don't know why you are sticking up for him. He's not even your father." I looked at Mama and replied coldly, "I know. I have known that all my life." Mama was stunned. "What? How could you know?" She was stammering and choking on the words as they came out. "When I was four, I heard you and Frau Israel talking in the kitchen. I heard her ask you when you were going to tell me that Uncle Leo was my father." Mama went pale and looked as though she were about to faint. "Mama, I learned to live with it. Let's go on with life and put it to rest." She said nothing more and walked away. The emotional gap between us had now become even wider. She was furious with me that I wouldn't do as she asked. I loved Papa, and I wanted him to be able to rebuild his life regardless of his past mistakes. He was the only father I had ever had, and he loved me as his son. I was proud of myself that I had stood up to my mother to do what was right. It was another step forward on my path to becoming a man.

The machinery went to Papa, including the drive shaft. Papa stored it in the barn until his new candy factory was built. I visited him and met the farmer, Mr. Wiesenhofer, and his family. Meanwhile, Mama and Sergio had started a new business. They had a portable kiosk at the streetcar junction, which was the perfect spot for sales. They sold hamburgers, bratwurst, and marinated fish from 8 p.m. to 2 a.m. every day. Business was booming. Unfortunately, while Mama was at the kiosk working hard, Sergio was in the pub drinking. He still treated her like she was his lowly servant and she accepted this treatment without protest. My beloved Oma was only a shadow of her former self. She had always been the heart and rock of our home. That heart, it turned out, was now broken. Every night I heard her endlessly praying, "God, take me away from this world." I was overwhelmed with waves of hopelessness as I listened to my beloved Oma praying for her death.

Soon, my former lifestyle came back to haunt me. I received a letter from the customs office stating that I owed them 52,000 marks. This was the consumer price in Germany of the cigarette papers that had been confiscated during our ill-fated smuggling trip. Added to this was another 52,000 marks for the customs fine. I stared unblinkingly at the figures. 104,000 marks! It would take me a lifetime, if not two or more, to pay off such a monumental sum. It seemed my luck had truly run out.

I immediately consulted a lawyer, Mr. Steinbach, who specialized in customs law. He considered the letter carefully before advising me. "Robert, this is the law, so you must pay it. However, I can set up a payment plan that they will have to accept because you have a family to support. I suggest you pay 20 marks a month, and state you have the intention to increase that payment later on." I was greatly relieved to find out that recurring payments were a possible option. Thankfully, the customs officials agreed to the proposal. On the first of each month, a man came on a motorbike to collect the payment. He was friendly and felt rather sorry for me. I knew that the only way to get out from under this enormous debt was to leave Germany altogether. However, I also knew that I could never leave as long as Oma was still alive. My savings were gone, and we were trying to survive on my meager wages from the mine. The pay was only 300 marks a month, which meant we had to be very careful not to overspend. I knew I could make more money working as a hard rock miner and sinking a shaft. In July 1949, I got a job at the Siegfried Lothringen mine in Bochum-Gerthe. The work was grueling and more dangerous, but now I made 600 marks a month. We didn't have to constantly fret over our finances any longer.

Being a father gave me the strength required to endure the hard work in the mine. I had matured and proved to my parents that I really could be a responsible family man. This recognition from them gave me a fulfilling feeling of self respect and pride. On my 22nd birthday, we visited my cousin Trudi. She was married to Hans Fischer, a man who owned a travelling carnival. Trudi was my favourite cousin and we were very close. She took a long, hard look at me. "Robert, you are going to ruin your health by working underground. You're smart and putting your intellect to waste. Come and work with us! You'll make more money and breathe fresh air instead of coal dust coating your lungs." I hated working in the mine, and I knew my fair share of miners who had died of silicosis. Trudi had it all figured out. "We'll give you a one man operation running the card game, Blinker. We'll go 50/50 on the profit. You can count on 50 marks a day, food included, and lots of travel. Emilie can come along and work as a cashier. Ask your mother to watch the baby while you're away. You would be working from Friday to Sunday." Hans encouraged me further by adding, "Robert, the mine is a murder pit."

Emilie and I looked at each other and nodded. This was a great opportunity to preserve my health. I had been in a deadly trap underground, but now I could be free again. Mama agreed to take care of Marie. A week later, we were officially on the road with the carnival. Trudi had a fantastic mobile arcade with shooting galleries, gambling games, a merry-go-round, games for children, and a big staff to work it all. Hans showed me the ropes and I caught on quickly. I enjoyed working with the public and my profits were high. We ended work at midnight each night and got together afterward for drinks. Emilie worked as a cashier and was happy with her job. We worked for three days and returned home to Herne for four days. My court notice came for me to serve my four month jail sentence. Once again, I went to see Dr. Hoppe, hoping he still loved his tea. He kindly wrote me yet another letter stating that I was still unfit to serve my sentence, and that I needed more treatment time for my kidney disease. The carnival travelled from the lower Rhineland, right across the Ruhr valley, stopping at each town. Business was good. Trudi was a lot of fun, but she was a heavy drinker, and I was only too happy to join her. It was life in the fast lane that paid with exciting and easy money.

CHAPTER 15

    We worked until Christmas, and then in January 1950, I received another court notice, and decided to finally serve my jail sentence. We now had enough money saved up for my family to live comfortably while I was in jail. I turned myself in to Herne jail, which had a reputation as the "fun" jail. The guards were mellow, and the inmates were all serving short term sentences for living common law or being gay. They took my information and one of the guards asked, "Do you want to be a kitchen helper and custodian of the second floor?" Lady Luck was smiling on me once again. When I met Richard, the cook, I found he was an old acquaintance from the black market. He was happy to see me and we worked well together. I had a private cell, and on Sundays I was part of a group that met in the tailor shop to play cards. There was the tailor, the cobbler, the cook, and the three custodians. We played Skat with pennies, told jokes, and thoroughly enjoyed our camaraderie. It was the good life.

    Visitors were allowed once a month, and Emilie and Trudi came to visit. After two months, I wrote an application to the court for a reduction of my sentence, which had to be approved by the warden. They kindly reduced my sentence by one month. While in prison, I met Conrad, Rudy, and Karl, who were all in jail for the "crime" of being homosexual. We shared our life stories and I found them to be caring, kind, and intelligent men. They had each been given a sentence of six months due to their sexual orientation. I felt this was a great injustice to them, as they would now have a criminal record. In mid-April, I was released and went home to my wife and baby. I felt that I would never return to jail again, and confident that I had given up my lawless ways. Marie had started walking on her own and was being spoiled by the whole family. Mama doted on her every wish while Oma knitted her outfits. I was happy to see that Marie had brought joy back into Oma's life. Marie seemed to be her inspiration to keep on living.

I went to see Papa on the farm. The factory was finished being built and they were in full production. I told him about my jail time and how joyful I was to be a father. Papa showed me the contract he had signed with Mr. Wiesenhofer. I noticed right away there was a serious problem in the paperwork. It stated that Papa's profit "should not exceed 50%." I pointed this out to Papa. "Yes, Robert, I get 50% and they get 50%." I tried to explain to him what it actually meant, but he didn't understand. "Papa, they can give you whatever they feel like. They could give you 5%, and it would still technically fulfill the contract." He still couldn't understand the insidious nature of this loophole and was too stubborn to listen to me. In his mind, he was getting 50%, and that was that. He had been tricked by this lingual nuance. A month later, he asked for some money from his profit to live on. He was given only a small amount in return. Papa, confused, asked about his 50% profit. Mr. Wiesenhofer replied, "That is not in the contract. Read the contract."

In response to Mr. Wiesenhofer's refusal to pay him, Papa went into a violent rage. He smashed a large chandelier on Mr. Wiesenhofer's head and beat him profusely. Mrs. Wiesenhofer phoned the police and an ambulance while trying her best to calm Papa down. Unfortunately, when Papa loses it, he becomes insane and totally out of control. Mr. Wiesenhofer went to hospital and Papa went to jail. A few days later, I received a letter from Papa. What a mess! I went to see him, and he ranted about the contract, still firmly believing that he was entitled to 50%. He had been a broken man since his marriage ended, and the new factory had given him a chance to rebuild his life. Now, even that hope was gone. Papa was sentenced to two years in prison for assault and disturbing the peace. He served one year in Luettringhausen prison, and one year in a penitentiary in Werl. I visited him every month and brought him money so he could buy supplies in the canteen. It broke my heart to see Papa in his prisoner's garb. I couldn't bear to look at this little broken man who cried the whole time I was there. I had always believed that Papa had a mental illness due to his inability to control his violent outbursts. He should have been in a psychiatric ward, not a prison.

After I got out of jail in April, Trudi had come up with a good idea. "Robert, since you know how to make candies, let's go into business together. I will lend you the money and you can start making lollipops. There is a huge demand for lollipops." I was over the moon with this offer from Trudi. I felt again that Lady Luck was sitting on my shoulder. We found a place to set up our business and were going strong by June. I couldn't keep up with the demand even though I produced approximately 2,000 lollipops in eight hours! The boiling of the sugar, mixing and pouring into the molds was all done by me, and I hired two women to do the processing and packing. I also hired a retired coal miner to work the night shift. I taught him the candy business and he caught on quickly. Two more women were soon hired for the night shift, which brought our overall production to 4,000 lollipops a day.

I worked seven days a week on my new business. We were always sold out. In late Fall, I bought a used car I could use for deliveries. I was happy to be my own boss and to have escaped the coalmine "murder pit." Financially I was doing well, and we were hosting weekend parties with friends. We were all still young and had survived the war, so we wanted to live life to the hilt. Our parties were rather wild. My friend, Erwin, had quite the sense of humour, and came up with an unusual party trick. He would take his prick out, put a lighted match in the opening, and walk around the table to light the ladies' cigarettes. This bizarre trick was a big hit. Not to be outdone, I also came up with a party trick. I filled up a one litre bucket with water from the sink, hung it on my erect penis, and walked around the table. This also was a big hit. There was a lot of drinking and noise and Mama would often shout up the stairs, "Robert, keep it down. It's past midnight."

In 1950, the Korean War broke out. As a result, wholesale sugar was rationed in Germany in the spring of 1951. I was "gebuegelt." That means I was flattened financially. I had to shut down the business, I had no other choice. Emilie was upset. "I wish you had kept the job in the coal mine!" She had a strong need for security. I didn't want her to be unhappy, and I knew she didn't want us to go back to carnival work where people looked down on us. I never cared what people thought, but

Emilie was always worried about it. Reluctantly, with a heavy heart, I went to Friederich der Grosse, the third coal mine in Herne, and got a job as a drift miner. It was tunnel work, and Emilie was happy to know I had a steady income. Marie was almost three and was the darling of the whole family. Mama spoiled her all the time, and bought her an extremely expensive dress for her third birthday. It cost 60 marks, which was a week's wage for a labourer. Marie wore it proudly at her party, and continued to wear it for a couple of days to show it off in the neighbourhood. Unfortunately, our road was being paved, and Marie went out to play with some other little girls. She was still wearing her new dress when they all decided it would be great fun to roll about in the freshly poured tar. She marched in proudly to show her Mom the beautiful new pattern she had acquired on her dress.

Oma had deteriorated rapidly over the past few months. She couldn't remember if she had eaten, saying things like, "I'm so hungry, I haven't eaten all day" right after Mama had just fed her. She could no longer control her bowels, and she had lost her concept of time. She would often wake us all up in the middle of the night. "You people are sleeping all day! It's time to get up." I heard her every night, praying and pleading the same has she had done years before. "Please, God, take me away from this world." She would weep so piteously. I hated to see her suffering, and wished her prayers would soon be answered so that she could finally feel at peace. On the morning of September 15, 1953, Mama called me to come to Oma's room. When I entered, Mama said, "Oma fell asleep forever." I looked down at my beloved Oma.

She had a beautiful smile on her face. I had vowed never to leave Germany until Oma was gone. Now, I felt that she was saying to me, "Robert, now you can go to the other side of the world! Nothing is holding you back." Oma had been my cornerstone, my safe nest, my wise mentor all these years. Now she was at peace and I was no longer tethered down in Germany. The family all came together to honour Oma. She was buried in Herne-Baukau cemetery near her husband, Wilhelm Kirschfink, who had died in 1901. He died young, but Oma lived until 93. I went to visit Papa in jail and told him of Oma's passing. He burst into tears. "She was like a mother to me." I remembered Oma's bravery when she refused to fly the Nazi flag. She had been the heart and soul of our entire family. Now, Oma had freed me to start a new life in a new country.

Shortly before Oma died, I had a surprise visitor from Australia. It was Gerhard Rosenberg, one of the sons of the family that Mama and I helped before they were sent to the concentration camp at Riga. He told me he was living in Australia with his sister, Irene, and his brother, Rolf. "Australia is a great country. You should apply to go there! If you come, I will help you. It is a progressive country and you will do well there." Oma was gone, and I could take Gerhard up on his kind offer. Gerhard was returning to Australia in a few days, and suggested that Emilie and I go with him to the Australian Embassy in Cologne and he would sponsor me. I talked it over with Emilie, and she was in favour of going. Some of her in-laws were Jewish and had been interred in a concentration camp. They survived, but the memories were still bitter ones. I now had an old Renault sedan, and we all took off on the autobahn for Cologne, Marie included. After a few kilometres, we had a flat tire. I had no spare tire, which showed how careless I could be at times. I had to remove the tire and roll it two kilometres to the nearest gas station. When it was repaired, we finally continued on our way. Twenty kilometres later, we got another flat tire! Gerhard came out to give me a hand and was shocked to see we had another flat. "Robert, all your tires are bald and you have no spare! I can't believe this. You have some nerve." I rolled the tire to the next village and had it repaired. Then, off we went. Ten kilometres later it started to rain, and…well, a third tire went flat.

Everyone, even Marie, became furious with me. They were all ready to strangle me and I deserved it. I was furious at myself for my lack of foresight, too, but their protests weren't going to change the past. "What are you complaining about? You are sitting in a nice, dry car while I have to roll this tire across the potato field in the rain!" When I returned to the car, they all stayed quiet the rest of the trip. They were so angry with me that it left them speechless. I couldn't blame them. I was holding my breath, waiting for the fourth tire to go flat. We arrived in Cologne very late at night, and, understandably, no one was in a good mood. I asked at the information office if there was a room to rent, but she told me there was a big exhibition in Cologne that had all of the hotels booked. A man overheard our conversation. He saw how tired we were, and how sleepy poor little Marie looked. "Would you mind sleeping in a jail? I am a guard, but I can rent you my bedroom and sleep on the couch." What luck! I thanked him, and off we went to jail. For 20 marks, we had a room and breakfast included. We went to the Australian embassy early next morning and the receptionist was friendly. "You usually need an appointment, but since you are here already, I will try to squeeze you in." Two hours later, we had an interview with the immigration officer. Gerhard signed as our sponsor, the doctor gave us all a checkup, and we passed the medical exams. The officer told us we were accepted for immigration, pending further investigation. I was fearful that my police record would cause problems, or that the 104,000 marks I owed to the customs would throw a monkey wrench in our plan.

We were all in a good mood on the return trip, thankfully. Then, close to home, the fourth tire went! Luckily, this time, it was right in front of a gas station. Emilie was furious. "Next time I go with you, I'll make sure everything is in order!" I was going to be in the dog house for a long time, and it was well deserved. A month later, surely by some miracle of inefficiency on someone's part, I was notified our applications for immigration were approved. They asked me to send in our passports to be stamped. Of course, none of us had passports. I had a good friend, Ernst, who had been in the Hitler Youth with me. Ernst had a high position as an investigator in the Herne police, so I asked him for advice. "If you can keep a clean record for three more years, you'll be able to get a passport, Robert." I was excited at this prospect. When I told Emilie the good news, she told me she had changed her mind. "Robert, I've thought it over, and I'm scared to go that far away from my family." I was devastated, as I knew this change of heart meant I had to give up my dream of going to Australia. "Would you go somewhere else, Emilie? What about Canada, the U.S., or South America?" She thought about it for a bit. "I would prefer Canada, as I've heard many good things about it." Immediately, I focussed on Canada and making that dream come true. I had a positive impression of Canadians from when I had bootlegged Schnapps to the Canadian soldiers after the war. They were all friendly, easy-going guys.

I focussed on a new dream. We could build a good life in Canada. By now, I was painfully aware of how mismatched Emilie and I were in so many important ways. She was a fearful person who craved security above all else. Conversely, I was a fearless person who thrived on adventure and challenge. I loved her, but it had become clear to me that Emilie didn't love me in return. When I would say, "I love you," she would reply, "Ach, you and your love. It's childish stuff. I wasn't brought up like that." She never once said, "I love you." When I kissed her, Emilie would turn her head and wipe off the kiss, an action that pierced my heart. All my life, I had loved to tell jokes and stories. Emilie never laughed at my jokes. Instead, she showed irritation and often disgust. She also never liked to hear my stories, and made it clear that she found me annoying. At times, I thought of Ria, and how much she had enjoyed my stories and laughed at my jokes. Ria told me constantly how much she loved me, and never wiped off my kisses. We had been a good match, both loving life on the edge, both always seeking new adventures. However, Ria was gone, and I was married to Emilie now. I was extremely lonely, but I was determined to make our marriage work for the sake of our child. My hope was that perhaps one day, Emilie would learn to love me, and our marriage would improve. My dream of a new and happier life in Canada kept me going.

In the fall of 1951, the sugar ration was lifted. I quit my job at the mine and returned to my lollipop business. Emilie, unsurprisingly, was not happy about this. The mine meant security to her, and she knew the lollipop business was more likely to fluctuate in its level of success. For me, it was freedom. It was freedom from the coal dust in my lungs, and freedom from the feeling of being trapped underground. Sadly, business slowed down in late fall, and I was desperate for supplemental income. I finally landed a job in the slaughterhouse in Recklinghausen. I was a cattle driver, my job was to unload the cattle from freight trains into the slaughterhouse. As an animal lover, I hated this job, but the pay was better than in the mine. In order to get the job, I had to bribe the head butcher by promising him I would give him my first paycheck. In March 1952, I started up my lollipop business again, as lollipops sold well during the warmer months. Papa got out of jail in April, and went to live with his sister, Antonia. The first thing he did was hire a lawyer to fight the farmer, Mr. Wiesenhofer, in regard to the contract. I knew Papa would not win this case, so I tried to help. "Papa, I'll be your mediator and save you lawyer costs. I'll go and talk to Mr. Wiesenhofer for you." Papa agreed. When I went to see Mr. Wisenhofer, it was clear that he wanted nothing more to do with Papa. "I want to end the contract and pay out your father with 20,000 marks." I thought this was a damn good offer. Papa could buy a small corner store with that amount and start his own business. I told Papa, and he stubbornly refused the offer. "No, no, no. I'm going to fight this and win." He spent all his savings on lawyers, and six months later, he inevitably lost his case. He was totally broke and deeply depressed. An old school friend gave Papa a job working in his bakery. Oh, how the mighty had fallen. The richest man in town was now the poorest, and the saddest.

Mama was doing well financially these days. She bought new machinery for the candy factory and had gained our old clientele back. She hired several women, and business was booming. Mama made me an offer to take the night shift and hire another team. I talked it over with Emilie and accepted Mama's offer. I still didn't want to have anything to do with Sergio, but working the night shift meant I would have little contact with him. He was drinking heavily and abusive to Mama. One evening Mama screamed for help and I ran downstairs. Sergio was beating her up. I grabbed him by the throat and pushed him hard against the wall. "If that happens again, Sergio, believe me, you are a dead man." Mama pleaded, "Robert, don't hurt him!" I was disgusted with both of them at this point. Her loyalty was to this bastard, not to her son or her own dignity. "Mama, don't let Sergio get away with this. Stop being his servant." Sergio never beat her again. He knew I meant what I said. Sergio and I avoided each other even more than we had before that confrontation. I only dealt with Mama, as I wanted nothing to do with this immoral man. He had betrayed everyone, Papa, who took him in when he was homeless, me, when he had sex with Alma, and his wife and two children in Italy, when he screwed around with Mama. My once headstrong mother let him treat her like shit and abuse her. I lost any respect I had for my mother because she allowed this to continue. Why had I opened the door to this viper who betrayed us? It would have been better if he had been shot by the Yugoslavians. They executed the wrong brother.

In the fall of 1952, I began working the night shift consistently at the candy factory. I shut down my lollipop business, as the winter season was coming and business would be slow. Mama had hired four women to work with me. I worked six days a week for long hours for a year before Mama and I had a falling out over Sergio. He was drinking heavily, and as a result, he fell negligently behind in his orders. Mama asked me to work on Sundays, my only day off, to catch up on Sergio's work. She wasn't even going to pay me for the extra time. She justified this by saying, "In the end it will all be yours, Robert." Again, she put Sergio's needs over mine. Why should I give up my day off just because Sergio is a drunk? I was furious with Mama. "I'm better off going back to the mine, at least I'll get Sundays off." I was finished with Mama. Sergio was all that mattered to her. "I quit," I said and walked out.

I was able to get a job as a shaft miner in Mont Cenis right away. Mama and I didn't talk to each other for a year, despite living in the same house. Emilie was happy that I had a steady job again in the mines, and I just had to set my mind to endure being trapped underground again. Marie was five years old now and in kindergarten. Every Saturday night, Emilie and I had our friends over for singing, music, and storytelling. Because

I spoke several languages, I had developed friendships with Italian, Polish, Russian, and French neighbours. By now, we had grown out of our silly party tricks and seemed to have matured. I played guitar while others played the fiddle and the accordion. On Sundays I put Marie on my shoulders, and we went to watch the local soccer games. She loved going with her Papa, and still has a love for soccer to this day. I kept working hard at the mine and made top money. My dream of going to Canada was keeping me going still. I knew that in July 1954, I could apply to go to Canada once my criminal record had been erased.

In February 1954, I was upstairs when Mama called to me. "Robert, please come quickly! Something has happened to Sergio." I went down and found him lying on their bed, all dressed up to go out for a night of heavy drinking. When I looked in his eyes, I knew right away that he was dead. "Mama, Sergio is gone." She screamed and cried out. "No, no, no!" She was in denial that he had died. I tried to calm her down until she finally accepted the truth and called the undertaker. The morgue employees came and took his body away. She turned to me. "Robert, you have to quit the mine. I have so many orders and I'm falling behind." Mama was always practical about financial matters. Her thoughts were focussed on keeping the candy factory going, not on the loss of Sergio. It was a great relief that he was gone, and perhaps now Mama and I could have a chance of a better relationship. I agreed to help her and quit my job at the mine. She needed my help, and it didn't seem that I had a choice. Of course, Emilie was angry with me once again. I began work in the candy factory the very next day and didn't get off work before midnight. I fell asleep right away out of pure exhaustion. Mama woke me up at 4 a.m. every morning to get back to work. The orders were overwhelming, and we struggled to keep up with the demand. I consoled myself with the dream of Canada. On July 1st, I sent the necessary papers to Canadian immigration. They told me they would inform me of a date for an interview. Mama and I were communicating about the business, but nothing else. Sadly, things had not improved between us. She was simply a business partner, and not a mother.

In September 1954, Marie entered grade one. She liked her teacher and enjoyed playing with the other children. Papa was still living with his sister and working in his friend's bakery. Every time I visited him, it was a depressing and sad experience. He remained bitter about Mama's betrayal and went on and on about what could have been. The only thing that brought him happiness was the fact that Sergio was dead. "I hope he rots in hell," he would shout. "Robert, throw that bitch out and take over the factory. It should be yours. I did it all for you!" Papa was a pathetic and tragic figure. He was furious that I was planning to leave Germany. "You don't have to go to Canada. I worked a lifetime for your future, and now you're leaving?" I hated these visits, but knew he needed me to come. He was the father who had raised me, and I loved him despite his many faults.

We received a letter in February for all of us to come to the Canadian Immigration office for our interview. We were to bring a letter from our local doctor about our medical history and a letter from my employer. The immigration doctor assessed us and we passed. All we needed now were passports. However, I still had a problem. How could I get a passport when I owed 104,000 Deutsch marks to the German customs? I pondered this and came up with a typical Robert plan that had a slight chance of working. I went to our local passport office. "We want to visit our relatives in Holland." By the next day, we had our passports. I sent them immediately to the Canadian immigration office to be approved for travel to Canada. A week later, we were approved, and I booked my passage on The Seven Seas, Holland America Line, for June 20, 1955. The plan was for me to go to Montreal, and once I was firmly established, to send for Emilie and Marie.

CHAPTER 16

Mama was already playing the dating game through friends. Two months after Sergio's death, she found a new man, Hans Neumann. A suitable name, as he was the new man in Mama's life. He moved in and Mama asked, "Robert, can you train him before you go to Canada?" Hans was a good man, and not a drinker. I felt that Mama would be safe with Hans. They seemed to love each other, and Mama was happy with him. However, he was not interested in being a candy maker. He told Mama, "I am not cut out to be a candy maker." He had worked in a shipyard most of his life and was now retired. Mama had just turned 57 and had been working since she was a young teenager. I thought it was time for her to retire, too, and enjoy life. "Mama, why don't you rent out the factory and the upstairs of the house? I know a couple who would like to rent the upstairs for 50 marks a month. With the rent and Han's pension, you could retire and enjoy your life, living comfortably." Mama was so used to working that this concept was totally alien to her. Hans was all in favour of the idea and backed me up. After a couple of days, Mama agreed to try it. She had no trouble renting the factory. On the weekends, I worked in the slaughterhouse, and soon got a job in a private coal mine in Bochum-Weitmar. I was happy at the thought of soon being in Canada.

Our plan was to sell all our furniture, and Emilie and Marie would stay with her mother until it was time to join me. I planned to take all my candy equipment to Canada and start a candy business there. As an immigrant, you were allowed a large container free of charge, so I packed it with all my candy making equipment. Meanwhile, my beloved Uncle Willy was in the hospital and near death. He had always been my fun-loving and beloved companion, the one that could always make me laugh. We had a sad farewell, and I left him with a heavy heart. I was still mad at Mama over all that had happened with Sergio. We had another argument, and I didn't even want to say goodbye to her. Emilie intervened. "Robert, you must say goodbye. She is your mother." On the last day before we left, I reluctantly went to say goodbye to Mama. She had tears in her eyes. This was unusual, as she seldom showed her emotions. "Goodbye Robert, and good luck. Don't forget to write me." We hugged each other. I am glad that I said goodbye to her, even though our relationship was not close. My friends all came to wish me luck.

On the night of June 19th, I went to stay at Emilie's mother's home. I gave Emilie an envelope filled with marks. "This is enough money for you to live comfortably on until I send for you." Her mother took me aside. "Robert, Emilie is my 'sorgenkind' and I want you to promise you will always take care of her." "Sorgenkind" means "sorry child," the one that the mother always has to worry about; the one that can't take care of herself. "I promise," I replied. "I will always take care of her." In the middle of the night, I woke with extreme pain in my left ear. I went to the ear specialist's home and woke him up. He examined me. "Robert, you can't travel with this severe ear infection. You have to stay in bed until it clears up." There was no doubt in my mind that I was still going. He gave me some pain killers. My train was leaving at 6 am for the coast. Papa was waiting for me at the railway station, and we had a sad farewell. He was a broken, old man. He cried profusely. "When you make enough money, Robert, come back so we can open a candy factory in Herne and work together." That was Papa's dream, it was not my dream. I felt guilty leaving this pathetic, sad man, but I yearned for the challenge and freedom of a new life.

We were waiting for the train when Heinz, my old school chum, turned up. He whispered in my ear that he was going to Canada to escape paying his taxes, because he owed so much money. I laughed and told him that I was in the same boat. We were both booked to Montreal on the Seven Seas. I saw this to be a good omen. As the train pulled out, I could see Papa sadly waving his white handkerchief and weeping. Somehow, I knew in my heart that I would never see my Papa again. I was still in extreme pain with my ear infection, and kept taking my pain killers and washing them down with red wine. We got off at Bremerhafen and went to the dock. When we boarded, we found there were 18 people to a cabin, tourist class. Heinz and I were nervous, as the German police were checking all the passports and asking questions. We were leaning over the railing when we heard an announcement that the following people were to report to the Captain's office. We held our breath and were greatly relieved when our names were not called. Later on, we saw several men being taken off the boat in handcuffs by the police. Then, they pulled up the gangplank, and the ship's horn sounded for departure. We could see the ship was moving. We were safely on our way to Canada. The band on the pier played "Auf Wiedersehn," which is the German version of "au revoir." That song never sounded so sweet as it did that day. I was absolutely elated to be starting this next chapter of my life. "Heinz, let's go down to the bar and celebrate!" So we did.

The price was right. For 5 cents, we got a shot of whiskey, and for 10 cents, we got a bottle of beer. Cigarettes were 15 cents a pack. In my pocket there was $50 U.S. dollars, and I felt rich and lucky. I was on my way to a new land and a new adventure. We explored the ship and discovered a library, casino, swimming pool, gym, movie theatre, and a large dance floor. Each night, two live orchestras played. I loved dancing, so I knew I would be spending time on the dance floor. When I saw the ship's doctor for my earache, he prescribed antibiotics and it healed quickly. The next day, we reached Le Havre, and more passengers came on board. Later that day, we reached South Hampton and took on many more passengers, which brought the total to 1,100. Within a couple of days, people formed groups. Our group included Italian, French, English, and Germans. We were all young people looking forward to making a new life in Canada.

An attractive English woman, Ruth, was part of our group, and we made a soulful connection that night on the dance floor. She was confident, tall, slim, and an excellent dancer. The next day, we ran in to each other by chance on the upper deck and had a game of shuffleboard. Afterwards, we sat and chatted. She was easy to talk with, intelligent and outgoing. She told me she was a doctor going to Montreal's Royal Victoria Hospital for her one year internship. "I'm a candy maker and plan to set up my business one day in Canada. I'm married with one child, and want to save money to bring my family over as soon as possible." That night, our group had dinner together, and some of us stayed to dance. Ruth and I became steady dance partners. During the day we took walks around the deck, played shuffleboard, and shared our life stories. We found we had the same interests and also shared a deep love of music. Ruth had a quick wit and our conversations were lively. Her sweetness and warmth drew me to her. She seemed fascinated by my life story and wanted to hear more of my adventures. We talked about what might lie ahead for each of us in Canada. We would often speak in French to practice for life in Montreal.

Ruth's girl friends started teasing me. "We lost Ruth to you, Robert, you took her away from us." I began to get an uneasy feeling in my stomach, and it wasn't from the motion of the ship. Ruth was so easy to talk to, that I found that I was enjoying her company a little too much. We never danced with anyone else, and that in itself was dangerous. I could tell she was starting to have feelings for me, but I made sure to keep a physical and emotional distance between us. She knew I was married and had a child. I found her enchanting, but I was not like my father, Leo. As a married man, I would never betray my wife. On July 1st, we landed in Quebec City, and immigration came aboard to stamp our passports and give us our landing papers.

That night, we sailed towards Montreal on the St. Laurence River. It was a beautiful, hot summer night, and the ship was lit like a giant birthday cake. Everyone was feeling heady with adventure and the thought of a new life. Ruth and I went for a last stroll on the deck. I could see she was feeling sad. It was our last night together. We stopped and looked out at the people on the shore. "We have to say goodbye, Ruth. I wish you all the best. Thank you for your company, I really enjoyed this time I spent with you." I knew she wanted more from me, but I couldn't let myself go there. When I reached my cabin, I was glad that I had remained loyal to Emilie despite this temptation. My marriage had serious problems. We were not a good match, and I often felt lonely. Emilie didn't show me affection, and I wondered if she even loved me in the slightest. Regardless, I had promised her mother that I would always take care of her, and I always kept my promises.

The next morning, I disembarked the ship and didn't see Ruth. I felt relief combined with a twinge of regret. Just before I left the ship, a steward gave me a letter from my cousin Elsbeth. Uncle Willy, her father, had died the day after I sailed. We had loved each other, and he had often raised my spirits with his jokes and camaraderie. They announced the order in which we were to leave the ship. First were Canadian citizens, then British subjects, Americans, the French, and finally the group I was part of, Germans, Poles, Italians, and Eastern Europeans. We each received a pink tag with our name and destination listed. On the pier, an immigration officer asked me how much money I had. "Five U.S. dollars." He was shocked by my response. "What?" He shook his head and gave me the address of the immigration shelter on Rue St Antoine. I said goodbye to Heinz, who was going to Port Arthur, Ontario. When I arrived at the shelter, I found out it had once been a prison, and we were all to sleep in cells. I found that amusing. "My first night in Canada, and I'm in jail already!" I thought. It was blazing hot and I was too wired to sleep, so I went to explore Montreal. The first Canadian I met was a homeless man. "Can you give me a smoke?" He told me he was a lumber jack from Ontario who had spent all his money on booze and women.

The immigrant families were given the bigger cells. I saw a woman crying piteously. "Why did we come here? We left our lovely home in Germany, and now we're in a jail." Her husband just sat there, head in his hands, looking depressed. They had been there a week, and he still hadn't found a job. Clearly, it had been the right decision to leave Emilie and Marie back home for the time being. Emilie would not have been able to handle this situation and would be faring worse than this man's anxious wife. I registered at the unemployment office. After three days in jail, I heard a man talking to the immigrants. "I'm John. I came five years ago from Slovenia. I have a room to rent for two men. It's a good start. It's $15 a week for room, board, and laundry. My wife is Italian and a good cook." I immediately grabbed a Romanian man in the crowd and asked him if would join me. He nodded. "We'll take it, but we don't have any money," I shouted. John looked us over. "I'll help you both find a job and you can pay me later." He took us to his home in the Jean Talon area. His wife, Francesca, was very welcoming, and they had two sweet children, Mario and Maria. It was an old house, and the room was small, but adequate for our needs. The next day I went job hunting early, and by noon I had a job in a window glass factory. It was a union job, which was lucky for me to have snagged, and by 4 p.m. I had started work. Even John was impressed. "You're making more money than me, Robert." My weekly pay was $60.00, which was good money for the time. Most average men were only making $30 a week. I wrote to Emilie that I had a place and a good job. "Within two months, I will have enough money to pay for your voyages to Canada." I was longing for my family. Perhaps, I thought, Emilie will have found love in her heart for me in my absence.

On my first day off, I went to see more of beautiful Montreal and ended my walk back at the jail. Some of the people from the ship were still there and feeling low because they hadn't found work. There was a letter for me from Ruth. "Dear Robert, I would like to see you again. I can't help but wonder how you are doing." She listed her phone number and I called her. It was good to hear a friendly voice. We chatted for a bit, and then she said, "I would love to see the movie, Lily, with Leslie Caron. Will you come with me, Robert?" I hesitated for a moment, but I felt I had made it clear to her that I was only interested in a friendship, so I agreed to go. Ruth was living in residence at the hospital and I picked her up. She looked lovely in a light blue summer frock. We went to the movie, which wasn't my cup of tea, but Ruth liked it. It was what they now would call a "chick flick." Afterwards, we went to a cafe and talked for hours. We ended the night with a stroll around Montreal. I told her how happy I was to have found a good job, and she talked about her experience as an intern. When I took her back to her residence, I knew I had to end things now. Her feelings for me were too strong, and that was not my path. "Ruth, I am working hard to bring my family over, so we can't meet again. It isn't right." Ruth looked up at me, burst out crying, and ran towards the residence. I also had tears in my eyes. What I had done was right, but I felt a great sense of loss as I walked the ten kilometers home through the hot Montreal night. We don't always get what we want in life. Sometimes we just have to make the best of what we have.

I got a second job on my days off, helping to build a house. With the extra money, I could bring my family to Canada sooner. My goal was to live frugally. I only allowed myself $2.00 a week for spending money. That covered the bus fare, 35 cents for tobacco, and 5 cents for the rolling paper. I spent no money on alcohol. At the end of August, I had enough money to book their voyage on the Arosa Star for the price of $250.00. They would arrive on October 31st, 1955. I felt proud of myself that I had reached my goal so quickly. At the end of September, I showed up for my shift, only to find a pink slip on my timecard which said, "travail terminee." Along with 60 others, I had been laid off because of production cutbacks. I was taken by surprise by this, but I knew I usually landed on my feet and would surely find another job soon.

The next day, I met an acquaintance who told me Pesner Meat Company was hiring European butchers. I immediately applied. The company was owned by a family of Polish Jews. I told them I was a butcher by trade, which was a lie, but Mama had taught me how to butcher pigs during the air raids, so I knew I could do the job. They hired me on the spot. I was assigned to be Eric's helper. As it turned out, he was also from Herne. He quickly realized the truth. "I can see that you are not a butcher, Robert, but don't worry, I'll train you quickly." Lady Luck had again smiled on me. My salary was $40 a week. Soon I would be picking up my family at the Windsor CPR Station. I was filled with excitement at the thought. They had disembarked in Quebec City and were arriving in Montreal on Halloween. My Romanian roommate had left, so Emilie could be in my room, and Marie could sleep in the children's room.

When the passengers emerged, I saw Marie looking like Little Red Riding Hood in a white fur coat and a red hat. It was absolutely wonderful to see them. Marie was shouting, "There is Papa, there is Papa!" She rushed at me and hugged me tightly. Emilie was exhausted but was happy when I held her in my arms. I gave her a dozen red roses, and we took a taxi to our new home. "Mama was worried that you wouldn't be there, but I knew you would be there, Papa." John and Francesca welcomed my family to their home. I hadn't had a drop of alcohol since coming to Canada, but that day we celebrated with a bottle of white Bordeaux. When we were alone, Emilie made it clear she wasn't happy with our living quarters. "Robert, couldn't you have found a better place than this?" My heart sank. I had done my very best, but she still wasn't happy. That was often the case. "For $15.00 a week, this is a great deal. I just wanted to save money so I could get you here quickly." I was upset by her reaction but kept quiet, as I always did. Why couldn't she just be happy that we were together again? Emilie didn't like sharing the bathroom and constantly complained about it with bitterness in her voice. "Robert, this is not good. You need to find us a better place." I gave in, and soon found a two bedroom apartment nearby for $70 a month, plus utilities. Emilie was happy with it, so we bought furniture and moved in on November 15th.

Then, I made one of the biggest financial mistakes of my life. I mentioned to Eric that I brought my candy making equipment. "Robert, let's not waste time in this job. Let's quit today and start our candy making business. Then we'll make real money!" I had already checked that sugar was selling for 5 cents a pound, and candy for 50 cents a pound. With these numbers, it seemed we couldn't go wrong. Like a fool, I listened to him. We both quit our jobs and found a place on St. Hubert Street in downtown Montreal, which we rented for $200 a month. Dumb and dumber then foolishly signed a lease for two years. Eric said he had connections with Steinberg, the biggest supermarket in Montreal. Within a week, we were set up and ready to start making candies. It was almost Christmas, so we made candy canes in all sizes and colours. We took our samples and went to Steinberg's for an interview. The buyer told us he was interested in our candy canes, but Canadian law called for the candy to be wrapped and labelled with the name of the manufacturer and a list of ingredients. We left like sad puppies with our tails between our legs. We checked to find out how much it would cost to do the wrapping and the labelling. To get an economical price, we would have to order 100,000 units. It was financially impossible for us to do this. We decided to try to sell to the European stores by going from store to store. By now we had run out of cash. We worked from early morning to late at night to have a good supply of candy for when our luck would hopefully change.

Now we were desperate, and went from apartment to apartment selling at a wholesale price. We felt like beggars, walking miles to sell our candy canes in 25 below weather. Sometimes I would go to an apartment with children who begged their parents to buy them a candy cane. The parents often had no money, so I would pull a Santa Claus and give our candy canes away. By now, I felt like a real schmuck. I began to berate myself. "Robert, how could you have been so stupid?" We realized we were in deep trouble and went to see the landlord to get out of the lease. "You signed a lease for two years and you are responsible for it. However, if you find someone to take over the lease, you are off the hook." I went to the employment office and got a job washing cars by hand for 75 cents an hour. The employment officer invited our family for Christmas dinner at the former prison, on Rue St. Antoine. Emilie was angry and distressed that I had made such a big mistake, and worried about what would happen to the family. Eric phoned to say he had found a religious group from Yugoslavia to rent the place. That was the first good news that I'd heard in awhile. On December 24th, I went to work to find out that I had been laid off once again. It was one blow too many, and it hit me hard. I walked miles through the snow to try to lessen my sorrow and depression. When I got home, I told Emilie the bad news. She began to cry and I tried to calm her. "I am sure I will find something." I had let my family down again, and I couldn't forgive myself.

We went to the Christmas dinner at the jail and met other immigrant families who were depressed and broke. It was a sad occasion, but at least we got a meal. I began looking for work on December 26th, but there was nothing to find. On January 1st, Eric tried to collect the rent from the religious group, but they stalled him. "Come back in a few days. The elders have to approve this first." I was penniless, so Eric paid the $200 rent. "Next time, you try to collect," he said. I went a few days later, and as soon as they invited me in, I realized they were actually gypsies. They had been masquerading as a religious group all along, and we'd likely never get a penny out of them. I also saw they had our gas stove on full blast and were all sitting around basking in the heat. I gave them an ultimatum. "If you don't pay within a week, I will get a lawyer and sue you." One of the young gypsy girls came up to mc flirtatiously. "Would you like me to read your palm?" She was exotically beautiful with dark hair and eyes. "No, thanks." She looked me over. "How would you like to come in the back? I'll show you a good time." I turned and left with a sense of despair. I knew I had to face the mess we had made. Now we would have to pay an exorbitant gas bill in addition to the $200 monthly rent.

In January, I found a job at a gas station on Mansfield and Burnside. It was a representative station for the British American Oil Company of Quebec. My pay was 90 cents an hour. You had to be bilingual for the position, and I was trilingual, which likely helped me get the job. I had some hope now that I might be able to get through this terrible financial disaster. Then, Eric phoned. "I have bad news. Our tenants left and turned off the heat. The pipes burst, flooded the place, and we are responsible for the damage." It was a devastating blow. The cost was $500, and I was only making $36 weekly. It was an absolute disaster. In order to pay the hefty sum, I sold all my candy making equipment to a scrap dealer. It was a sad day for me. So much for my dream of becoming a candy maker in Canada.

In the Summer, we found someone who needed a warehouse and was willing to pay us $100 a month. We took their offer. I found two German immigrants and I rented the second bedroom to them for $15 each a week, including food and laundry. By then, I had realized there was something corrupt going on at my work. Every time there was a delivery of oil, I was told by the boss to put some aside. It was obvious there was double book-keeping going on. He confided in me and told me the truth. "Robert, I trust you. This account is for our drinking money." He invited me to an employee party at a nightclub called the Cavendish Bar. The customers left tips and I was getting at least $20 a day, so financially I was doing much better. Without those tips, my family would not have made it. Unfortunately, that is when I started on the road to self destruction. I began drinking heavily at the parties and coming home late from work. Alcoholism had been the curse of our family for generations, and I was no exception. I began to realize I had a problem, but I wasn't ready to face it.

Within six weeks of arriving in Canada, Marie had become fluent in both English and French. Obviously, she had inherited my gift for learning languages. Marie made new friends at St. Roche Catholic School and was happy to be in Canada. I was proud of her progress. Emilie was also learning English and French. We had made some German, Polish, and Jewish friends and started having parties every weekend. It was similar to what we did back in Herne, taking turns hosting the parties. We always took Marie along to the parties where she was treated like a little princess. As the only child at the parties, she got a lot of attention and seemed to thrive on it. I now had enough money to buy a 1948 Ford for $75.00. My drinking, however, was causing problems. I was a happy drunk, not a mean drunk, but when I overdid it, I became foolishly generous and paid for everyone's drinks. I lost all judgement and began driving home from work drunk. Emilie was terrified. "Robert, either stop drinking, or sell the car." In response, I sold the car. My addiction had taken control of my life.

Emilie never learned to love me. She likely married me out of a need for financial security and because she was pregnant. I foolishly thought I could win Emilie's love by buying her expensive gifts when I could. I bought her a fur coat, a diamond ring, and designer evening dresses. I chose these gifts because she liked to dress up and show off. She loved the gifts, but she still didn't show any love for me. It wasn't until later that I realized I was following the hopeless pattern of my parent's marriage. Papa was always trying to buy Mama's love with expensive gifts, too. The only difference was Mama never accepted his gifts, whereas Emilie was more than happy to accept my gifts. I kept this expensive and futile habit up for all the years of our marriage. It never made Emilie love me, but it kept my pockets empty.

In early December 1956, I had a terrible accident at work. I was replacing a truck tire with a snow tire. There was no gauge on the air compressor, and it blew up from all the pressure. The rim hit me with explosive force, breaking all my ribs on the right side and subsequently piercing my lungs. My right wrist and forearm were shattered from the impact. I was taken by ambulance to Queen Elizabeth Hospital and had surgery to repair my arm. Afterwards, Dr. Ostapowich, the surgeon, said, "Robert, you were very lucky you didn't lose your arm. Your heavy parka likely saved your life." I was in the hospital for three long weeks and was discharged just before Christmas with a large cast. My company topped up my Workman's Compensation benefits to make it my regular wage, but I really missed having those supplemental tips. In January, my cast was removed, and I was assigned to a rehabilitation clinic. It was six months before I was able to return to work again. When I came back, I found out the corruption had spread. Now they were not only ripping off the company, but also ripping off the customers. This did not sit well with me. It was one thing to rip off the wealthy, but another to lie to unsuspecting clients. I felt guilty, but I really needed the job. I started looking for another job but couldn't find anything that was as secure and paid as well. I felt trapped.

CHAPTER 17

In January 1958, we found out that Emilie was pregnant with another child. I was over the moon with joy and it made me reflect on my lifestyle. I was deeply ashamed of my excessive drinking and made the decision to finally quit. I also wasn't able to live with the corruption at work, and knew I had to leave. Montreal was too expensive for us to buy a house. I wanted my children to have a yard to play in, and I wanted them to be proud of their father. It seemed to me that I had to make a clean break and start a new life somewhere else. My friend, Heinz, was living in Fort William, Ontario, which later became Thunder Bay. I wrote and asked him if I might be able to find a job there. He replied, "You are taking a risk because unemployment is high here, but knowing you, Robert, you will likely find a job. I am willing to assist you." Emilie reluctantly agreed to the plan. I quit my job, sold the furniture, and we moved to Fort William. On the train I started chatting with Eric, a CPR train conductor from Sweden. We hit it off right away, as we were both jokesters. At one point, he cracked me up by lustily singing improvised lyrics to the theme song from, "The Bridge on the River Kwai," the fine British movie that came out in 1957. The lyrics were: "Hitler has only got one ball, Goebbels has one that is too small, Himmler has something similar, but Herman Goering has no balls at all." We sang that song all the way to Fort William.

Heinz picked us up at the train station and took us to an old apartment that he had found for us. It was much worse than our place in Montreal, and Emilie began to cry bitterly at the sight. The next day, I went job hunting. After ten days, I found a job at Thornes Manufacturing. They built 16-foot aluminum boats and my job was riveting the sheet metal together. The pay was $1.00 an hour and it would increase as I improved my skills. A letter came from Worker's Compensation that I was entitled to a lifetime pension of $40.00 a month for my permanent partial disability. They also gave me the pension retroactively from June 1957, to May 1958. With this money, I immediately made a down payment on a house at 120 North Selkirk Street in Fort William. Emilie's outlook on life quickly improved with this turn of events. For $8,500.00, we had a double story house with a yard for the children and room for a garden.

I went to work in the morning singing like a kid strolling through a park on a breezy summer day. It was a family atmosphere at work, and the company was kind and compassionate to their employees. Within a month, I had my first raise, and was moved up to $1.25 an hour. Unfortunately, I soon started to drink again by going out with some guys after work to the Victoria Hotel. I had not yet learned that alcoholism is a disease, or that I needed help to control it.

On September 25th, 1958, our son was born, and I was feeling on top of the world. When we brought him home, Marie made us all laugh by asking, "Can we keep this baby?" All the neighbours came to see our son and congratulated us on how handsome and big he was. We named him Robert, but he soon picked up the nickname Bobby. He was a good natured baby and rarely ever cried. Even though we were estranged, I wanted Mama to meet her grandson. I wrote to her and asked her to visit us. When Bobby was eight months old, she came to Canada. It had been almost four years since I had seen her, and I was happy she had come. She looked unwell, and it soon became apparent that something was wrong. I arranged an appointment with a doctor who spoke German, but Mama refused to see him. "I am fine." Things didn't go well between Mama and Emilie. When I came home from work, Mama would complain, "I haven't eaten all day, your wife never gave me anything to eat." Emilie was busy with the baby, so she had told Mama, "Help yourself, the food is in the fridge." Mama, however, was German, and her belief was that you would never go into anyone else's fridge. It was clear that Emilie and Mama were not getting along, and it didn't help that I would often arrive home from work drunk. Our old wounds had never healed and had been festering all these years. One night Mama and I got into a terrible argument about Otto and Sergio. I stuck up for Otto, which she didn't like, and she stuck up for Sergio, which I didn't like.

The next day Mama told me, "I'm going to see Heinz and his wife." She had known them in Herne. They picked her up, and she later phoned to say she was going to stay with them for a week. She promised me that she would come back for the final week of her visit. A week later, Heinz phoned me. "Robert, I took your mother to the airport. She said not to tell you until she was gone." I was dismayed to hear this news and berated myself for not being there for her during her visit. I carried that guilt with me for many years, especially because of what happened next. My cousin, Elsbeth, phoned me two weeks later to tell me Mama had died. "She went from the plane in an ambulance to the hospital. They operated and found she had advanced liver cancer, and today, she died. I'm sorry, Robert. Now she is at peace, at least." No one had let me know what was happening with Mama. I felt great sadness and guilt, and blamed myself for causing her distress. Why had I fought with her? We weren't close, but she was still my mother and the woman who had given birth to me. A few days later, I received a letter from Otto. "Hooray, hooray, the old whore is dead! May she rot in hell." I burned the letter upon reading it. I knew his hatred for Mama would never end, not even in the wake of her death. My childhood came back to haunt me, and I began to drink even more in attempts to forget the past.

In July 1959, Mr. Thornes assembled the staff. "I'm sorry, but the bank will not back me up, and I had to sell my company to a larger company in Windsor. You can all keep your jobs, however, if you're willing to move to Windsor." It was a tremendous shock that none of us had been expecting. I had a mortgage, a large debt, and my family to support. I couldn't move to Windsor because of the house. Times were bad economically, and there was no hope of selling the house. Instead, I managed to find a job with TransCanada Pipeline. This meant that I would be on the road a lot of the time, away from my family. I was just happy to have found a job at all, as unemployment was high. Because I already had trained as a heavy equipment operator, my pay was $2.00 an hour. In order to get ahead financially, I worked a lot of overtime, from sunup to sundown, seven days a week. Three weeks later, I was able to see my family for

24 hours and gave Emilie a large sum of money. It was a lonely life, but at least I could support my family and see them on occasion.

In September, we found out that Emilie was pregnant again. I was happy, because I always wanted eight children. Emilie said, "Robert, when will you become a mensch and learn how to control your drinking?" I knew she was right, and I tried my best to keep my drinking under control, but I always slipped back into chaos. Today, I understand that I had inherited the genes that predisposed me to becoming an alcoholic. Both my maternal great grandfathers had been alcoholics, as well as most of their male descendants. My maternal grandfather died at 38 from kidney failure due to alcoholism. Uncle Willy was the alcoholic who got me drunk on my fifth birthday. My cousin Trudi was also an alcoholic. I had never lost a job because of my drinking, and my friends liked me drunk because I would amuse them with my boisterous jokes, but it wasn't fair to Emilie or the children. I wanted to stop, but found myself feeling powerless. I still didn't understand that I was in the control of a terrible addiction, and that I desperately needed help to escape it's clutches.

I informed my boss that I wanted to take my two weeks holiday to help Emilie when the baby was born. Emilie went into labour on April 5th, 1960, and we went to the McKellar hospital in Fort William. They told me to go home and wait for them to call me once the baby was born. I went home to take care of Bobby, who was 18 months old. The next morning, the nurse called. "Congratulations, you have a little boy, and a little girl." I thought I hadn't heard her correctly and asked her to repeat herself. She told me again and I was overjoyed. I had won the baby jackpot. Twins! The doctor never realized that Emilie was pregnant with twins. Marie was at school, and I asked a neighbour to take care of Bobby so I could go to the hospital. When I came in the room, Emilie was sitting in the bed with a baby on either side. She looked worried and anxious. "What are we going to do with all these children?" The little girl had a beautiful delicate face. The boy was big and strong, with a broad face and good lungs. I held each of them tenderly and was euphoric. This was cause for a celebration! When I left the hospital, I went straight to the liquor store for a bottle of whisky to bring to Jim's house. He was an old drinking buddy, and we celebrated my good news. I drank all day, getting more bottles as needed. What an idiotic thing to do. That night, Jim drove me home. He helped me into the house, as I was too drunk to navigate on my own, then left. The children were still at the neighbour's house. I climbed the stairs with significant difficulty, then suddenly slipped and fell backwards. My head hit each step as I went down, then struck the hardwood floor. The next morning, the neighbour came over with the children and found me unconscious at the bottom of the stairs.

I was taken by ambulance to McKellar Hospital. Dr. Augustin, our family doctor, was called to treat me. I was floating in and out of consciousness. He had a worried look on his face. "You have a severe concussion, Robert, and a brain bleed. This is extremely serious." They found blood in my spinal fluid for four days. After that, the fluid was clear, and the doctor told me, "Well, now I have hope. I didn't know if you would make it, Robert. You could have become a paraplegic, or worse." I made a slow recovery. My headaches were severe and I was vomiting without an end in sight. After six weeks, the doctor thought I was recovered enough to go home. I had vertigo and great difficulty walking. Emilie was so disgusted with me that she had refused to go to the hospital and refused to talk to me when I returned home.

Dr. Augustin gave me a stern lecture. "Robert, you have damaged your brain. Even one drink would be dangerous for you now. You must stop drinking!" This warning made me afraid to drink, and I didn't touch a drop. I knew I had made a mess of everything. We decided to name the twins Gloria and Barry. I helped as much as I could with the babies so Emilie could rest and spent time with little Bobby. My recovery took over three months, and in July I was finally able to return to work. Emilie was happy that I wasn't drinking and began to forgive me. I worked the whole day and felt fine. At the end of the day I thought, "If I'm well enough to work, I must be well enough to drink." I started drinking again, but with more restraint. I foolishly made myself believe that I could drink in moderation and not get into trouble. In reality, alcoholism is a progressive and insidious disease. It wasn't long before my drinking became out of control again.

On August 15th, we got a new boss who cut out all the overtime. I knew I had to find another job that would let me work overtime, as that was the only way I could support my family and pay off my debts. I found a job at a road construction company that allowed you to work 16 hours a day, seven days a week. It was 600 km east of our home. We were building the road connecting Rossport to White River. I lived in camp and only went home once a month. Marie was 11 now, so she took over some household duties, like grocery shopping and helping with the babies. Bobby enjoyed playing with the twins, who were lively and good natured. My pay was $1.50 an hour for operating a dump truck. I quickly realized that the equipment was run down and in a constant state of disrepair. One day, I ended up with a truck that had no working brakes, aside from the emergency brake. "This truck is unsafe, and I refuse to operate it!" I told my supervisor. He fired me on the spot. I was pissed off, but I also knew I couldn't risk working for a company who put their employees in danger. Immediately, I came up with a plan. There were two copper mines, Gico and Villroy, 200 km away in Manitouwadge, Ontario. With a packsack and a few bucks in my pocket, I hitchhiked east. I applied to both mines, but there were no jobs available. Finally, I gave up and hitchhiked to where I could hop a freight train to Port Arthur. I walked home and arrived there at 3 a.m.. I hadn't been drinking for awhile, and Emilie was happy to see me. I began looking for work again the following day, but there had been so many layoffs that it was impossible to find a job.

In early October, a man came to our door selling the Encyclopedia Britannica. He had a friendly face and a nice atmosphere about him. "I'm unemployed, I can't afford it," I told him. We could both tell by our accents that the other was from Germany. He told me his name was Franz. "I've been unemployed too, and simply took this job because I couldn't find anything else." I asked him in for a cup of tea. We chatted and hit it off, and he eventually came up with a good idea. "I have an old car that we could use to travel into the bush where the logging camps are and find work there. We could split the cost of gas to make the travel affordable for us both." I agreed it was worth a try, talked to Emilie about it, and I was headed for the bush and saying goodbye to my family the very next day. We found jobs at Black Sturgeon Lake, Camp #9, and were put in a bunkhouse with 20 men, mostly Finnlanders. Our job was cutting pulp wood for $8.50 a cord. We heard that some men cut up to six cords a day, which was equivalent to a week's pay in town. The strip boss showed me the ropes, and I felt confident that I would learn the necessary skills to be successful. The first day, I only managed one cord, but was getting better every day. Soon, I was up to three cords a day. We worked six days a week. I picked up the Finnish language quickly, and built a rapport with the Finns. They were hard-working during the week, and drinking hard on the weekend.

After work on Saturday, four of us went home in Franz's car. Emilie was glad to find out that I had found a job. The children were happy to see their Papa again, and seeing them brought joy to my heart. Gloria had beautiful blonde hair and fair skin, just like her mother. Barry had darker skin and hair that resembled my own. It was a joyful family reunion. That night, Franz phoned. "Robert, I got a job in Fort Francis and start on Monday. You need to look for a ride to get back to camp." I found a ride with one of the Finnlanders. I had managed to stop drinking, but quickly fell off the wagon. My new travel companions were heavy drinkers, and there was always a stop at the hotel in Dorian. Alas, I joined in, knowing it would lead to problems. I justified my drinking by telling myself, "You worked hard all week, you deserve it." Alcoholics can always find some sort excuse to drink. I came home with fish and the excess food from the kitchen, but I came home drunk. Again, I let my wife and children down. I began to hate myself for my repeated failures at sobriety. By Christmas of 1960, I was catching up on my debts, but I was in for another blow. The company brought in a new logging system, mechanical logging. Now, all staff were compensated with a flat rate of $18 a day, when I had previously been making $25.50 per day with my three cords.

I was becoming more and more disgusted with myself, but was powerless to stop drinking. One night, we were going to a dance, and I felt confident that I would not drink. "Tonight, I will prove to you that I will refrain from getting drunk at the dance. I promise you, Emilie." That night, I got so drunk that I couldn't even recall how I got home the next morning. I felt totally worthless. "You're just a piece of shit, go hang yourself," was the thought that just kept repeating in my mind. I didn't want to live any more, but I looked at my beautiful children and knew I couldn't kill myself. They needed my support. By chance, the local paper was on the table and I noticed an ad. "Alcoholics Anonymous, if you need help, call us." I phoned the number listed, and a friendly male voice answered. I just blurted out, without context, "I need help!" He asked for my address. "Okay, hang in there, someone will come to see you within the hour." Ten minutes later, there was a knock at the door. When I opened it, I found two well-dressed men standing there. One of them looked like the actor, David Niven, and introduced himself as Johnny. They sat down with me and I told them my story. I didn't have a clue about AA and asked, "Are you social workers?" Johnny smiled. "No, we're alcoholics. I spent 32 years on skid row, lost my family, my job, and my health, but I recovered with the help of AA. I'm confident that you can too. You have everything going for you, Robert. You have a nice family and a job. There is an AA meeting this afternoon in the Masonic Hall. Join us, Robert."

They left, and I told Emilie that I was going to the meeting. "I don't care what you do, I've had it." She didn't see any hope or use in this AA idea. There were about 60 people at the meeting, drinking coffee and chatting. It was a happy atmosphere. Johnny introduced me to several people. To me, they all looked like doctors or lawyers, besuited and confident. I was overcome with a powerful surge of optimism and hope for a new life that was not controlled by my addiction to alcohol. If they could do it, so could I. To my surprise, I saw my paymaster, Tommy. When we chatted he told me, "Robert, you can ride with me to camp, and that will keep you away from the drinkers." I went home on a high and knew I would be able to do this. I told Emilie about my new hope, but she was still angry. "Do whatever you want, I don't care anymore." She had every right to be angry. I had let her down so many times, and I only hoped that I might earn her forgiveness with time. Every Sunday, I went to an AA meeting. I learned the 12 step program and followed it faithfully. In the evening, at camp, I studied the AA literature. After a few weeks, Emilie started to believe that I might make it. Now that I was sober, I was more rational, and realized I was in serious trouble when reviewing my debts. We cut corners wherever we could. In October, there was a slump in the pulp market, and we were all laid off. My unemployment insurance was $36 a week. We could buy food for the family, but I couldn't pay my bills. I looked for work everywhere, but there was nothing there to find. My creditors were losing their patience, and I was desperate.

I went to every AA meeting I could, and they taught me how to deal with the creditors, in addition to providing me with spiritual and emotional support. After six months of not working, I couldn't stand it anymore. I went to the unemployment office determined to get work. "I want to talk to the manager here, and I won't leave until I do." Several hours later, I was called to talk to the man in charge. I told him my story and my financial situation. "I feel like writing a letter to President Khrushchev, telling him that I am a young man with four children, and begging him for a job, any job. You North Americans are so afraid of communism. And yet, you don't realize that you are creating communism in your own country by not providing enough employment for a man to support his family." He looked at me in amazement. I think he had never heard such a rant before. Luckily, he realized how desperate I was, and decided to help me. "Have you had any mining experience?" My heart leapt, and I told him of my mining experience in Germany and Belgium. "I advise you to go to Le Pas, Manitoba, to Inco's hiring office. The mine itself is in Thompson, 200 miles North of Le

Pas. I can't promise you a job, but this is the only possibility I can see for you. There is no housing. You would have to live in a tent for six months." I was overjoyed. "If there are others living there and surviving, so can I. Thank you, thank you."

On the way out, I met three men who were going to Le Pas, and we agreed to travel together. When I got home, I told Emilie the news, and gave her half of the $36 stipend. The other half I would need for my trip. The next morning, I kissed Emilie and the children goodbye and joined the other men in an old car for our trip to Le Pas. The car broke down in Winnipeg, and the owner sold it for $50.00. We had nowhere to sleep and ended up at the police station on Rupert Street. The next day was April 1st, a real April fool's day for me, as I was once again in a Canadian jail. We had just enough money to take the Greyhound Bus to Le Pas. It was 20 degrees below freezing when we arrived, and we had no choice but to go to the jail and ring the bell. The jailer showed us where the Salvation Army office was, and the officer there immediately gave us tickets for supper, room and breakfast, with no questions asked. In the morning, we went to the Inco hiring station to find a long queue of other people waiting. People from all over Canada had lined up overnight in attempts to get hired. One man in the lineup shouted, "Join the slave market in Canada!"

Three hours later, I was finally at the front of the line. A medic was checking each man for hearing, vision, and any other obvious health problems. Only men between 19 and 35 were being accepted. About one third of the men in line were turned away. I knew my right eye was going to be a problem. Ever since my bad concussion as a child, I have only had very little vision in that eye. Luckily, the doctor checked my left eye first, and I cheated by memorizing the letters on the eye chart. I passed, as did my three travelling companions. We were given train tickets to Thompson. It was an eight hour trip, and we were starving, but no one had money. The train finally stopped, and there was only a pole with a sign saying, "THOMPSON". The pole was surrounded by hundreds of men waiting to get the train back to Le Pas. I got off the train and immediately ran into Mirko, an old buddy from camp 9 at Black Sturgeon, Ontario. He grabbed me by my coat sleeve. "Robert, this is not a place to make money. I was lucky and I won $5,000 in a poker game. I can escape this place. Come with me, I'll pay for everything." "No, I can't, I have to make money to support my family. Good luck." "You're making a mistake, Robert. Don't you see how many people have quit? This place is the shits."

That news was a bit depressing, but I still needed a job. Our luggage was put on a big truck and searched for anything suspicious, and we were all frisked. I felt like I was back in Germany heading for the POW camp. Only after this full inspection were we allowed on the bus. At the camp, we were assigned to tents, each of which housing three men. I was faint from hunger and could smell the food from the cook house. The food was excellent, and we all gorged ourselves like eating was going out of style. The next day, I was interviewed. I mentioned shaft mining, and was told I could start that night as part of the shaft inspection crew. "It's the highest paid job in the mine." I felt like doing a handstand I was so happy, and went back to my tent to write Emilie about the good news. It was an important job, as there was only one production shaft, and I was essential for it to be kept in safe condition. Over the next week, I met men from every corner of the world. Out of 2,000 employees, there were about 800 Germans, 600 Poles, and 400 Italians. The rest were from everywhere, even Jamaica and Hawaii.

We were allowed overtime, and I worked seven days a week. I was so proud to send my first paycheck to Emilie, and to let her know that I had already put in my name for a company apartment in town, six miles from the mine. Mother Inco was a good company who supported their workers, especially if you were a family man. Construction in Thompson was going on 24/7 to build houses for the workers. I saw a note posted on the bulletin board saying, "TWO MEN WANTED TO WORK PART TIME IN THE CAMP POST OFFICE." I jumped at the job and was hired, along with a Ukrainian man. The law stated that they had to hire Canadian citizens, but they couldn't find any who wanted the job, so they took us. The postmaster said, with a wink, "You two look Canadian to me!" Now I was making $3.00 an hour at the mine, and $1.50 an hour at the post office. I saw a notice for a weekly AA meeting in the camp, and I started going faithfully to meetings. It wasn't long before I had made good friends with the other AA members. They gave me wise advice on how to deal with my creditors, as they had also been in financial trouble. I began paying off my debts. Finally, I was able to have peace of mind about my money problems.

The Thompson Shopping Centre was completed before the beginning of summer. It was the most modern centre in Canada, and even had a German bakery. I bought furniture from the Hudson Bay Company for the two-bedroom apartment I had rented. I wrote Emilie, and told her to request that the real estate company holding our mortgage to sell the house for a fair price. "You can come any time now, Emilie, as the apartment is ready for the family." On August 2nd, my family arrived by train. This was one of the happiest days of my life! I couldn't stop smiling while greeting my family in our new hometown. Marie was a beautiful girl of 14, so grown up. Bobby was full of energy, and the twins were all tuckered out. I had a beef roast in the oven, and Emilie's favourite wine, Mazel Tov. We had a delicious celebratory dinner with lots of laughter and joy at being together again as a family. I had taken the weekend off, and the next day we went on a picnic at Paint Lake. My cup runneth over that day.

In order to be with my family during the day, I worked night shift. I showed them the new shopping centre. Emilie was delighted, as shopping was her favourite activity. Marie quickly made friends with other teenagers at school. We only associated with AA members, and our parties were now family oriented and alcohol-free. There was a big turnover at the mine, because the single men didn't stay long. The first night of frost came in early September. On Halloween, our children couldn't go trick or treating because of the deep blankets of snow. I made igloos with them in the yard to make up for it. Almost every day, I took them tobogganing. The kids all loved being outdoors, just like their Dad. Emilie didn't join us, preferring to stay home to have some peace and quiet. For the first time in ages, I felt good about my life. I was sober, had a steady job, was paying my debts, and we didn't have to pinch pennies anymore. Being a father brought me my greatest joy. Some nights, Emilie and I walked through the snow and watched the magical Northern lights together. I had never seen anything so mystical and majestic in all my years. The only downside was our attempts to acclimate to the harsh cold. At times, the temperature dropped as low as minus 50 degrees Fahrenheit.

Robert at Burntwood River, Thompson Manitoba, July 1962

Christmas in Thompson Manitoba 1962, L to R,
Robert, Bobby, Emilie, Barry, Marlies, Gloria

CHAPTER 18

In January 1963, my world collapsed. Things were going so well, and I once again deluded myself into thinking I could drink in moderation. I decided I deserved to celebrate our new life, and I bought a bottle of vodka. Soon, I was drunkenly walking around in circles in the snow. I was completely disgusted with myself and threw the bottle with the remaining vodka away in the bush. There was no way I could go home and face Emilie like this. Cecil lived nearby. He was the most senior AA member in our group. I went to his home, and when I saw him, I started to cry profusely. He listened to me and phoned Emilie, explained what was happening, and asked her to come to pick me up. Cecil told her that relapses happen and reassured her I would get back on track. When she came to get me, I just kept weeping and saying, "I'm sorry, I made a mistake, I really screwed up." Once again, I made the promise to never drink again. By April, I had been at Inco for a year, and I had to take my two weeks holiday. I decided to find work instead of taking a vacation, so I applied for a job in the German bakery. Luckily, I was hired at $3.00 an hour, which was the same pay I received at the mine. I had never had a savings account in my life, but I opened my first one in Thompson. At 35, I was the oldest man at Inco doing the underground work.

In May, Inco offered me a company house with no down payment and a mortgage of $110.00 a month. It was a three bedroom house with a spacious recreation room in the basement. I jumped at this opportunity and we moved in on June 1st, 1963. One morning, I came out of the cage after my shift, and the next shift all congratulated me. "Robert, you've been chosen Father of the Year," one man shouted. I didn't know what he was talking about. They all gave me a cheer. When I came home, I found out that the Thompson Chamber of Commerce had an annual contest to pick the Father of the Year, and I had won. Every store had a box for people to put in their nomination. I was surprised and felt proud to be chosen by my community. The big prize was a suit, shirt, shoes, and necktie at Tip Top tailors. I also received a $50 grocery voucher from Shop Easy. Summer came and I spent every spare moment with the kids, fishing and swimming. I was in a state of contented sobriety. Most of the employees were heavy drinkers, especially the single men, and this caused a lot of problems at work. A new AA group was formed, and I was asked to make 12 step calls with another member. It was rewarding because I felt I owed so much to AA, and I wanted to give back to the community. I gave AA credit for my recovery. I was in the AA family, and they cared for and supported me.

At AA, I heard of a respected person in Thompson, a Catholic priest of the St. Laurence Parish. His name was Leon Levasseur. I was eager to meet him because he was so revered. I called him, we chatted, and I invited him for tea. He was a charismatic and handsome man in his late thirties with a warm and humorous manner. We talked for hours, and I found him to be one of the wisest men I had ever met. He also had a loving heart and an open mind. Leon was born in Quebec, one of 13 children, and was a socialist and activist. The locals also called him "The Rebel Priest"

312

because he spoke of much needed reform in the Catholic Church. Leon and I felt a strong connection to each other in both heart and mind. He was full of jokes and had a hearty laugh. Soon we started attending his Sunday services as a family. Emilie was devoutly religious, but I had lost my faith a long time ago. This was the first time in my life I had heard a priest speaking from his heart with both humour and wisdom. Father Levasseur was full of surprises. After the service, he invited everyone to stay for lunch and a dance in the church hall. He always had a live band playing and made sure we were connected with other German families. Soon Leon and I became close friends, spending hours talking history, politics and, of course, religion.

One day Emilie said, "It would make me very happy, Robert, if we got married in church." I had never wanted to be married in a church, but I could see it was important to her, and now that I had become so close with Father Levasseur, I was willing to do it. We arranged to be married in the sacristy in St. Lawrence Parish. The children came, and two AA friends were the witnesses. Emilie was delighted that I agreed, because she had always felt we weren't truly married without the blessing of the church. Shortly after this, Father Levasseur received our three younger children into the Catholic Church. Marie, however, wanted nothing to do with the church. She argued with Father Levasseur and refused to come with us to Sunday services. She was going through a rebellious time as a teenager, and didn't want anything to do with religion. A few weeks later, however, she walked into the service with a girlfriend and sat down. Father Levasseur greeted Marie and knelt on the floor in front of her. "I am so glad to see you here in God's house, and I welcome you."

This was a happy time for our family. Father Levasseur helped many families in the community and was a mediator between Inco and the workers on numerous occasions. He was so well loved that even Protestants attended his services. I was happy with my life, but I was terribly lonely in my marriage. Long ago, I had realized that Emilie didn't love me, and had married me for security. I always kept a faint hope in my heart that one day she would love me. One day I was upset and said, "Emilie, I love you very much but you have never once said that you love me." She looked at me with irritation. "Ach! As I've told you before, our family was never into romance and kissing. I just wasn't brought up that way." I was so lonely that I would honestly go into the woods and find a tree to hug at times. My only source of joy came from my children, who I knew loved me.

Christmas, 1963, was a time for celebration. My debts were all paid, and I finally felt free again. Life was good, but I was having serious concerns about raising my children in this rough community of heavy drinkers and gamblers. I also began worrying about what the future held for my children once they were of working age. If I stayed in Thompson, the only future for my sons would be to work in the mines. I had been forced into work underground, but I was damned if this would be the fate for my sons. Additionally, I had concerns about them staying in a town where the nine-month-long winter conditions were so bleak and severe. I'd met several people from the West Coast, and they always talked about how beautiful it was, with such a mild climate. Sadly, they also mentioned how hard it was to find work out there, because everyone wanted to live in beautiful B.C too. A man mentioned the copper mine at Britannia Beach, just north of Vancouver. The idea began growing in my mind to find a way to get a job there and move my family away from Thompson. At first, I couldn't see a way to do this, and I just kept working long hours and saving money as the time passed. It was clear to me that Emilie would not want to leave Thompson. She was always fearful of change, and her constant anxiety made it hard for her to adapt to new places. Papa's words came into my mind. "You will never reach a green branch with her." My green branch was B.C. It became my dream to reach that green branch, and I was determined to fulfill it.

At the end of June, the snow had finally melted. Bobby was five, and we were playing ball outside when he pointed to a weed that was peeking through the gravel. "Papa, is that a flower?" It was a stab in my heart. I thought, "Poor boy, he will never see flowers or fruit trees if we stay here." I knelt down, took him by the shoulders, and said to my son, "I promise I will take you to a place where there are many flowers." I felt a surge of conclusive certainty rush through my body. Now I knew I was taking my family to beautiful B.C., and nothing could stop me. I went into the house, phoned Britannia Mine, and asked to speak to the Personnel Manager. "I'm Robert Middelmann. I'm calling from Thompson, Manitoba, where I work for Inco as a shaft miner. Are you currently hiring?" A friendly voice replied, "Not at the moment, but if you are nearby in the future, make sure to drop in to see me." I felt confident that I would get a job there. I knew the only way I could convince Emilie to move to B.C. was to lie and tell her I had a job. "Emilie, I have good news! I got a job in Britannia Mine near Vancouver." She looked at me with a glare of suspicion. "You're lying to me, Robert." My heart began to flutter and I broke out in a cold sweat. "No, no, I just got hired over the phone and they're waiting for me to start." She looked around sadly. "You realize we'll never get a house like this again." She was right, but we would never get to see the beautiful flowers, the magnificent Pacific Ocean and the majestic mountains of B.C. if we stayed here.

I phoned work, told them I was quitting, and wanted to pick up my pay. They had many men in line waiting to take my job. I went from door to door and told my neighbours that I was selling everything to the highest bidder. "At six pm there will be an auction sale in my house." At six, the house was packed, and I auctioned everything off within the span of two hours. Marie was thrilled at the thought of going to B.C., and the young ones were excited at the prospect of a new adventure. On Friday, I picked up my paycheck and bought CNR train tickets to Vancouver. We left Saturday to head toward Le Pas, and changed trains to go to Hudson Bay Junction, Saskatchewan. We slept on our packsacks at the open train station, and in the morning took the train to Saskatoon. From there, we caught the TransCanada train to Vancouver. We woke to the awesome majesty of the Rocky Mountains in Banff, Alberta.

At 11 p.m. on July 1st, 1964, we arrived in Vancouver. We were totally exhausted from our travel. We rented two rooms at the Grandview Hotel for $20, and woke the next morning to a beautiful, sunny Vancouver day. We went to the head office of AA, and the women there were very friendly. I told them we had just arrived from Thompson. "We'll take you to Stanley Park. The children will love it." As we strolled through this enchanting park, I knew I had made the right decision. These kind-hearted women took us for lunch and drove us to the bus station to go to Squamish, as there was no hotel in Britannia Beach. Emilie was terrified by the winding road from Horseshoe Bay to Squamish. The kids thought it was great, like being on a roller coaster. By now, I had convinced myself that I already had the job. I not only lied to Emilie, but I lied to myself and believed my own lie. When we got off the bus in downtown Squamish, Emilie and Marie were both terribly disappointed. For two years, they had only seen young people and brand new houses. Squamish seemed to have a lot of ramshackle houses and elderly people. The residents were not friendly and looked at us as though we came from another planet. I took rooms at the Garibaldi Motor Hotel, for $10 a night, and found a Chinese restaurant nearby called the Caribou Cafe. It was run by Caribou Jack, a Chinese man in his 80s. He was the first person in Squamish who was welcoming to us and was generous enough to give us a deal for the whole family to eat there for just $10 a day.

The next morning, I hitchhiked to Britannia Mine and asked to see the personnel manager. I still felt confident that I would be hired. "My name is Robert

Middelmann. I called you from Thompson about a job."
He was awestruck. "I never promised you a job, Mr.
Middelmann." "That's right, but you said if I was near
here in the future, to come and see you." He chuckled.
"You've got some nerve. Wait a minute I'll see what I
can do." He returned in a few minutes. "Man, you are
one lucky fellow. We just lost a man to a bad accident in
the shaft and need a replacement. Are you a shaft
miner?" I nodded. "Can you start tonight?" "You bet I
can!" I hitchhiked back to bring Emilie the good news.
Lady Luck was rooting for me once again. On the way
there, I decided to come clean and tell her the truth.
When I told her that I was starting work that night, she
was very happy. I quickly ruined her approval with the
truth. "Emilie, please forgive me. I lied to you in
Thompson that I had the job. I knew you wouldn't want
to give up your secure life there unless I told you that I
had a job." She was stunned. "You lied to me?" Now she
was furious. I had a job and we were in beautiful B.C
now, so I hoped she would accept it. "We can build a
wonderful life here, Emilie." She gave me the silent
treatment for quite some time, but I had achieved my
dream of reaching a green branch.

I packed my lunch and hitchhiked to the mine to
meet the crew. They were old timers, burned out from
mine work. The pay was $2.17 an hour, and my shift was
from midnight to 8 am. I quickly arranged to carpool
with another miner. The next day, an older couple from
the Squamish AA group came to our motel. The AA
grapevine was working well. "If you need help, let us
know." I began going weekly to the meetings. Soon
enough, I found a cottage with two bedrooms on

Garibaldi Street for $120 a month. It was too small for all of us but would do for now. We moved in and furnished the place with second-hand furniture. Emilie and Marie were both furious at me for bringing them to Squamish. Thompson had been an international and progressive community. Squamish, on the other hand, was like an old backwards Western town right out of a movie. It was isolated geographically, and the residents seemed judgemental and close-minded. We were looked at as unwanted outsiders by most of the residents.

Emilie turned to religion as a source of comfort, and we began going to St. Joseph Parish. At church, we finally found some acceptance and sense of belonging. We both joined the choir, led by Peter Bukowski. We had picnics with the other AA families, and made friendly connections with the Squamish Nation. In fact, our closest friendships were with people on the reserve. They also felt ostracized and were treated as second class citizens by the town. One day, Bobby came home from kindergarten very upset. "Papa, what is a Nazi? Some kids called me a Nazi!" I was shocked. I told him about the Nazis and explained that our family had been enemies of the Nazis. Marie hated Squamish and became increasingly miserable. We loved the mountains and beautiful setting, but we felt as though we had regressed in time. We were stuck in a conservative town that didn't want us there. It was sad and depressing to be treated as unwanted foreigners.

In September, Bobby started grade one, Marie entered grade nine, and the mine went on strike. The union warned us it would be a long strike. They were asking for a 25 cent an hour increase. Immediately, I found a job as a contract worker, clearing building lots in Garibaldi Estates and Highlands. I received $30 a lot and was able to clear one a day. Always looking for better employment, I put my name in at Woodfibre, a local pulp and paper plant. They hired me as a longshoreman on call at $3.50 an hour. I kept the clearing job and hoped to get a permanent job at Woodfibre. Financially I was doing well, so I put a down payment of $1,500 on a lot I cleared in the Highlands with which to build our new home.

On April 1st, 1965, I got a job as a wood plant operator at Woodfibre at $2.25 an hour. In May, we moved into a new three bedroom townhouse on River Road, $115 a month. I continued going to AA meetings because I knew I needed the guidance and solidarity to keep me sober. In the summer, we received a letter from Father Levasseur. He wrote he "was tired of running up against the concrete wall of the Catholic Church." He had left the priesthood. It seemed he had met a woman, fallen in love, and married. "I am going on my honeymoon to Victoria and would like to visit you while we're there." We were happy for him, and a week later, he came with his lovely new wife. They seemed well suited for each other. She was captivated by the scenery, and asked Leon if they could move there. He replied, "No, they need me in Winnipeg as a social worker." I knew he would be a caring and compassionate social worker and help many people.

I bought a 1958 Oldsmobile for $100 and started taking the children to all the beautiful lakes and rivers in the area. Like their Dad, they loved nature, hiking, camping, and roughing it. In March 1966, I heard about a house for sale on 39764 Government Road. It was a three bedroom house on two acres, selling for $15,000. I needed money for the down payment and sold my lot. When we moved in, the whole family felt as though we had won the jackpot. The bush started right behind the house and was great for exploring. Work was going well, and in 1966 I was promoted to the managerial position of head sawyer, a position which usually requires 20 years of experience. I began clearing some of the bush so that I could make a garden, and I traded the Oldsmobile in for a brand new Volkswagen Beatle, $1,800.

I began taking the kids, their friends, and a couple of dogs to Brohm Lake for the day. People couldn't believe that I could get so many kids and dogs into my small Beatle. Emilie was not an outdoor person, as she had sensitive skin that burned easily and a terrible fear of insects. Bobby was now in grade two at Mamquam School. He was a quiet and sweet natured boy, and well liked by all of his teachers. Barry and Gloria started grade one in September 1966. Gloria was happy and enthusiastic about going to school. Barry, on the other hand, came home on his first day and announced, "I quit school. This is not for me. I can't learn anything there." With great effort, we finally convinced him to return. Barry loved to go to the reserve to go fishing with the kids there. He was hard to handle, mischievous, marched to the beat of his own drum, wild, and frustrating at times for his parents. He reminded me of myself when I was his age. I had driven my mother to distraction with my antics. Now, in return, Barry did the same to me and Emilie.

In the fall I planted apple, cherry, and plum trees. My garden produced a bountiful crop of potatoes and Dutch pole beans. I joined the Brackendale Farmer's Institute and went to monthly meetings where we shared our gardening knowledge. At the fall fair, I won first prize for my potatoes and beans. I dug a pond for ducks, built a tree house, bought a small goat for Bobby, and began raising rabbits and chickens. Barry wanted hamsters, gerbils, a large tortoise, and an alligator. Soon the basement was a menagerie, much to the delight of the children. Emilie and I had different ideas of parenting. Whenever the children asked if they could go somewhere or do something, Emilie would automatically say, "No." She likely did this because of her deep-seated fear and anxiety. Then, they would come to me, and I would always say, "Yes." She was upset that I let them have all the pets they wanted. She was right. I just couldn't say no to my children.

Emilie still avoided going to town because of the way our family was treated by its residents. We all felt unwelcome in Squamish. Renovations were needed on the house, and it was expensive. I always paid my bills, but in November 1966, I didn't have enough cash to pay for the oil delivery. The oil dealer said he wouldn't deliver unless I had the cash. There was another oil provider who allowed credit. I called them next, and told them I would pay the bill in a week when I got my pay. They also turned me down. It was terribly cold, and there was nothing I could do. We just had to suffer it out. I felt I was being discriminated against in an attempt to run me out of town. I knew other people were paying on credit on a regular basis without issue. The injustice hit me hard and made me furious. My children were freezing, and I was powerless to help them. I had to ensure that I would never be in a position where I needed to ask for credit again in this backwards town that bothered us.

Barry started getting into trouble with some of the neighbours. He started to get a reputation as a "bad kid," and the RCMP came to our door several times. The complaints were that he had allegedly thrown a rock at a barking dog, trespassed through properties in order to take a short cut to the river, and had stuck his tongue out at a neighbour who scolded him. I was always at work when they came, and these police visits thoroughly upset Emilie. I asked Barry why he was acting out this way. "People are always calling me a Nazi, and it makes me mad!" How sad it was, that my children were being punished for what the Nazis did. As Germans, would we ever be accepted in Squamish? I went to Parents Day, and his teacher told me that Barry often left school at recess, never did his homework, and showed no interest in school. The teacher said that in stark contrast, Gloria was a responsible and sweet little girl and no trouble. Bobby's teacher commented that he was a well behaved boy and quiet in class. Bobby was also getting the Nazi insults, but he bottled up his reactions to them and avoided trouble. I felt trapped in the financial necessity of this job, but I wished we could move to cosmopolitan Vancouver where we would be more accepted, instead of being treated as unwanted outsiders. In an attempt to minimize the insults to my children, I told them to stay on our property of two acres when they weren't at school. "You can bring your friends here to play."

In early 1967, an RCMP officer came to our door again. "Mr. Middelmann, we are getting more complaints about Barry from neighbours, and we need you to do something about it." I took him to the backyard and showed him the playground I had made. "They don't need to go anywhere; they play right here on my property." He looked around. "They've dug holes in your lawn, what about that?" "This is my lawn. What do you want them to do, dig holes in someone else's lawn?" He didn't like how I had talked back, and my remark put me further toward the top of the troublemaker shit list. I had a flashback to the feeling of powerlessness I had felt in Nazi Germany. We were branded as the "Bad Middelmanns," and I was once again trapped. Young American men started coming to the Squamish area as draft dodgers to escape being sent to Vietnam. I sympathized and identified with them. In World War II, I was forced into the army, and lied in order to avoid a suicide mission. The actions of these American men seemed no different to me. Several of the draft dodgers were camping along the Mamquam River close to our home. In the evening, I took the children and joined them around the campfire. I played my guitar and sang their protest songs. One night, two RCMP officers came. "This is illegal, you have to move on." One of the officers then said to me, "What are you doing here with your children? That is disgusting behaviour." I just kept quiet in response, not wanting any more trouble. Being with the draft dodgers didn't help improve my reputation in Squamish at all. Most Squamish residents hated them and didn't want them there.

From 1967 to 1968, there was a slump in the pulp market, and Woodfibre closed several times. Employees went on unemployment insurance. Because of this, I fell behind in my debt payments. There were no other jobs available, but in the fall, I managed to find a job planting Douglas fir seedlings with the Department of Forestry. It paid minimum wage of $1.00 an hour, but this work was the most satisfying work of my life. I love nature, and I felt I was creating future forests. At 6 am I walked to the forestry camp, where the workers were transported to the Macmillan Bloedel area to plant our seedlings. I averaged 600 seedlings per day, seven days a week. It was exhausting and backbreaking work, but I loved it, and made friends with my fellow planters. We were paid for ten hours a day. It kept me barely alive financially, and I was still falling behind in my debt payments. The children were all in school, and it would have tremendously helped if Emilie had a job. She refused to even consider the idea. The financial responsibility was all on my back. In December, we got snowed out, and the planting job ended. I was in a state of exhaustion and heading for a complete breakdown.

CHAPTER 19

I felt heavily burdened by my debts, and at the age of 42, I just didn't have the energy I used to have. The constant stress of dealing with Barry's reckless behaviour was getting to me. We were socially isolated, and it was only our close connection with our friends of the Squamish Nation that helped us to survive. They were treated even worse than we were and knew all too well what it felt like to be a second class citizen in Squamish. Barry spent a lot of time at the reserve and was given the pet name of "Barry the Indian." I worked hard at my job, and then came home to more work. My large vegetable garden took a lot of time and energy. One day, Barry fell ill with a high fever. After two days of fever, we called Dr. Rimmer to make a house call. He told us to keep Barry in bed until he was well, and confirmed it was a case of the flu. Just after the doctor left, an RCMP officer was at the door. "There was a break in at a store in town, and someone reported that he recognized Barry as the suspect." I couldn't believe it. "Barry's been ill in bed for two days, so there is no possible way for it to have been Barry. Ask Dr. Rimmer, you just missed him." We had been labelled as the black sheep of Squamish, and there was no escape. We just had to stay and deal with being treated like dirt. It wore me down. I had always been an optimistic person, but once again I felt trapped, just like I had in the army and in the POW camp. Unfortunately, this was a trap I couldn't escape.

In early 1969, another two month shut down came, and I was devastated. Luckily, my garden kept us going, and gifts of fish from our Squamish Nation friends helped as well. I was able to barter with them with my garden produce to get smoked salmon at a good price. Again, I fell behind in my debts. In March, the shutdown ended, and I went back to work. In early July, I was going for my afternoon shift, and I suddenly felt short of breath. I collapsed on the stairs, certain that I was having a heart attack. The medic sent me by ambulance to the Squamish Hospital. Dr. Redford did extensive tests and came to my bedside. "You are healthy as a horse, Robert. You must have a big load on your mind." I told him about my financial worries and the ongoing stress of how my family was being treated with hatred. "Robert, go home, and I'll make you an appointment with Dr. Slade. He is a highly recommended psychiatrist, and I think you would benefit from speaking with him."

The next day, I went to see Dr. Slade, an elderly English doctor who turned out to be a very wise man. I told him my story. "When was your last holiday?" I had to stop and think. "The truth is, I have never actually had one in my entire life." He shook his head sadly. "It is high time for you to take a holiday." "I have no money to do that." "You have to take a holiday. Go to Skaha Lake, you can camp there for $3.00 a night. All you need is a tent and a motor car." "I have a car, but no tent." "Go to the Army and Navy, they have a sale on." For $20.00, I was able to buy a tent big enough for the family. I phoned Woodfibre to tell my boss I was taking my two week holiday, filled a tank of gas for $2.00, dug up a bag of potatoes from the garden, and we took off to Skaha Lake with everything tied up on top of the Beatle.

That psychiatrist knew exactly what I needed. His common sense approach saved my body and my mind. Marie was working at the Royal Bank for the summer, so she stayed home.

The closer we came to Penticton, the better we all felt. We got a spot right by the beach and pitched the tent. Farmers came every morning with fresh fruits and vegetables for sale. We made friends with the neighbouring campers, and luckily the band that had just played at Grouse Mountain was also camping there. They played every night for the campers. We went swimming, fishing, and canoeing. It was a physical and emotional healing for both me and my family. We were no longer the outcasts, the hated Middelmanns. At Skaha Lake, we were amongst friends who treated us with affection and respect. It gave us new strength to go back and deal with our life in Squamish. We felt we could now rise above these narrow-minded and mean-spirited people. Marie turned 21 that summer and fell in love with Mike, an American draft dodger. Six months later, they moved to Vancouver together. His mother supported them, as neither of them had been able to find a job. One day she phoned to say, "We've gotten married, and I'm pregnant." It all happened very fast, but I hoped they would be happy, and I was thrilled at the thought of becoming a grandfather.

Gloria was in grade four now, and a delightful child that was sweet and full of fun. She was strikingly beautiful with her white blonde hair, and she always found joy in life. One day she came home crying. "The teacher made me sit in the cloak room all day, separated from the other kids, just because I smelled of garlic."

328

She was heartbroken. I tried to comfort her. "The teacher is wrong and ignorant. She shouldn't have done that to you. I will talk to her about this." I couldn't take time off work to go to the school, but I made sure I went to the parent's night to speak to the teacher. How could the teacher have done this to my sweet little girl who only brought joy into the world? I told the teacher how upset Gloria had been by being cast out into the cloak room. "We are a family who use garlic in our cooking. It is tasty, and also very healthy." The teacher looked at me coldly. "Not in our culture."

She then proceeded to go on a long rant about Barry. "He doesn't care about school. His homework is never done. This outlook and behavior has to change." I was fuming about the way she had mistreated Gloria, but I replied, "I'll talk with him," knowing full well it wouldn't make a bit of difference. Barry would do whatever he damn well pleased, and there was nothing anybody could do to stop him. I left the school infuriated at this mean-spirited teacher who felt justified in punishing my daughter unfairly. It filled me with sorrow that my sweet and gentle daughter had to go through such mistreatment in Squamish. That incident has affected Gloria until this day. In grade six, Barry had a nice male teacher who was being driven crazy by Barry. One day, the harassed teacher told me, "Barry is going to drive me to quit my job! I can't take any more." Bobby, on the other hand, was now in grade eight. His report card stated, "He is very obedient, helpful, easy-going, friendly, and an ideal student overall." Barry and Bobby were raised by the same parents but grew up to be very different boys. It puzzled me. How much is nature, and how much is nurture? Bobby had been quiet and obedient since he was born, and Barry had been a wild child since his birth.

I was still struggling financially but managing to keep my head just above water. With the support of AA, I now had ten years of sobriety. Papa's weekly letters were an ongoing source of stress for me. He was in a terrible state, living in a room in the cheapest area in Herne, and surviving solely on social assistance. I sent him money regularly. When I received his letters, I dreaded opening them, as there would be pages and pages of vitriolic hatred towards Mama. I would force myself to read them, but it brought me down emotionally. In one letter he wrote, "I went to the cemetery and was happy to see Marie and Sergio's graves being used by dogs as a shit house." On the last page of each letter, he would suddenly become spiritual. "I am praying to God to protect Robert and his family." I had to burn every letter after reading it, because each one was so full of hatred that it felt like drinking poison.

In early 1971, I was in a state of exhaustion and stressed out. A fellow worker, a friendly young hippy, said to me, "Robert, you look terrible, I can help you." He invited me to his house and offered me a toke. "This will help you to relax, try it." I smoked it, and soon I was completely relaxed and felt freed from the burdens I carried. He gave me some to take home, and Emilie decided to try it. Her constant anxiety dissipated, and she felt quite happy and content. I had never seen her that way, it was miraculous. The marijuana he had given me had seeds in it, which gave me an idea. "I'm a gardener. I could grow this stuff myself." Soon, I had the seeds in small planters on the windowsill, and eagerly watched them sprout. I tended them lovingly, and soon it became part of our nightly routine for Emilie and me to smoke and try to forget all of our worries.

On February 3rd, 1971, Marie gave birth to a beautiful baby girl they called Kirsten. We were thrilled to become grandparents. Now there were three generations of Middelmanns in Squamish. A dynasty. In May, I planted marijuana in my garden, hidden between the corn and tomato plants. It was a hot summer, so I had a bumper crop. I made friends with the hippies at work, and liked their philosophy of "make love, not war." Before long, I was a welcome member of the Squamish subculture of hippies and draft dodgers. At the age of 44, I became the oldest hippie in Squamish, and grew my hair long to fit my new status. By doing this, however, I gave the established Squamish society even more reason to view our family as outcasts. Emilie hated my new look, but for the first time in years, I felt that I belonged and had friends who understood and accepted me.

It was around that time that I decided to write my memoir. In order to travel to work, I had to take a ferry. Every day, on the ferry rides to and from work, I would sit alone and write. It was important for me to leave my children the story of my life and the history of our family. It was that summer that Emilie and I decided to quit smoking tobacco. Even though we had both smoked for almost 30 years, we quit "cold turkey" and it worked. We preferred marijuana, and believed it was healthier. We began biking and swimming in order to be more active. Also, we started driving to Vancouver to go dancing at Johann Strauss on Robson Street. It was a good time in our marriage. Unfortunately, the mill had another shut down in September. As we had never learned our lesson that we needed to save money for unexpected events such as this, we were caught in a bad financial situation once again. My hippy friends were more than willing to buy some of my marijuana crop, and I sold it for $5.00 an ounce. When Emilie found out, she became paranoid. She was constantly worried the police would come to the door to arrest me. I decided that it wasn't worth the stress, and we both quit smoking marijuana.

In 1971, new neighbours moved into a house two doors from us. This would prove disastrous for our family. Mr. and Mrs. Tinker were an English couple in their 50s. Mr. Tinker was a quiet, unobtrusive man, who seemed beaten down by life. Mrs. Tinker was an athletic, stocky dynamo of a woman, who had been a sergeant in the British military police, and well versed in martial arts. She hated Germans and began harassing our family. I could take it, but it was very hard on our children. When they got off the school bus, she would be walking up and down, giving the Nazi salute and shouting, "Heil Hitler, Heil Hitler, you bloody Nazi brats!" She frightened them, and they would run into the house to escape her. When I was working in the garden, she would frequently come and scream at me. "You fucking Nazi! My husband was torpedoed twice by your Nazi U-boats, you bastard!" I would go into the house and try to ignore her. Then, she would walk up and down doing the Nazi salute and shouting, "Heil Hitler!" This barrage of verbal attacks went on for a year. It never occurred to me to go to the RCMP and make a complaint. I didn't feel

332

they would listen to me, as they already saw my family as being counterculture troublemakers. I was associating with the local hippies and American draft dodgers, which did not go over well in the right wing, conservative town of Squamish. My long hair and the peace signs my kids were painting in our driveway didn't help, either.

Our family was singled out and harassed, not only by Mrs. Tinker, but also by the Squamish RCMP. I was often stopped for no reason by the RCMP and questioned while driving. One day I was driving on Cleveland Avenue and saw Bobby standing against the wall of Stewart's Drugstore with his hands up against the wall. Two police officers were frisking him from head to toe. Bobby was never in trouble, but he was now 14 and had also grown his hair long, so he was a target for profiling. I had a flashback to Nazi Germany where we were powerless against Hitler's thugs. I parked just as they let him go. He was calm. "They just frisked me, Dad. It's okay." Many of the RCMP officers hated hippies. One time I was in a Squamish café, and heard a RCMP officer telling two other men, "We were breaking up a hippy party in Stanley Park. They were having a Smoke-in. I wish I could have shot all those goddamn hippies." I felt a terrible jolt tear through my body. He sounded just like the SS men from the war. I felt nauseated to hear this in Canada, especially from someone who was supposed to protect us.

I had found acceptance in the hippy community, but at home I was feeling more and more rejection. For over two decades, I had kept the hope that, one day, Emilie would find love in her heart for me. Now I knew that hope would never be. Emilie made it clear that she didn't want anything to do with me. She ignored me, and still wiped my kisses from her mouth with a grimace of disgust. I craved affection and began going into the bush for solace. On my trips I would hug trees, just to feel that I could hug something. It brought me some peace to do that, and nature helped to restore me. Emilie was a good woman, she just didn't love me. Why didn't I accept that and not expect more? You can't make someone love you, but I foolishly continued buying her expensive gifts in a futile effort to buy her love. Like father, like son.

Barry was still making trouble, and I had to spend much of my energy and time rescuing him from his scrapes. He hated school and skipped most of his classes. His friends mainly consisted of kids from the reserve. Barry was dark-skinned and was often mistaken for one of the kids from the reserve. That is where he most felt at home and accepted. He was proud to be called "Barry the Indian." When he was in grade six, his class went on a field trip for a couple of days at Evans Lake. His teacher was young and quite pretty. When they returned, she dropped him home. "I call him Barry the Brave now," she said, with a sheepish smile. "Why?" "Because last night, he came into my tent and asked if he could sleep with me." Emilie wasn't too impressed by this news, but I thought wryly, "Looks like he's a chip off the old block."

Bobby was 14 and decided to join the Air Cadets. He enjoyed the discipline and comradeship, and within a few months, he was promoted to Lance Corporal. I was happy that he had found this outlet. At the end of June, Barry went to play with two kids who lived next door.

They were having fun and making noise. Mrs. Tinker came to the fence and shouted, "Keep quiet, you rotten brats!" The three boys all spat at her. She immediately went to the RCMP station, showed the officer the spit on her coat, and said that Barry had spat on her. She didn't mention the involvement of the other boys because their father was an RCMP officer, and her primary goal was to get Barry in trouble because of his German background. An officer came to our door and questioned Barry. He admitted he had spat at her. "But so did the other boys!" Barry was charged with assault and was told he had to go to Juvenile Court. I was shocked by the severity of the charge, and how Barry had been singled out for punishment while the other boys walked free. This shook our family to the core.

A few days later, an RCMP officer phoned and told me that I had to see Mr. Paulsen, the social worker who would testify at Barry's hearing. He was also a Baptist Minister. I was so angry at the unfairness of the situation that I had lost my sense of reason and made a serious error. If I had calmed down and thought it through, I would have realized that I needed to make a good impression on Mr. Paulsen in order to protect my son. Mr. Paulsen held our son's fate in his hands. When the day came, I went to the meeting determined to convince Mr. Paulsen that Barry was a good boy from a good family. Mr. Paulsen interrogated me at great length about our family life. I told him I took my kids camping, hiking, and swimming. Also, I told him we were loving parents who devoted ourselves to our children and encouraged them in their sports and hobbies. Mr. Paulsen listened, but he was only really interested in one thing. "Do you go to church?" That would have been a good time to lie to him, but I didn't. I told the truth. "I am not a church goer. We don't attend church." I had lost my faith years ago and believed that religion was the cause of much suffering in the world. I had no idea that by telling the truth, Mr. Paulsen would use my statement to try to remove Barry permanently from our family. Talk about history repeating itself! The Catholic Church tried to remove me from my family back in Herne in 1933. Now, a Baptist minister would try to remove Barry from his family in Squamish in 1972.

I went to court in July with Barry, and Mr. Paulsen was called to the stand to give his assessment. "Barry Middelmann should be removed from this family and placed in a home where he would receive a proper Christian upbringing." He continued to speak, but I felt as though my heart had stopped. Barry looked terrified. Would we lose Barry? Can they actually take him away, just because I admitted we were not attending church? Why didn't I lie when he asked me? I had lied all my life in Germany to get out of bad predicaments, and like an idiot, I told the truth this time. As a result, we might lose our son. I struggled not to fall to the ground in despair. The thought of losing my son was just too much for me. I felt as though I had failed him as a father. Mr. Paulsen finished his testimony and the judge turned to look at Barry. "Did you spit at Mrs. Tinker?" Barry was shaking, staring at the floor, and he struggled to answer. "Yes," he stammered, "but so did the other two boys." The judge gave me a stern look. "Do you tolerate this kind of behaviour?" I felt that we were already judged as guilty. "Of course I don't." I tried to point out that Mrs.

Tinker had been harassing the boys and shouting abuse at them before all three spat at her. The judge brought down his gavel. "You are out of order." I wasn't allowed to continue. I couldn't do anything to protect my son. The judge sentenced Barry to six weeks in the Juvenile Delinquency Detention Centre at Porteau Cove. I was choking on my tears and Barry looked up at me with a hopelessly sad face. We couldn't believe this was happening. He was just 12 years old and being shipped off for one provoked mistake. My only comfort was that the judge didn't agree with Mr. Paulsen's suggestion to remove him from our home permanently.

I had to deliver Barry to the detention centre in three days. When we got home, I told Emilie, and she almost fainted. It was one of the most terrible days of our lives. We had been labelled as unwanted foreigners and heathens that were unfit to raise our children. Barry reacted to our collective grief by putting on his tough guy act. "No problem, Papa, I'll show them." I think he saw how sad I was and wanted to make his Papa feel better. We travelled to the detention centre three days later and I handed my child, my beloved son, over to the guard. Barry tried to put on a brave face, but I could tell he was scared, more scared than he had ever been in his life. It was one of the hardest things I have ever done. Emilie was weeping and literally on the verge of collapse. I was worried that I might have to call an ambulance. They told us there was no visitation allowed, and to pick him up in six weeks. I was filled with anguish as we drove home. What would happen to Barry there? Would he be safe? I turned to my AA friends for support, but it was the worst summer of our family's life.

All of us were devastated by the injustice that had been meted out to Barry.

Two weeks later there was a loud banging at the door at 3 a.m. I opened the door, and there was Barry. He had walked 15 km from Porteau Cove, along the railway tracks, to come home. I had to laugh. He was an escape artist just like his Dad! You can't keep a Middelmann locked up for long. I woke the family and they were delighted to see Barry. It was a special family reunion. He was hungry, thirsty, and needed a bath. I cooked him a good meal and put him to bed. We were together again as a family. Early in the morning, Emilie and I drove him back to the Detention Centre. I talked to the social worker in charge to ask if Barry would be punished for running away. He was quite kind and reassured me. "This often happens, and it is all about learning for the boys. Barry won't be punished this time." At the end of the six weeks, we went to pick him up. They had a special closing ceremony for everyone. The parents were all there, and the boys put on a show. They made pyramids with their bodies and showed us the huts they had built. On the drive home he said, "Papa, I enjoyed myself and learned a lot." Then he looked up at me again with great sadness on his face. "Papa, I don't understand. All the other boys were law breakers and what did I do? I didn't break the law." It tore at my heartstrings to see his face. "Barry, what happened to you was an injustice. It was wrong. I am so sorry that I couldn't protect you, my son." Barry hung his head. It seemed to me his spirit had been broken. I had failed to protect my son from this unwarranted bias.

This experience changed Barry and our family. Barry lost his self confidence and felt as though he were now branded as a "bad kid." He no longer felt safe in Squamish. Our entire family felt unsafe by this point. We believed there would never be justice for the Middelmanns in Squamish. We felt as though we were walking on eggshells and had to be vigilant all the time. We did everything we could to ensure we weren't targeted and victimized again. I made certain that the children never went anywhere near Mrs. Tinker's place. We all just took her insults and abuse and remained civil toward her. For the next few months, she kept on with her insults and harassment. One day I was in my yard and she arrived with a machete in her hand. "You fucking Nazi bastard," she shouted, "you're all murderers!" She was waving the machete around in a dangerous way and Emilie saw her from the window. She begged me to come into the house. I had finally had enough. "Phone the police, Emilie." I gave these instructions in German so that Mrs. Tinker wouldn't understand. She was crazy, not stupid. I wanted her to stay on my property so that the police could see her threatening behaviour. She kept screaming abusive insults and threatening me with the machete. When an officer arrived in his car, she was completely taken off-guard. He saw what was happening and immediately intervened. He charged her with assault with a deadly weapon and told her to return home. Emilie and I went to court as witnesses, and Mrs. Tinker was ordered not to go near us or our property and was given two years probation by the judge. He told her that if she broke this condition she would be sent to a psychiatric hospital for assessment. Our family was tremendously relieved to see the end of the abuse. Mrs. Tinker never came near us again. It felt as though we finally had some justice and we could breathe easier. It brought some comfort to Barry that Mrs. Tinker could no longer hurt our family. I was proud of Barry for having forgiveness in his heart for her. He told me, "Dad, I feel no hatred towards her. She is a sick woman and needs help."

I kept the kids busy with hiking, fishing, camping, and the healing power of nature. Unfortunately, there was another shut down of the mill that spanned through September and October. It was always one step forward and two steps back for us financially. I could never get on top of my debts. However, being an Opa brought me great joy. Emilie and I both doted on Kirsten, who was a beautiful and happy child. Emilie called me "The teenage Opa," as I was still in my hippy phase with long hair and a big Kaiser-style moustache. I worked as much overtime hours at the mill as I could manage. At 45, the changing shifts were taking a heavy toll on me. I worked as hard as I could, only to come home to another mountain of responsibilities. The kids, the garden, and constant repairs to the house also took a toll. As a result, I had lost a lot of weight and was skin and bones. I think I was in a constant state of exhaustion but didn't realize it. My friends at work were worried about me. One of them said, "Robert, you are too skinny, you need to build yourself up. Drink a bottle of Guinness stout before dinner, and you will get your strength back." Foolishly, I took his advice, even after 12 years of sobriety. I let

Emilie down again. I felt great shame for my lapse, but kept on drinking for the next year.

On June 26, 1973, Marie gave birth to another beautiful daughter. They named her Corrina, and we were delighted to be grandparents again. I did gain my weight back with the Guinness stout, but I lost my self respect. I hated myself for being weak. A letter came from Papa's cousin saying that Papa had died from an infected appendix. He was 82 years old. The news absolutely devastated me. I was filled with guilt for not having seen him since I left Germany in 1955. Now he was gone, and there would never be another chance to see him. I cried for three days, consumed by overwhelming grief. Otto had not been my biological father, but he loved me as a son. He had suffered from untreated mental illness that had made him violent, and my mother had grown to hate him. He was also violent with me at times, but I loved him all the same. When my mother died, I didn't shed a tear, but for my Papa, I wept endless tears. One day in November, I hit emotional rock bottom. I despised myself for having relapsed, and my grief at losing Papa was too much for me to bear. Suddenly, I collapsed on the living room floor. I was taken by ambulance to the hospital and was sure I must be dying. By the time I reached the hospital, I was vomiting violently. I had every diagnostic test in the book performed on me. After 24 hours, Dr. Dundas, our GP, came to talk to me. "Robert, you are a very healthy man. There is nothing wrong with you. I know you have a nice family, home, and a good job. Why are you drinking?"

The next day I went to an AA meeting. My friends welcomed me back and offered emotional support. I was glad for the support, but ever since I had quit smoking, the second-hand smoke made me feel ill. I had to leave the meeting. There were no smoke-free meetings in Squamish, so I gave up my support network once more. I began using marijuana on occasion, as it reduced my stress. To save money, I decided to grow my own marijuana in logged out areas in the mountains. With marijuana, I could try to stay relaxed, and not end up having another nervous breakdown. I planted in the spring and checked my crop as much as I could. In the fall, I went to harvest my crop, and found half of it had been eaten by deer. I can only imagine that there must have been a lot of stoned deer in the forest! Thankfully, I still managed to harvest several large garbage bags of B.C. bud. After drying them at home, I looked for a good hiding place to put my stash. The Squamish River had rocky banks, and I thought that would be a safe place. I buried the bags under huge rocks which were about 100 kg each in weight. Every time I needed a monthly supply, I had to move one of those damn rocks. One day, I was heading for my supply and heard loud noises. When I got to the river, I saw big bulldozers building a dike and raising the banks of the Squamish River for flood control. My heart sank. My crop was buried under tons of rock. I felt "gebuegelt," once again. That is a German word that means you are finished. I thought of all the hours I had climbed mountains, planted my crop, harvested my crop, dried it, and hidden it in what turned out to be the most stupid place possible. I couldn't help but laugh at myself for being such a fool.

In the seventies, Squamish began to change as new people and more industries furthered the development of Whistler. There were different RCMP staff, and it seemed as though the witch hunt on the Middelmann family was finally in the past. We had a new mayor, Pat Brennan, who was progressive and put in great efforts to improve Squamish. He gave the hippies a rock festival in Paradise Valley and had a big recreation centre built. Additionally, he encouraged sports, and Squamish then became a place where BC tournaments were held. Our marriage had improved since I stopped drinking, and I was determined not to relapse again. Smoking marijuana helped us to relax, and we smoked together in the evening after the children were in bed. Bobby graduated high school and got a job as a boom man at Woodfibre. He wanted to get out of Squamish, and at 18 he made the wise decision to join the Canadian Navy, where he trained as a marine engineer on the supply ship, The Provider. They went to Hong Kong, Philippines, Japan, Australia, Hawaii and Fiji. When he came home, he was confident, mature, and physically fit. He had left as a boy and had returned as a man.

As soon as Bobby joined the navy, Barry quit school and took a job at Woodfibre as a boom man. He was only 16, but he was a natural at it due to having grown up by the river and knowing how to balance on logs. President Carter announced an amnesty for the U.S. draft dodgers on January 21st, 1977. Mike soon decided to leave Marie and the children in order to return to Tacoma and his parents. Marie and the children then moved in with us. This made Emilie happy and gave her a new lease on life. We weren't being harassed any more by the RCMP, and began to feel safe again. When Barry started working, Emilie told him he had to pay $50 a month for room and board. Barry refused, and Emilie informed him he had to move out if he wasn't going to pay his share. Barry went right out and bought a trailer for $500. At the age of 21, Barry came home and announced, "Mom and Dad, I want you to meet my wife." A blonde and attractive young woman walked in. "This is Pat, my wife." We thought it was one of Barry's jokes, but it turned out to be true. They had married at the registry office about an hour prior to stopping by. Barry worked hard, renovated the trailer, put on an addition, and added a wood stove. Our wild boy was now a married man.

At Home, Squamish, British Columbia, 1970, L to R, Gloria, Barry, Bobby and neighbour's children

Robert and one of the many farm animals 1970

CHAPTER 20

My cousin Elsbeth wanted us to visit her back in Germany, she informed me that my 104,000 marks fine had expired some years before. With the fine gone, I knew I could safely visit Germany without financial or criminal consequence. In May 1979, Emilie and I flew to Germany to visit with Elsbeth in Dusseldorf. She gave us a royal welcome and treated us well. Elsbeth had never married and had a high paying job as a secretary at Veba, one of the largest energy companies in the world. She graciously paid for us to stay a week in a five star hotel in Herne. We visited all our relatives there, and I soon realized that after being away for 24 years, I felt like a stranger in my own hometown. The best moment for me was when we went to see my cousin Trudi. She almost dropped with joy when she saw me. Like me, she was an alcoholic, but she had finally quit drinking and was now able to afford a brand new Mercedes. Everywhere I went, I was offered a drink, but I stayed strong and refused. People were surprised by that. I felt claustrophobic in Germany, there were so many people. I could never find a peaceful place to relax, and it brought back bad memories. We flew home, and I realized I lived in paradise. I had a renewed appreciation for this magnificent and vast country. In Germany, I couldn't breathe, but in Canada, I felt invigorated with every breath. This was my true home.

Unfortunately, both Emilie and I looked at our house, and were no longer happy with what we saw. We had seen the homes of our German friends and relatives that were newer and well maintained. Now, our old and worn house made us feel discontent. We talked it over and decided to renovate and modernize it. Of course, I had no savings, so I foolishly took a loan. That was the beginning of our financial downfall. The pulp market looked good, and I had established an excellent credit rating. In Germany, what I did would have been called "leichtsinnig." In English, that translates to being irresponsible and not thinking about the needs of tomorrow. By the time the renovations were done, and I had a double garage completed, the expense was exorbitant. Also, the basement flooded and was not covered by our insurance. I was keeping up the payments, but then I made another mistake. In 1981, I invited several German relatives and friends to come for a visit. I wanted to show them this wonderful country of Canada. For some idiotic reason, I decided to treat them all and got myself into heavy credit card debt. I was showing off, I suppose. To make matters worse, I took six weeks of unpaid leave in order to show them around. Perhaps I was trying to prove to the Germans that I had made it in Canada. Whatever the unfathomable reason, it had terrible financial consequences for us.

In early 1982, the Woodworker's union and affiliated unions called a strike. The strike lasted five months, and that was the final financial blow. I was already $62,000 in debt to the Squamish Credit Union, and a month behind in my mortgage. Strike money was $5.00 a day if you went on the picket line twice a week. We were not eligible for UIC as strikers. I went to the credit union and explained my situation, and they gave me an extension of two months. Three months later, I was in foreclosure. The judge gave me six months to catch up with my payments. All the men from Woodfibre were looking for work. Alas, it was impossible to get hired. I knew that I had only one option to save us. I had to sell the house. The kids were all gone, and Emilie and I could manage in a small apartment. Brand new houses were going for $32,000 at the time because many other homeowners in the area were also desperate to sell. I put a big sign on my front lawn. "HOUSE FOR SALE BY OWNER, COME IN AND MAKE AN OFFER."

Not one person came to look. Finally, my next door neighbour, Quido, agreed to purchase the house and he paid the $62,000 that I owed. Emilie was in terrible distress by the loss of our house. She was crying all the time and it took a huge emotional toll on her. As a born optimist, I was able to swallow the bitter pill and keep going my merry way. I had lived through worse than this and had always survived. In August, Woodfibre called the senior workers back, and I was one of them. At the end of August, Emilie and I moved into a basement apartment in Tantalus Manor. Six months later we could afford to move to a nicer apartment on the second floor. I said to Emilie, "You see, we're on the way up again." She seemed to finally be recovering emotionally from the loss of the house. Two months later, the most appealing apartment, the one on the top floor with a lovely view, became available. We moved in there. Emilie was very happy with this new home. I was managing financially. We kept healthy by swimming and biking. Life was good.

Emilie and I started reminiscing about Herne, our childhood and the war. I began thinking of Leo's son and daughter, who were my half siblings, and wondered what happened to them. Leo had been wise to get his children out of Nazi Germany in 1938 through the Youth Alia. I recalled seeing the photo of them in the kibbutz in Israel. I had thought of them many times over the years, but my life had always been too busy to take any action. Now, however, my heart was yearning to find them. I phoned the Jewish Community Centre in Vancouver and talked with Dov Efron, the new ambassador from Israel. I told him I wanted to find my half siblings. "Come anytime and see me." "What about in one hour?" I replied. "I'll get the tea ready," Dov said with a laugh. So, at the age of 58, I began the search for my half siblings.

Dov welcomed us with a big smile. He was an intelligent and handsome man. I shared details of my background and explained why I wanted to search for my siblings, Benjamin and Ruth Neuberger. Dov told us his mother had come to Israel through the Youth Alia in the same year as my siblings. He told us that most of the newcomers changed their names to Hebrew names when they got to Israel, which made it very difficult to trace relatives. Dov also pointed out that Ben and Ruth could have ended up in the military, where they might not have survived. He promised he would do his best to help me all the same. Two weeks later, I got a letter from the Israeli government that the search for Benjamin and Ruth was underway. Dov and I developed a close brotherly bond. He suggested that I study Hebrew through Langara College, as this would help me in my search when I went to Israel. "Many of the older ones remember those who came through the Youth Alia in 1938. They will be helpful to you." I signed up for the

349

Hebrew class, which was held in the Jewish Community Centre. I knew my gift for languages would be of great aid. Leah Benron was our teacher and made the course a most interesting and joyful experience. The students were from all over the world.

For the first time since 1943, I felt I was with my "people" again. It reminded me of the time during the war when I was helping Jewish families in our neighbourhood. I quickly made good friends amongst my classmates. I was determined to learn Hebrew and taped the class to keep as reference. All week I would play this tape while en route to and from work, both by car and on the ferry. When I went to bed, I put my headphones on and played the looping tape. In the morning, I would wake up speaking Hebrew. It felt good to be returning to my roots and learning the language of my ancestors. I was on day shift, and twice a week I would leave work and drive to Vancouver for my four hour class, arriving home at midnight. In my second semester, we had a new teacher, Shoshana. At the end of a class she announced, "Robert, you are my best student." I felt proud, but uncomfortable. Praise can cause jealousy. The search enacted by the Israeli officials was not successful. They had found no trace of my siblings. I was now on my own in this reunion endeavour. This only made me more determined in my quest, and I devoted all my spare time to learning Hebrew. For several years, I had been suffering severe back pain. I could only make it through work by taking heavy doses of pain killers and sheer will. Finally, at age 60, I went on long term disability, which took me to age 65 and retirement. After four years of classes, I was now fluent in Hebrew. I felt intertwined with my Jewish heritage. I celebrated Jewish holidays, attended synagogues in Vancouver, and concerts at the Jewish Community Centre. My family also took part with me and learned about their Jewish heritage. I made plans to go to Israel to find my brother and sister. My long time dream was about to be fulfilled.

Shortly afterwards, Emilie and I were having dinner when she suddenly had a seizure. I called Gloria to come for help. She was an excellent nurse's aide and had a great deal of experience from having worked at Hilltop Care Centre. I told Gloria what had happened, but Emilie stubbornly denied it. "What are you talking about, Robert?" She was angry with me for having suggested such a thing. Emilie refused to go to the doctor, and her seizures started happening several times a day. Gloria and Marie observed her seizures personally, they assured their Mom that it was happening. Emilie was in denial, and became incensed with them, too. "What, is the whole family against me now?" Finally, we were able to convince her to go Dr. Raymond, her GP. Gloria and Marie came with us and told the doctor about the seizures. Emilie was furious. "It's not true. They are all plotting against me!" Dr. Raymond sent Emilie for a series of diagnostic tests, but they all came back negative. At that point, she was sent to a neurologist in Vancouver where she was again thoroughly tested, but the cause remained a mystery. Her seizures increased in frequency, and finally the neurologist put her on Dilantin to try and control them. It worked, but it made Emilie feel drugged and nauseated, so she refused to take the medication. The seizures came back even worse than before. She still couldn't come to terms with the reality of her vulnerability. The doctor put her on Tegretol, which completely controlled her seizures. Always the contrarian, Emilie would only take half of her prescribed dose, so the seizures inevitably returned. She'd been having eight of them a day, but now she was down to four a day. One day during her seizure, she pulled the tablecloth, bringing our dinner and all of our dishes down with it. I left it there to show her when she woke. "Who did that?" she asked angrily, refusing to accept that it had been her.

This period was the most frustrating and desperate time of my married life. I realized I had to give up my dream of going to Israel to find my siblings, and instead take care of my wife. Emilie's refusal to accept her condition and take the medication made me feel powerless to help. I knew I was headed for another downward spiral. Then I remembered the "Serenity Prayer" I learned in AA, "God grant me the serenity to accept the things I cannot change, courage to change the things I can, and the wisdom to know the difference." I hung onto that prayer, and it comforted me when I felt I just couldn't go on any longer. Gloria and Marie helped when they could and tried to give me respite at times. I would go to the Squamish River or Brohm Lake for healing. Being alone in nature gave me strength to endure this sad and impossible situation. To add to our stress, new tenants soon moved in to our complex, causing problems. Emilie couldn't tolerate the trouble they instigated, so in 1993, we moved to a new and modern condo in Diamond Head Village. With the ongoing stress and now the added burden of the move, I had a complete physical collapse. I went to see Dr. Kindry and told him what was happening. "Robert, you are completely exhausted. You need sleep. Go to bed and stay there." Gloria came to take care of her mother and I went to bed for a long and healing sleep. Emilie continued to be in denial of what was happening to her. I think she had now realized the truth, but she didn't have the courage to admit it. I could never leave her alone with her ever-present risk of seizures, so I just made up my mind just to face whatever came and take care of her the best I could.

Emilie was examined endlessly, and still the doctors were not able to find the cause of her seizures. In 1995, Emilie had a seizure in the car. While seizing, she grabbed the gear shift and put the car in neutral. Thankfully, I was able to grab her hand from the gear and stop the car safely. Otherwise, it could have been a deadly accident. A week later, we were crossing the Burrard Bridge when she opened the door and tried to get out. I traded the car in for a new one that had a master switch, where I could prevent her door from opening from the inside. Our whole family was suffering from this terrible situation and it continued for the next nine years. By 2001, her mind had been significantly affected, and she couldn't tell the difference between a toothbrush and a comb. Dr. Cutmore referred her to another neurologist, Dr. Cameron, at Lion's Gate Hospital. Gloria came with me and we waited eight hours in the emergency room. Emilie could barely stand, but we held her up as best we could. Dr. Cameron ordered a brain scan, and finally we discovered the insidious cause of her ailment. "I've discovered a cancerous tumour in her brain, about the size of a golf ball." We were stunned, but also relieved that they now knew what was causing her seizures. "I have a bed for her, and you can meet the surgeon in the next few days." We couldn't understand why this hadn't been discovered earlier.

We went home and phoned everyone in the family with the sad news. The next morning, I drove to Lion's Gate Hospital at 5am, only to find Emilie in the hallway crawling towards me. She was covered in feces. I called a nurse, and they got her back in her room and helped her to shower. I was upset and demanded to speak to the head nurse. "Why was my wife in the hallway in this condition?" "We're on a slowdown strike, resulting in our being overwhelmingly short staffed." Three days later, I met with Dr. Mutant, the surgeon. Gloria, Bobby, and Marie were with me. The doctor gave us terrible news. "The chances are less than 0.09 % that she will survive this cancer, and I'm being optimistic with that percentage. If we leave her, she may live three months. If we operate, she may have six or more months, if we're lucky. The decision is yours." We asked for some time to discuss this as a family before making the decision. Emilie was so far gone that she didn't understand anything the doctor had said. We talked it over and decided to go for the surgery. It might give Emilie some more time. It was a Hobson's choice. We informed the surgeon of our mutual conclusion. Afterwards, we all went for a walk on the hospital balcony. Emilie looked at Bobby and said, "Calgary is such a beautiful city." In her delirious state, she thought we were all in Calgary, where Bobby lived.

The next day, Emilie had the brain surgery. Afterwards, the surgeon came to talk to the family. "She survived and is in recovery. Come back tomorrow to see her." We went back the next day, and Gloria realized that her mother must have had a stroke, as she was now paralyzed on one side. We couldn't understand her at first, but later on Emilie said, "Where am I?" She didn't realize she was in hospital. Gloria and I talked softly to her and kissed her, trying to calm and comfort her. Bobby had to fly back to Calgary for work, but Marie and Gloria went with me every day to the hospital. Eight days later, Emilie was extremely distressed when we came in to visit. Gloria rolled her mother over, and found hardened old feces smeared on the bedding. Gloria was absolutely livid. "My mother is sitting in shit. This is totally unacceptable!" The only reply the nurse could muster was, "We're sorry, but we're understaffed." Gloria began taking care of her mother herself, washing her, changing the bedding. We were all horrified at the bad care Emilie was receiving in the hospital. I knew I could give her better care than what she received there and informed the nurse I wanted to take Emilie home. The next day, the doctor signed the discharge papers for her to go home. It seemed she had suffered another stroke around this time, because she had now completely lost the ability to speak.

We took her home, and Gloria came every day after work to help me. I knew the end must be near because the doctor announced that the cancer was spreading. Our family physician, Dr. Cutmore, told me, "keep her at home as long as you can, but be sure to take care of the caretaker. There is a bed reserved in the palliative care unit for her when the time comes." I was able to fulfill her care needs at home for four weeks. After that, the day approached when I knew I couldn't do it anymore. I called Dr. Cutmore, and Emilie was admitted to the palliative care unit of the hospital. The nurses were excellent, and I knew she would be taken good care of there. It was estimated that she had one more week or so to live. I phoned Bobby, and he flew in from Calgary. We made sure Emilie was never alone and that a family member was always with her to keep her company during her end days. Bobby never wanted to leave his mother, and we had to force him to take breaks. We played her favourite music, Chopin, Tchaikovsky, and songs by Nana Mouskouri.

Friends came to say their goodbyes. Sarah, Emilie's closest friend, came to visit her. Afterwards she told me, "Robert, Emilie told me a few years ago that she could never find it in her heart to love you before, but that in these last years, she was able to find love for you." Perhaps Emilie realized that I had taken good care of her during her long years of illness, even though she refused to admit she was ill. Barry came, and when he saw his mother, he started weeping freely. "Mom, I am sorry I was such a bad kid, please forgive me, I love you." It was touching to see that Barry was able to realize he had been unkind to his mother at times and had made life difficult for her. On September 2nd, Bobby had to return to work. The next day, it was my turn to sleep at the hospital, and around 3 a.m. I felt a strong force wake me from my deep sleep. I went to Emilie and saw that she was gone. Her body was still warm. A peaceful feeling came over me then, and I felt relieved that her suffering was over. She was my wife for 53 years and the mother of my children. Emilie had been a loyal wife and had a kind heart. I had loved her even though I knew she didn't love me. It was of some consolation to discover that she finally was able to find some love for me in the end. I called all my children to let them know their Mother was gone.

The funeral was held in the Squamish Funeral parlor and Father Angelo from St. Joseph's parish officiated. More than 200 people attended. Her death was a liberation for Emilie, as well as the whole family, because her illness had been so long and so tragic. I recalled what Emilie's mother had asked of me when I left for Canada. She had asked me to promise that I would always take care of Emilie. I had kept that promise. Emilie's long illness had left me exhausted and on the verge of collapse. I realized it was now time for me to take care of the caretaker. When my health improved, I knew I wanted to travel. Traveling the world had been my dream for over 60 years. I gave notice at my apartment and called the family to take the furniture and Emilie's belongings. I moved in with Gloria in October. Australia was a country that I had always wanted to visit, so I phoned the Rosenbergs, who were living in Sidney. They were the Jewish family that I had helped as a teenager before they were sent to concentration camps. Irene, the girl that I had been infatuated with, had survived, along with her two brothers. Unfortunately, both brothers had passed away recently. She was sad to hear of Emilie's death, but encouraged me to come and visit. I made the decision to go and told my family of my plan. I thought they would be happy for me, but Bobby was bewildered by the news. "You can't go, Dad, you are the head of the family. Please don't do this." I was surprised by Bobby's intensely negative reaction to my decision. "I'm coming back, Bobby," I reassured him. "I'm not moving there."

On January 10, 2002, I flew to Sidney. Irene was meeting me at the airport. I recalled her being a beautiful and willowy young woman with dark curly hair who loved to dance. I looked down from the top of the escalator and saw an elderly woman, obese and paralyzed on one side. She seemed to be waiting for someone. After a moment, I realized that someone was me. As the escalator descended, I had a desperate thought. "Oh, no, can this escalator be reversed?" Instantly, I was deeply ashamed of that thought. Irene greeted me, and we hugged as old friends who had both survived. I realized that she had been through so much turmoil, and it had taken a great toll on her life. We drove to her lovely condo, located close to Bondi Beach. Over tea, Irene shared what she had been through since we had last seen each other. She had divorced her first husband, the man she had married because he saved her life in Riga concentration camp. She had not loved him, but felt she owed him her life. Later, she married a wealthy man in the clothing business with which she had two sons. Irene was a talented designer, and she became very successful. Her husband died, and Irene was in poor health, having had two strokes and several cancer surgeries. She was extremely happy to see me, and I was grateful to be in sunny Australia. I knew I would never want a romantic relationship with Irene, but we could at least be companions in this beautiful country together.

We were survivors and shared a common history. After arranging to pay half of the expenses, I settled into a relaxing daily routine. A big breakfast, a trip to the beach, home for lunch, a siesta, dinner, and then off to Hakoah Club, a Russian Jewish club for dining and dancing. Irene had a large circle of friends, mainly older Jewish women, who came to accept me as part of Irene's inner circle.

Irene lived in a Jewish enclave. Everyone in the condos seemed to be retired millionaires. Here I was, a half Jewish Canadian labourer, hanging in the same circles as millionaire Jews. Irene warned me. "Robert, don't tell anyone that you have worked in the bush and the mine." "Why, is it a shande to be a malocher?" I asked. In English I was asking her, "is it a shame to be a hard working labourer?" She replied, "It is not a shande, but they will all think you're a schmuck." Being called a schmuck essentially means that you are as useless as a tit on a bull's ass. "If anyone asks what work you did in Canada, tell them that you were an amber salesman." There was a slight sliver of truth to that, being that I had worked briefly at my friend Andre's Amber and Silver store in Britannia Beach. Irene then pointed out another problem. I was not really considered a Jew, because the lineage must come from the mother's line. She advised me, "Don't bring that up, as far as everyone else is concerned, you are a full Jew." I felt uncomfortable with these deceptions, but Irene insisted it was necessary, so I played along. In my soul, I felt Jewish.

I fell in love with Australia, and spent most of my time swimming at the beach. After three months, Irene said, "Robert, I love you and I would like to share my life with you. I feel I have such a mazel late in life to have you." Mazel means "luck." Sadly, I didn't feel the same way. For me, what we had felt more like a close friendship. I didn't want to bring her spirits down after seeing how she was so happy. Her doctor had even told me, "Irene's health is much better since you came." However, I knew the right thing to do was be honest with her. "Irene, I am also enjoying the time we have together, but I don't feel the same way. I just want a friendship. I have a large family in Canada, and I will have to return eventually." She was not happy with my response but seemed to accept it for the time being. We lived together as companions and had separate bedrooms. I would leave in the morning for the beach to swim, and our shared life was in the evening at the club for dining and dancing.

After six months, my permit to be in Australia expired, and I had to leave. Irene said, "Robert, please promise me you will come back." It was a wonderful life there, and I truly did want to return. I worked in the gold and amber shop for the six months I was back in Canada. In November 2002, I returned and resumed my life with Irene. I spent most of my time at Bondi Beach and found it healing for me, both physically and emotionally. As time passed, Irene was becoming more controlling and manipulative. One day she announced firmly, "Robert, I don't want you to return to Canada. I want you to stay with me in Australia. If your children want to see you, then they can come here." I was alarmed by her possessive attitude. My family was of the utmost importance to me. "I am going back to Canada. My heart belongs with my family in Canada." She became terribly angry. "Then you can just stay there!" Our relationship was never the same after that. Irene began ordering me around and making demands. I felt as though I was living with a sergeant major. Towards the end of the six months, Irene told me, "Robert, I want us to get married, and I want to be buried beside you. I will buy two grave sites for us. Don't go back to Canada. As my husband, you can live in Australia. You don't have to ever return to Canada." The nonchalance with which she said these words horrified me. It was as if she felt that if she couldn't possess me in life, she wanted to at least possess me in death. "I can't do that to my family, Irene. I'm returning to Canada." I decided I would never return to this woman who wanted to control and possess me. Our friendship had taken a toxic turn, and there was no recourse.

My family was happy to have me back and I again returned to work at Andre's gold and amber store. Six months later, Irene's best friend, Marika, phoned. "Robert, Irene is very ill and depressed. Please come back for a visit. It would mean so much to her." Irene had been through so much. Perhaps I could help her spirits by going for a short visit. I talked it over with Gloria and asked her if she would come with me. "Yes, Dad, I've always wanted to go to Australia!" I phoned Irene to tell her. We booked a six week trip there. In November, 2003, we flew to Sidney. Gloria was a big hit with the whole Jewish community. Her beauty and amicable personality enchanted them. She made connections easily and became a popular dance partner at the Hakoah Club. Karl, Irene's younger brother, who had been saved in 1938 by going on the kinder transport to England, came to visit. One night, at dinner, Irene began making demands of me in her usual militant manner. Karl was appalled. "Irene, are you talking to a dog, or to Robert?" Gloria, too, was very uncomfortable with the belittling way Irene spoke to me. Irene was even jealous of my own daughter. "You spend more time with Gloria than with me!" she complained.

After a month in Australia, Gloria turned to me and said, "Dad, I feel like going home right now. The way Irene orders you around is unacceptable and I just can't stand it anymore." An immediate wave of relief surged through me when I heard those words. "I feel the same way. Let's get out of here!" Half an hour later, we had changed our flights and were booked to fly back that very evening. We went back to Irene's to pack. Irene asked me why we were packing our belongings so soon. "We are returning to Canada. I will write you a letter to explain it all." Off we went, in a fashion not dissimilar to Hansel and Gretel escaping the wicked witch. We were inexplicably happy to be going home to Canada. When I arrived home, I wrote a letter of explanation to Irene and every member of her family. I told Irene that my family came first, and I would not be returning. I respectfully thanked her for welcoming me to Australia and wished her the best in the future.

My children were all happy to have me home to stay. However, I missed my relaxing and healing beach life in sunny Australia, and I became restless. In April 2004, Marie phoned. "Dad, why don't you come to Campbell River? Rent is cheap and you can get a place by the beach!" This was very tempting as I had a lot of family there; Marie and her husband Bert, Kirsten and

Corrina, and their families. I was great buddies with Bert, who was from Holland, and enjoyed his company immensely. Also, I could be near a beach again, albeit not as lovely as the one in Australia. So, ever the impulsive one, I packed up and moved to Campbell River. Right away, I found a nice apartment within walking distance to town and the beach. Two weeks later, I met Janet. Her father was Haida, and her mother was English. She was an attractive woman in her late 60s, and I asked her to come dancing that night. We had a romantic evening, and not much time passed before we were together every day. A short time later, we moved in together. Unfortunately, and possibly on an unrelated note, I was once again drinking heavily and not making the wisest choices.

At first, all seemed well. Janet behaved like a geisha every evening. She would dress like one and then serve me, lighting many candles, playing soft romantic music and drawing my bath. It was an exotic new experience for me to be catered to in this way. However, there was another side to Janet that soon came out. It was a side that was filled with anger, primarily directed towards men. It all came to a climax one night when we were watching a rather ridiculous Hollywood movie about World War II. Janet started shouting, "The Germans are all rotten murderers. We should have killed all of them!" I was astonished by her words. Her face was contorted with anger, and she kept shouting insults at me. Always the pacifist, I have always hated confrontation and anger. My childhood had been full of it and I had tried to avoid it all my life. Now, somehow, I was living with an extremely angry woman, and I realized what a terrible mistake I had made. "Sorry, Janet, I have to leave. This is not going to work." Janet continued ranting and throwing insults as I packed. I found an apartment, but soon Janet was at my door and begging me to come back. "I'm so sorry, Robert. I love you, and I want us to be back together. Nothing like that will ever happen again. Please give me another chance!" Every day, she came back with food and gifts and pleaded for a second chance. A week later, I succumbed to her wishes, and moved back in with her.

All was well for a few days, but soon Janet started going into rages completely unprovoked. She would be so apologetic afterwards, promising it would never happen again. Each time, I would forgive and believe her. Looking back, I believe I was a victim of emotional abuse. I felt I had made a mess of things and was permanently trapped in a cycle of anger and remorse. This toxic relationship mimicked the pattern of my childhood. Depressed and drinking heavily, I lost control of my life. Janet kept pushing for us to get married, and despite warnings from multiple members of my family and hers, I married her on December 28th, 2005. The rage Janet felt for all the men who had abused her in the past was now directed toward me. Though I had never treated her poorly, and more abuse was not going to help solve her pain, I served as her scapegoat. I grew up with Papa's rage, and now, towards the end of my life, I was married to a woman who was filled with rage. Walking alone in the bush was my only escape and refuge for healing. I felt like such a "schmuck" that I hadn't listened to others, and I was angry at myself for being so stupid. My sense of self worth was diminished, and depression took over.

One day, on my walk, I saw a tree and said to myself, "That would be a good hanging tree for me." Every day I would visit that tree and think of ending my life. I bought a rope that would hold my weight, and I began to see this as the only way out. Each passing day brought me closer to suicide. How ironic that I had survived so much, and now I was contemplating suicide because of someone I had welcomed into my life as family. I was no longer thinking rationally. One day, however, as I was walking to my tree, I remembered that AA had saved me many times and I decided to seek help. For some reason, I phoned the Senior Help Line instead of AA. Interestingly, that turned out to be one of the best decisions of my life. A woman answered, and I told her my situation and that I was thinking of ending my life. She listened carefully to everything I said and then spoke emphatically to me. "Robert, do you have any relatives?" "Yes." "Can you go to them?" "Yes, I can." "Then get out of there as soon as possible and don't marry any more of these women."

The next morning, I was on the road to Red Deer to stay with Bobby. That wise woman at the Senior Help Line had saved my life with her advice. I got a divorce and vowed never to make such a stupid mistake again. In 2007, I returned to Squamish. I tried one more relationship with a woman I met on a trip to Germany. At first it seemed fine, but as time went on, she became more and more controlling. She didn't want to share me with my family and became outwardly jealous if I spoke to other women. My family has always been the most important thing in my life, so I ended the relationship before it could spiral further. Although my love life was not doing so well, my work life since my retirement had been quite successful. At 82, I got a job at the Helping Hands Foundation, a homeless shelter in Squamish. I worked from 8 am to 8 pm making meals, checking people in and out, doing laundry, and cleaning. I met many interesting people and it made me feel good to be helping others. Since retirement, I also worked as a paper carrier, an amber jewellery salesman, vitamin salesman, Okanagan fruit distributor, gardener, landscaper, sold my homemade Kombucha, and delivered phone books for TELUS. I missed the thrill of the black market, but life was still exciting and full of new challenges.

Robert on the Woodfibre Ferry 1979

*Hiking up the Chief, Squamish, British Columbia
1990*

Gloria and Marlies 1997

Squamish, British Columbia 1997

*Selling Amber, Silver and Gold Jewellrey,
Britannia Beach, British Columbia 2002*

*Red Deer, Alberta 2006, 3 Generations Robert,
Bobby and Kelly*

CHAPTER 21

Bobby had found a lovely American woman named Melanie. He'd fallen madly in love and was planning to marry her. After I broke up with my German girlfriend, Bobby came to me with a serious look on his face. "Dad, Melanie and I met a wonderful woman last fall on the Sunshine Coast, and we both think she would be a perfect match for you." I didn't want to hear that after all of my relationship mishaps. "No, I'm done with women. I'd rather be a monk than have another woman!" My last two experiences had been disasters, and I'd made up my mind that my time with women was over for good. Even so, Bobby wouldn't give up. He explained that Bobby and Melanie had attended a spiritual retreat at a place called Halfmoon Haven. While they were there, they met Dorothy, whose son, Chris, was the owner of Halfmoon Haven. They spent a lot of time with Dorothy and were impressed with her wisdom and loving heart. At one point Melanie said to Bobby, "Dorothy would be perfect for your father." Dorothy seemed interested until Bobby had told her I was seeing a German woman. Bobby waited until I ended that relationship and made his move. They wanted me to meet her. Of course, I was not interested. I had been hurt and trapped too many times. But Bobby, who had never done this before, kept on bringing her up over and over. He wouldn't give up, and neither did Melanie. When I wouldn't budge in my response, Bobby looked her up on the internet. "Look, Dad, she is a Cancer." He knew that I had always had a soft spot for women of the Cancer sign. I had always found them to be warm, loving, and family oriented. Next, he showed me her photo. She was an attractive woman with a red rose in her hair, a rainbow-hued flowing scarf, and sparkling brown eyes. I could see she had an aura of joy and that there was sweetness in her eyes. My stubbornness began to waver.

Bobby would simply not relent in his requests for me to meet her. Finally, I said, "Okay, okay, I'll meet her." I hoped agreeing to meet her would get Bobby off my back. When I got home later, Bobby told me that he had called Dorothy and left a message. "I told her you had broken up with the German woman, and that Melanie and I would like the two of you to meet." Five days later, the phone rang and I answered. "Hi, Bobby, this is Dorothy returning your call." She sounded confident, kind, and had a soothing voice. I replied, "No, this is his father, Robert." She was surprised, and had no idea that Bobby was living with me. We had a long conversation and I felt very comfortable talking with her. She sounded intelligent and well read. My inner voice said, "Robert, this is an interesting woman. You should meet this woman now!" I took a chance and blurted out, "I would like to meet you." Dorothy replied cautiously, "Well, perhaps when you are coming to Vancouver sometime in the future, we could arrange to meet." "What about tomorrow?" She seemed surprised, but didn't turn me down, and we arranged that I would come to her house on Zero Avenue, in Surrey, for tea at 3 p.m.

Dorothy gave me explicit directions, which of course I ignored, so I became lost. I was actually very close to her home, but as I have no sense of direction, I couldn't figure it out. There was a young woman at a bus stop, and I asked if I could use her cell phone. She graciously agreed, and I called Dorothy. She quickly realized I was only a few blocks away, but also realized that I was geographically challenged. "Can you see a large Pink Hotel near you?" I looked and it was just a block away. "Go there and wait for me to come." The young woman, Sina, was a youth pastor from Peru. She had to get to the border to renew her visa and didn't realize the bus didn't go there. I asked Sina to come with me to the Pink Hotel, and soon a car drove up and parked beside mine. Dorothy got out, and I had an overwhelming feeling of deep recognition, as if I had known her in the past. We smiled, I took her in my arms, and we had a lovely embrace. "How long have you two known each other?" Sina asked. "We just met," I replied. "It seems to me that you must have known each other before and were reuniting just now!" When Dorothy found out Sina needed to go to the border, she kindly offered to drive her there. "Robert, you follow me, I will take Sina to the border, and then we'll go home for tea." Dorothy lived right beside the beautiful U.S. Peace Park, and the ocean was nearby. We had a delightful tea and chatted on the sofa in the living room after. She shared that she had been a social worker and journalist before her retirement and was now trained as a Hospice volunteer.   At one point, I was feeling close to her, so I reached out and took her hand. Dorothy gently pulled her hand away so as not to hurt my feelings. She seems to be an old fashioned girl, I thought. I liked that.

She suggested we go for a walk in the Peace Park to continue sharing our life stories. I was becoming more interested in her by the moment. It was obvious from the way she spoke that she deeply loved her four sons and four grandchildren, and that she had a kind and compassionate heart. I was happy to learn she was so close to her family and valued the bonds of kinship as much as I did. She told me she had been separated from a marriage of 33 years and was soon to be divorced. When we got back, I asked if I could see her again. We had already expressed that we both shared an affinity for nights of music and dancing. "There is a dance this Sunday at 2 p.m. Would you like to go with me?" I jumped at the chance. "Yes, but will you make a reservation for me at a motel nearby? I can't drive back in the dark. I will pay for it, of course." She agreed. I drove home to Squamish feeling young again and hopeful that a beautiful new chapter in my life was about to begin. I told Bobby about my visit. "Dad, didn't I tell you she was a special lady?" When I phoned to tell Gloria and Marie, they were not pleased about my level of enthusiasm and warned me to be careful. Gloria scolded me, "Dad, take it easy. Don't move too quickly with a woman you've only just met. Haven't you learned your lesson yet?" Marie gave me the same well-intended warning. They had seen me burned multiple times, and they were concerned that I was once again impulsively jumping into the dangerous frying pan of love. My mind was focussed on Sunday, which was Mother's Day, as well as our first date. The four days of waiting for Sunday to arrive seemed to take forever. Sunday came and I put on my best suit and Florsheim dance shoes. When I arrived at her home, she looked enchanting in a pale rose and gold dress accompanied by a scarf she had bought when she had lived in India. There was a live

Dixieland band and we danced all night with abandon. I couldn't help but admire that Dorothy had voluptuous breasts, so much so that I wondered if they might be enhanced. I have always been a "breast man." What can I say? I appreciate the art that is a woman's body. As we danced a close tango, my questions of enhancement diminished. Those beauties had to be real. We had dinner at Little India on Marine Drive, followed by a romantic stroll on the White Rock pier.

Dorothy had rented me a room in a motel in White Rock, and I invited her to come join me for tea. I'd brought damask teacups, cream, sugar and biscuits, and served her a nice tea. She confessed that she was impressed by my thoughtfulness. Dorothy apologized for her choice in motel, as the place was quite derelict. She thought she was renting the one up the street that featured much better amenities. The motel seemed to be filled with people who had drug problems and big dogs. I reassured her with a chuckle, "Don't worry, I've lived in worse dumps than this." I dropped her off at home, and as we hugged, I felt enveloped by her sweet and loving heart. My last thoughts that night were of her and the flickering hope of what might come. When I got home the next day, I called her. After that, there wasn't a day where we didn't talk, and our closeness increased. Not only was she well-read and intelligent, but she had an empathetic and open-minded attitude that impressed me. We were able to discuss politics, religion, and philosophy, and found we had similar values. Bobby and Melanie were thrilled that we were getting along so well. They were my snadchan. In Hebrew, that means matchmaker. Meanwhile, the rest of the family thought I was out of my mind.

Dorothy mentioned she was going to drive up to her timeshare in Whistler soon, and asked if she could drop by to see me in Squamish. On Saturday, May 19, she arrived at my apartment. Bobby was delighted to see her again and we all had tea together. When she was leaving, I went with her to the parking lot. With a shy smile she asked, "Would you like to join me in Whistler on Wednesday when my family goes?" I stammered back, "Yes," like a lovesick schoolboy. On Tuesday evening, however, Dorothy called. "Robert, you shouldn't come, I've got the flu." She sounded terribly ill. Not to be deterred I firmly replied, "Nonsense. I will come and bring my Jewish penicillin to help make you better." Jewish penicillin, or chicken soup, is my speciality. I drove to Whistler with a song in my heart, and vitamin C, Buckley's cough syrup, and Fisherman's cough drops in my bag. She was quite ill, feverish and coughing. I served her many bowls of my healing chicken soup. That night, I slept in the second bedroom and could hear her coughing. In the morning, however, I was happy to find that she was much improved.

I did my best to nurse her to health. My feelings were becoming stronger for this kind, sweet, and wise woman who was entrancing me. On Friday, Dorothy felt much better, and we made a plan to go to nearby Brandywine Falls for a picnic. It was a beautiful day, sunny and warm. We had our picnic and started walking up the path to the falls. I had a strong urge to kiss her and finally found the courage to ask. "Can I kiss you?" I was afraid she would say no, just like the time she

375

slipped her hand away. She looked up at me with a teasing smile in her beautiful brown eyes. "Yes." I held her in my arms and kissed her passionately. When we broke apart, we saw two young and petite nuns walking by and smiling sweetly at us. We felt we had been blessed by these little angels. Frequently on our journey up to the falls, we would stop and kiss, and our angels blessed us again and again with their smiles and giggles. When we reached the top, we marvelled at the spectacular falls as they thundered down in all their glory. We kissed again, and our angels, hovering nearby, once more blessed us with their sweet smiles. It felt like an auspicious beginning to our romance.

We returned to the condo and sat down for afternoon tea. As we talked, Dorothy suddenly reached over and touched my hand. She looked directly into my eyes and said something that totally blew my mind. "Don't you think it's time we made love?" It was so unexpected that I was in shock. I stood up in disbelief. "Could you repeat that?" She repeated those magic words, and I responded with an enthusiastic, "Yes!" We went up the stairs to her bedroom. Soon, I discovered that Mother Nature had endowed this lovely woman with the most beautiful breasts, and there was absolutely nothing false about them. Several hours later, we surfaced to forage for food and marvel at the bliss we had just shared with one another. I was in awe and wonder at the power of love, a power that was stronger than any other force. Dorothy was also feeling strong emotions, and we realized we had fallen in love. Dorothy said later, "Perhaps we had just fallen in lust." Lust or love, or both, we were like a couple of infatuated teenagers the next day when I left to drive to Squamish. As soon as I walked into my apartment and saw Bobby, I blurted out, "We're in love!" He was delighted to find that his sneaky matchmaking endeavour had been so successful. Our pairing was almost like an arranged marriage, but in reverse. In our case, it was the kids making the arrangements. I wanted to share our good news with Gloria, so I asked her to come over. When she arrived, I happily announced, "We've fallen in love." Gloria looked deeply concerned. "Oh, Dad, take it easy, don't rush into anything like you usually do!" She was worried, and I could see that she thought I was about to make another mistake. Bobby, however, had a big grin on his face. "No, Gloria, this time is different. Dorothy is a really kind and loving woman who is a wonderful match for Dad." But Gloria had seen too many disasters with my other relationships, and it would take more than that to convince her that my heart was safe.

Dorothy and I visited each other regularly and talked for hours on the phone. It was quickly apparent that we had common values and interests. Family is important to us and we both highly value loyalty and kindness. We were both socialists, agnostics, world travellers, and avid lovers of nature and animals. My mother taught me to love history, and Dorothy shared that love. To our joy, we discovered we were both passionate about books and music, especially classical music. Hours were spent in lively discussions about history, politics, feminism, and the sad plight of the environment. We shared our dreams and our most intimate secrets. I had never had such a deep and meaningful relationship with any other woman in my life. A few weeks later, I made a decision. In July, I would turn 85, and she would turn 73. We had fallen passionately in love. At our age, that was unquestionably a miracle. I saw Dorothy as a beautiful karmic gift I had received for having done some good in my life. I picked up the phone. "I love you, I want to be with you for the rest of my life. I think we need to be living together. No more of this long distance romance. What we have is rare and special, and at our age, we shouldn't dare wait." She agreed without hesitation. I immediately started packing. My family, except for Bobby, were all worried that I was rushing into what would turn out to be another disastrous relationship. On July 22nd, I moved into Dorothy's home on Zero Avenue. It was the best decision I ever made.

We enjoyed being together and delighted in our love. She found me quite amusing and laughed at my jokes. Most of them, at least. One day she said, "Robert, you have given me a precious gift, the gift of laughter." We began going to concerts and dances, and I met her many friends. Her family accepted me with open hearts. My family was finally realizing that Dorothy was a good woman and began to relax. On top of all this happiness, there was another source of joy for me. I could have a garden again! The loss of my garden in 1982 had been a long source of grief for me. Now I could plant a large vegetable garden to provide for myself and my sweetheart. I thrived most when I could watch my hard work develop into blooming life.

I greatly admired Dorothy for her altruistic efforts to make the world a better place. As a social worker, she had run a psychosocial rehabilitation program for people with mental health issues and had helped many of her clients to rebuild their lives. Now she was retired, but she continued a special personal project that she had begun 50 years ago. Instead of celebrating her birthday, Dorothy held a fund raiser to raise money for famine relief and to help children in third world countries.

Shortly after I moved in, Dorothy had her annual fund raiser. It was held in her lovely front garden and began with a delicious potluck. Almost 90 people came, and after the lunch, the fundraiser began. Before the event, Dorothy asked her friends and family members to offer their talents for this good cause. Numerous people responded. Her sons, Chris and Lee, then auctioned off these talents to the highest bidder. You could purchase a massage, a yoga class, high tea, homemade wine, a motorcycle ride, a movie night, car wash, and more. Dorothy's friends offered a birding adventure and it raised a great deal. It was one of the more popular activities that many people would bid on every year. Her sons all offered their talents as well. Colin offered computer training, Chris offered a stay at his beautiful Halfmoon Haven, Lee offered a forest adventure, and Dan offered drum lessons. Even I participated, offering a cooking class to learn how to make my famous Jewish penicillin. When Dorothy's fundraising party was over, she had raised a total of $4,000. She immediately arranged for the Canadian government to match it, and a large company to also match it, adding up to a total of $12,000. She donated the money to World Vision for famine relief in Africa. I was immensely proud to be with this amazing woman who helped so many people. A month later, I had my cooking class with six of Dorothy's friends attending. All went well, until I turned my back for a moment, and a big dog that was staying with us jumped up and ate almost all of the chicken that had been in the bowl on the counter. Dorothy and I decided it was best to keep quiet about it and just serve the chicken soup, even though there was very little chicken in it. Canadians are so polite that no one said a word. Germans would have complained loudly. "Where the hell is the chicken?" The Jews would have used humour in such a situation. "It tasted all right, but can you put some chicken in next time?"

I was struggling to find the courage to tell Dorothy that I was an alcoholic. My fear was that she would end the relationship upon such a discovery. We were becoming closer each day, and I knew I had to be honest and tell her about my long struggle with alcoholism. I did not want to lose this woman who was the love of my life, and knew I had to return to AA and quit drinking. When I told her, she was supportive and understood that alcoholism is a disease. She had been in charge of an alcohol and drug program in Ontario for 13 years. I went to a meeting that day, and with AA's help, I was able to quit drinking. It has now been over six years, and I haven't had a single drink. Now that I was sober again, I started to think about the memoir I had written in German many years ago. I wanted to try to get it published in Germany. Regina, my nephew's wife, lived in Germany, and offered to edit the book and find a publisher.

In 2013, I sent her the manuscript. She began editing, and we were in constant touch about the manuscript. Her son, Sascha, helped with the layout, the photos, and the covers. Her daughters, Vanessa and Tanya, also helped with the editing and layout. It was a real family affair! They also came up with a great title for the memoir. I had told them that one of my Oma's favourite sayings had been, "Kinder betet, der Vater geht stehlen." That translates to, "Children pray, your father is out stealing." This meant that the children should pray for their father, to protect him when he was stealing to provide for them. Oma would say this as a prayer and as an ironic comment when there was something taking place in our family that was unlawful, which was quite often. We worked on the book until 2015, and it was ready to send to publishers. Several publishers were interested, and we chose Asaro Verlag. The book was published in January, 2016. This was the greatest accomplishment of my life, as I had recorded our family history and my personal journey. I felt proud to have a book published at the age of 88.

Since I moved in with Dorothy, our love has become deeper, and we marvel at the fact that we found each other so late in life. We both feel that our love is a precious gift given to us for being loving and kind people. I have always tried to help others, such as the Jewish families and the French POW's during the war. Dorothy was raised by a mother who taught her three daughters to make the world a better place by living their lives with kindness. Like me, Dorothy had been in a loveless marriage. I was married for 53 years to a good woman who didn't love me. Dorothy was married to a good man who tried, but just couldn't find it in his heart to love her. Finally, after 33 years, he found the courage to tell her the truth. He offered her a companionship marriage, but she didn't want to settle for that. She was devastated, and went into a deep depression, but her many friends and family encircled her with their love and she was able to slowly heal.

Dorothy always encouraged me to spend time with my family, and she suggested we go to visit our matchmakers, Bobby and Melanie. They were now happily married, living in Virginia, and delighted to see that we were so much in love. While we were there, Bobby took us to Mom's Organic Market. I was looking lovingly at the large and healthy looking leeks with great interest. I am especially fond of leeks, as I use them in my soups. Bobby turned to me. "Dad, when are you going to ask Dorothy to marry you?" He put me on the spot and it dawned on me that my matchmaker was right. I had been holding back on asking her, due to my rash impulsiveness and moving forward too quickly in relationships in the past. With sudden clarity, I realized that marrying this woman would not be another mistake, rather, it would be the best decision of my life. I took her in my arms and looked at her sweet face. She gave me a shy smile in return. "Will you marry me?" She nodded, and we shared a passionate kiss in front of the lovely leeks while Bobby looked on, beaming.

On February 8th, 2014, her divorce became final, and we married the next day. We had decided to have a large wedding reception in the summer and marry in a simple ceremony at our home. We chose a friend of Dorothy's as our minister. Her name was also Dorothy, and she was spiritual, feisty, and humorous. We thought she was a good choice for what we hoped would be our playful and fun wedding. Our dear friends, Sarah and Jeff Neff, were delighted to be asked to help out. Jeff would be my best man, and Sarah would be Dorothy's bridesmaid. Dorothy chose Felix River Beavington, her 11-month-old grandson, to give her away. Since he couldn't walk yet, his father, Lee, offered to carry him as they escorted the bride through our living room towards her beloved. As Felix was still nursing, Jenn, Lee's wife, also attended. It was vital that she was there in case Felix needed a snack. Laughter is a daily part of the life that Dorothy and I share. She finds me funny, even when I am not trying to be funny. I can be myself, telling jokes and humorous stories, and Dorothy is always an appreciative audience.

We had no idea that our wedding day would turn into a hilarious "Comedy of Errors." The first error occurred when our minister, normally a very organized woman, realized she had forgotten her robes. She became flustered, and Jeff had to drive her home to retrieve them. She finally returned, Felix did an excellent job of giving his Grammy Dot away, and the minister began the ceremony. All went well until the phone rang. Lee, who is also known for always being organized and well-prepared, had turned the ringer off on his phone, but didn't realize there was an answering machine. We all stopped and listened as a voice came on the machine. It was a friend asking Dorothy if she would like to go to a movie, while giving a detailed description of the plot. We all started to lose it, trying valiantly to suppress our giggles. Felix then decided he wanted to nurse, and Jenn proceeded to oblige. The minister asked Jeff for the ring. Jeff went white and started rummaging frantically through his pockets. He couldn't find the ring. Sarah tried to help. We began giggling some more. The minister began shaking with repressed laughter. Finally, Jeff found the ring, and the minister pronounced us man and wife before mirth overtook us all. I happily kissed the bride. It was the most amusing wedding I had ever attended, and I wouldn't have had it any other way.

In the summer, we had a large wedding reception in our front garden. It was the most beautiful sunny day and we couldn't have asked for better weather. Chris, Dorothy's eldest son, was the Master of Ceremonies. Our families and many friends were in attendance. We planned to have two flower girls proceed us, and we would enter through a small pathway into the garden. Annika, Dorothy's granddaughter, and Sarah and Jeff's daughter, Aryana, were chosen. As we were about to proceed, we heard an explosion of laughter coming from the guests. We came into the garden, only to find everyone convulsed in laughter. Chris had been given a huge zucchini by one of the guests, and he had placed it on the head table where I was to sit. Somehow this tickled the crowd greatly. Chris did this in all innocence, which made it even more amusing. We had a delicious potluck lunch, toasts to our future, and musical entertainment by our many talented friends. We ended with a song circle and a bonfire in the backyard. It was a perfect day, filled with love, music, and laughter. Dorothy and I know how precious this late life love affair is, and treasure our love like the priceless gem that it is. I have never been this happy in my life previously, and we both felt truly blessed to have found each other.

Our deepest wish is only that we will continue to have many more years together.

A month after the reception, my doctor told me he had some concerns about my heart, and referred me to a cardiologist. There were many tests done and I had to wait until December for the appointment. I was not worried, as I felt well and was swimming, walking the dog, and gardening without any obstacles. Dorothy and I were not expecting bad news. However, it was very bad news we soon received. Such is the roller coaster of life, I suppose. The doctor informed me that my aortic valve had to be replaced with a porcine valve, and that I needed a triple bypass surgery. We were stunned speechless. "Robert, you need open heart surgery as soon as possible, and there is a long wait list in line before you." He looked right at Dorothy with a penetrating look. "The only way to get in quickly would be if Robert collapsed, and you called an ambulance." Dorothy felt he was giving her permission to do whatever necessary to ensure that I had my heart surgery done in haste. It was transparent to us that the doctor believed I could die any day.

Dorothy was racking her brains about what to do, and then my heart solved the problem. I have always been a good problem solver. Three days later, I was getting ready to go swimming when I suddenly collapsed in the kitchen. Dorothy called an ambulance, and I was taken to Peace Arch Hospital. After two weeks of hospitalization, I was transferred to VGH for my surgery. I was fortunate to get the top heart surgeon, Dr. Skaarsgard, and was not afraid of having the surgery, as I trusted him completely. He looked like a gold medalist alpine skier and had twice the confidence. Who wouldn't trust someone like that? When I came out of the anaesthetic, I thought I had died. Two beautiful angels in white were there to welcome me to paradise. "At least Dorothy gets my survivor's pension," was my only thought. Then one of the angels spoke softly in my ear. "Robert, you are doing fine and recovering well." A pig died to save my life. I am incredibly grateful to that pig, although as a half-Jew, I suppose that I am not kosher anymore. I recovered well, and at 87, I felt that I had been given a second lease on life. I cheated the devil once again.

I value family above all else, and my life has always centred on my children. It was important to me to give them an appreciation of the beauty and healing power of nature. Also, I tried to instill in them the qualities of kindness, loyalty, and integrity. I am so proud of my children for all that they have accomplished. They have all made happy marriages and created beautiful families. They are good people who have always helped others while living their lives with loving kindness. I tried to be a good father, and in many ways I succeeded. However, in one way, I failed. I have apologized to my children for the years that I couldn't control my addiction, the years when alcohol took over my life. They have forgiven me and remain close to me, which brings me immense joy. I am now a Great-Great-Opa, and I'm filled with pride to be the patriarch of the Middelmann clan.

Dorothy and I continue enjoying our rich and interesting life together. Our families say we still act like two madly-infatuated teenagers. We are romantic and kind to each other, and are delighted to wake up every morning to find we are still alive, and can be together for one more day. Dorothy and I both find joy in the small, magic moments, such as watching the feisty hummingbirds at our feeders. There is a bench in the Peace Park where we go to hold hands and watch the sunset over Semiahmoo Bay. I have never been happier and more at peace. There was just one thing that had been bothering me. Even though I had published my memoir in Germany, I realized that almost none of my descendants could read German. Foolishly, I had written my memoir in the wrong language. I wanted my family to know about my life and their history, so I made the decision that I would now write my life story again, but in English this time. I knew Dorothy had been a journalist, so I asked her if she would be willing to help me write my memoir in English. She agreed, and we began this book. It is not a translation of the German book, but an entirely new book. In the German book I wrote about the events of my life but didn't speak of my emotional life or share my sexual adventures. I have no computer skills, so I thought I would be handwriting the book like I had done with the German version. Thankfully, Dorothy came up with a better plan. "You are a natural storyteller, and I am a writer and editor. I will sit at the computer, and you will sit beside me and tell me the story of your life. There are three conditions. You have to be totally honest, describe the emotions you felt, and share with me all the juicy, sexy bits of your life that you left out of the German book." I agreed, and working on the book has brought us even closer. We met too late to have children, but this book has become our child, a true labour of love.

On July 10th, 2017, I turned 90. There was a beautiful birthday celebration with our families and many friends. My life has been an amazing adventure and I regret nothing. For some reason I was fearless, even as a half-Jewish boy in Nazi Germany. Many times I escaped death because I was able to keep a cool head during a crisis. As a child, Oma was my safe nest. Now, my safe nest is the vast and beautiful Canada. This peaceful country is my beloved home, and the birthplace of my 26 descendants. I feel "kinderreich," which means my life is rich with children. I have always tried to live with honour, integrity, and kindness. My reward has been the love of a wise and amazing woman. Each day is filled with our passion, laughter, and the sheer joy of being alive. I am the luckiest of men.

Dorothy and Robert's Wedding, February 2014

Robert's 90th Birthday 2017, Brackendale,
British Columbia

Robert's Family, Brackendale Art Gallery

FIN

Made in the USA
Middletown, DE
04 January 2020